AutoCAD® 14

Instant Reference

George Omura

B. Robert Callori, A.I.A.

San Francisco • Paris • Düsseldorf • Soest

SYBEX®

Associate Publisher: Amy Romanoff
Acquisitions Manager: Kristine Plachy
Acquisitions & Developmental Editor: Melanie Spiller
Editor: Alison Moncrieff
Technical Editor: Andy Hill
Book Designer: Patrick Dintino
Electronic Publishing Specialist: Bill Gibson
Production Coordinator: Amy Eoff
Proofreaders: Charles Mathews, Duncan Watson
Indexer: Nancy Guenther
Cover Designer: Design Site
Cover Photographer: Mark Johann
Cover Art Direction: Ingalls & Associates

Screen reproductions produced with Collage Complete.

Collage Complete is a trademark of Inner Media Inc.

Sybex is a registered trademark of SYBEX, Inc.

TRADEMARKS: SYBEX has attempted throughout this book to distinguish proprietary trademarks from descriptive terms by following the capitalization style used by the manufacturer.

The author and publisher have made their best efforts to prepare this book, and the content is based upon final release software whenever possible. Portions of the manuscript may be based upon pre-release versions supplied by software manufacturer(s). The author and the publisher make no representation or warranties of any kind with regard to the completeness or accuracy of the contents herein and accept no liability of any kind including but not limited to performance, merchantability, fitness for any particular purpose, or any losses or damages of any kind caused or alleged to be caused directly or indirectly from this book.

Library of Congress Card Number: 97-67761
ISBN: 0-7821-2129-2

Manufactured in the United States of America

10 9 8 7 6 5 4

Although this project was a welcome and challenging experience, it took many hours of research, hard work and dedication. I accepted the responsibility because I know that the contents of this book will facilitate and enrich your understanding of the AutoCAD release 14 program. I wish to dedicate the book to individuals in my life who I know face some extraordinary challenges in their lives every day. So, in dedication, Michael Calafati, Rose Vigdal and Kathy Callori, I admire your strength, patience, and endurance in always being there and helping others deal with the turmoil of life and living.

Acknowledgments

It took the expertise and support of trained professionals to make this project successful. It started with brief conversations, then detailed guidance from Melanie Spiller, Acquisitions and Development Editor, and George Omura, with whom I proudly share authorship. Next, it required the talent and delicate scrutiny of Alison Moncrieff, Editor, and the acquired AutoCAD knowledge and technical skill of Andy Hill, Technical Editor. The process also required contributions from AutoCAD's technical support team member Cathleen Jones, whose quick response to questions helped me meet tightly scheduled dead-lines. My appreciation goes to Dominic Panholzer for inviting me to be the author of the bonus menu help file. Finally, a special thanks goes to all my colleagues and friends from the San Francisco AutoCAD User Group, who provided welcome encouragement and support to complete this book. Finally, I would like to thank Electronic Publishing Specialist Bill Gibson, Production Coordinator Amy Eoff, and Indexer Nancy Guenther.

Introduction

How This Book Is Organized

This book presents commands and features in alphabetical order. Most entries adhere to the following structure:

1. The *name* of the command or feature appears as a heading.

2. A short paragraph or two follows the command heading, explaining the command's *purpose*.

3. Unless the procedure is completely obvious, *instructions* on using the command follow a head that takes the form *To Do Such-and-Such*. The instructions take you through the prompts and/or dialog box settings that AutoCAD displays. The instructions tell you what information AutoCAD requires to complete the command.

4. Many AutoCAD commands present choices, or options. Short descriptions of these options and notes on how to select them are presented in the *Options* section.

5. *Notes, Tips,* and *Warnings* identify command restrictions and short-cuts, as well as pointing out possible trouble spots.

6. *See Also* directs you to related entries for further information.

We have also used the following typographic conventions. Command prompts are generally displayed in numbered sequence in boldface. Command options and system variables are in italic. Prompts that appear after commands are given are in quotes, and file names are in program font (Acad.PGP, for example).

Working from the Command Line

All AutoCAD commands can be started by typing the command at the command prompt. They can also be selected from a pull-down menu or picked from a toolbar. Not all commands are available from the pull-down menu or a toolbar. Most commands will either execute immediately or prompt you for further information in the floating (or docked) command window or in a dialog box that pops open. If you prefer the command-line approach, you can use the *Filedia* or *Cmddia* system variables to turn off the dialog box in most cases. *Filedia* controls the dialog boxes pertaining to file and directory management, and *Cmddia* controls the dialog box for plotting as well as external database commands. To turn *Filedia* off, simply type *Filedia* and set the value to zero (0). You can change *Filedia* or *Cmddia* as often as you wish, according to how you want to work.

INTRODUCTION

Some commands, such as **Layer**, **Bhatch**, **Linetype**, **Pan**, and **Xref**, display a dialog box instead of prompts at the command line. If you wish to use one of these commands at the command line, enter it by typing a hyphen in front of the command, such as **-Layer**. All hyphenated commands have been included in this book.

Working with AutoCAD Dialog Boxes

Dialog boxes allow you to see all the options necessary for an operation at one time. Make sure that *Filedia* and *Cmddia* are set to ON (1). If *Filedia* is OFF and you only wish to override it for the current command, type a ~ (tilde) at any prompt asking for a file name.

When a dialog box opens, the cursor changes from a crosshair to an arrow, which you position on the item you want by moving and clicking the mouse (or some other point-and-click device) or by pressing the Tab key on your keyboard. You can also press and hold the Alt key on your keyboard and type the letter that is underscored in the item you want to pick. For example, typing Alt+P will activate the Pattern edit box for keyboard entry. The following dialog box operations are standard throughout the AutoCAD dialog-box system:

- To make a cursor pick, click the arrow on the item you want to pick.

- To type information in an edit box, click the arrow inside the edit box to place the cursor where you want it.

- To move a slide bar, drag the arrow in the direction you want (hold the mouse button down while moving the mouse).

- To toggle a radio button or check box, simply click on it.

- To select a specific tab in a dialog box, click the tabbed section name.

- To expand a pop-up or drop-down list, double-click on it.

- To view an image tile, double-click on it.

- To pick an icon button, click on it.

- To stretch a column heading or drag a division, press your cursor over the vertical line to the right of the column until an anchor symbol appears, then drag to expand or shrink its size.

- To expand or restore dialog boxes containing a Details>> or Details<< button, click on the respective Details button.

• To display a cursor menu inside a dialog box, press your right mouse button. This feature is available for dialog boxes such as Layer and Linetype.

• To toggle a command at the status bar, double-click on it.

Working with the Windows Toolbars

AutoCAD release 14 comes with a set of standard toolbars. Frequently used commands are grouped on the toolbars for easy access. Toolbars can be docked on any side of the AutoCAD window or left floating in the drawing workspace. Each command (or subgroup of commands) is represented by a distinctive icon or button. To identify a command on a toolbar, rest your pointing device on the icon. A *Tool Tip* will appear below the icon showing the icon name. This setting can be turned off in the Toolbar dialog box by unchecking *Show ToolTips*. At the same time, a short description of its function appears in the status line.

To start a command, simply click on the icon and follow the prompts or provide information as required in the dialog box. When you click on an icon with an arrow in the bottom-right corner, yet another nested toolbar (called a flyout) appears, offering more choices within the command group. Note that any flyout icon you choose becomes the "default" and will appear on top of the flyout in the future. This setting is controlled by checking *Show This Button's Icon* in the Flyout Properties subdialog box. To display the Flyout Properties subdialog box (in the Toolbar dialog box), right-click the specific fly-out button twice, pausing between clicks.

New Features with Release 14

AutoCAD release 14 comes with the following new features:

Paper Space   Elimination of regenerations in paper space following a **Zoom** or **Pan**. Transparent Zoom and Pan and Realtime Zoom and Pan are now allowed.

Lightweight Polylines   Polylines are now 2D lines composed of line and arc segments stored as single objects, and occupy less space in your drawing database.

Hatching   AutoCAD now stores hatch patterns as a single object instead of an unnamed block. A new solid hatch pattern allows you to create areas with a solid fill. Use the **Bhatch** command and click the Pick Points button to define the area. If you wish to view available hatch patterns, click the Pattern button to open the Hatch Pattern Palette, then double-click an image box to select it.

Application Demand Loading The 3D features—ACIS solid modeler, Image Support Module, **Draworder** command, Multiline Text Editor, external databases, Match Properties, Internet Utilities, and Render—are now demand-loaded ARX applications. Calling or executing the command loads the specific application into your drawing session.

AutoSnap AutoSnap is a new running object snap feature that identifies your snap modes by displaying a unique colored graphic symbol and tool tip. Pressing the Tab key allows you to cycle through all the snap modes available on the object. Use the Osnap Settings dialog box to set controls for your desired object snaps.

Object Snap The Osnap button on the status bar allows you to temporarily toggle your object snaps on and off.

Plot Preview Allows you to preview, as well as use realtime Zoom and Pan, a drawing that you wish to plot using the Microsoft-standard layout format. This feature has been incorporated in the full preview section of the Plot dialog box.

Tracking Tracking has been added to help users select orthogonal points relative to another point in your drawing, similar to X and Y point filters, as a quick and simple operation.

Realtime Zoom and Pan The **Zoom** and **Pan** commands have now been activated as Realtime Zoom and Pan. Once executed, right-click your pointing device to display a cursor menu with options to switch between the commands.

Zoom Dynamic If Fast Zoom is enabled, you'll be able to use the Dynamic option of the **Zoom** command to change the current drawing view without regenerating the drawing. Otherwise, the drawing causes a regen. Fast Zoom in controlled with the **Viewres** command.

Command Line Window Editing Place your pointing device over the command line and right-click to display the cursor menu, offering such options as Paste to Cmdline (command line), Copy, Copy History, Paste, and Preferences. Use the Up arrow and Down arrow keys to retrieve previous keyboard entries, then press ⏎ to reissue the command on the current line.

Dialog Boxes Several dialog box commands have been introduced to help you manage information easier. **Layer** and **Linetype** have been combined in a single dialog box with separate tabbed sections. The **Xref**, **Xbind**, and **Image** commands now display dialog boxes. In some cases, you have the ability to sort, rename, and delete using standard Windows methods. A Ctrl+right-click or Shift+right-click in many cases, displays a cursor menu for additional information control and selection. The **Style** command displays a new and improved dialog box and allows you to select from any registered True Type fonts installed on your system.

Toolbars   Toolbar display has been enhanced and simplified. A right-click over any icon continues, as in previous releases, to open the Toolbar dialog box. However, picking one or more check boxes adjacent to toolbar names automatically displays the toolbar. The Object Properties toolbar has been streamlined and contains commands to help you view and edit an object's properties more productively. New icons, such as Match Properties (**Matchprop**) and Make Object's Layer Current (**Ai_molc**), have been added to improve your efficiency.

Multiline Text Editor   The Multiline Text Editor dialog box offers a Microsoft-standard Windows interface to create and edit paragraph text. AutoCAD standard SHX and True Type fonts are now available to users within your drawing session.

Start Up and Setup Wizards   A new AutoCAD release 14 Start Up dialog box offers you a variety of ways to begin a new drawing. You can use a Wizard for a Quick Setup or Advanced Setup to set units of measure, drawing limits, and paper space. Prototype drawings are now stored as Templates (with a .DWT extension) with descriptive text to help you organize your work habits. Use the **Saveas** command to open the Save Drawing As dialog box and pick the Drawing Template File (.DWT) option in the Save as type pop-up list to assign a description and unit of measure to your template.

Internet Browser   Launch your system's default Internet browser within an AutoCAD session by picking the Launch Browser icon located in the Standard Toolbar and connect to any Web site you choose. Use the Files tab in the Preferences dialog box and double-click on Menu, Help, Log, and Miscellaneous File names to set your Internet location.

Windows OLE   Support for printing OLE metafile objects, such as line drawings and spreadsheets, as well as control for visibility and printing order, on nonsystem printers has been added as a new AutoCAD release 14 feature. You also have more control over proportional scaling of OLE objects and can change them into AutoCAD raster objects during a copy and paste operation.

Reduced File Size   AutoCAD has been able to reduce the size of drawing files by introducing such elements as the lightweight polyline, hatching, and the new **Xclip** command. **Xclip** allows you to specify an irregular-shaped clipping window, providing you with a cleaner drawing and reduced memory usage.

Bonus Utilities   A number of bonus commands and utilities can be installed from the CD-ROM to help users work more efficiently. Review the list of bonus commands described in Appendix A to learn how they can make your work more productive.

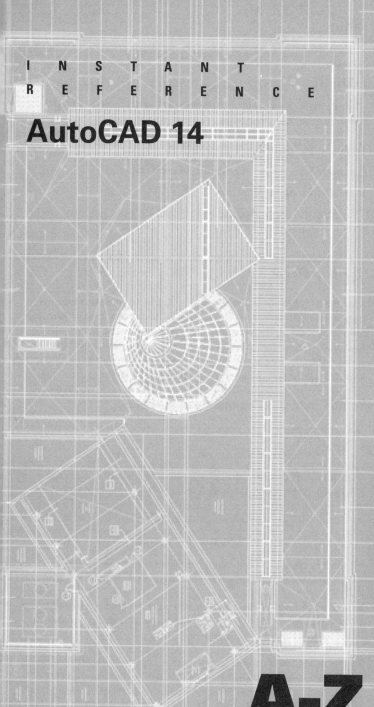

INSTANT
REFERENCE

AutoCAD 14

A-Z

About

About identifies your AutoCAD version and serial numbers, and displays the Acad.MSG message file.

To Access AutoCAD Information

Command Line: **About** (or **'About**, to use transparently)

Menu: Help ➤ About AutoCAD

The Acad.MSG file can be customized using any word processor that saves files in the ASCII format.

Acad.PGP

Acad.PGP is the ProGram Parameters ASCII file that contains information in an ASCII file needed to launch a DOS program from within AutoCAD; it is also the location for command alias definitions. Most of the commands in the Utility-External Commands menu need this file. For example, if you use a favorite DOS program, specifying the alias in Acad.PGP allows you to execute it as an AutoCAD command.

To Add External Commands and Aliases

NOTE Each external command has a maximum of four parts—each separated by a comma.

The following describes the entry for **Catalog**, which has already been assigned by AutoCAD to represent the DOS command DIR/W in the Acad.pgp file. DIR/W executes the DOS Dir command and uses the /W switch allowing you to view or list a directory in "wide format."

Catalog,   DIR /W, 0, File specification:

- The first item is the command name you wish to use at the AutoCAD command prompt—**catalog** in our example.

- The second item is the actual command as it would be entered at the DOS prompt. The drive letter and directory path name can also be included—*DIR/W* in our example.

- The third item is the amount of memory in bytes allocated to the command. AutoCAD Release 12 and earlier do not use the value of this field—it is retained for compatibility with previous releases and should always be set to 0.

- The fourth item specifies the prompt (if there is one) that appears after the command is issued. An asterisk (optional) preceding the prompt tells AutoCAD to accept spaces within the user's response. If there is no prompt, this item can be blank—"File specification:" is the prompt in our example.

- The command alias format is simple.

AR, *ARRAY

The first item, *AR,* is the alias or command that you would enter at the command line. It is followed by a comma, a space, an asterisk, and the name of the command being aliased. The Release 14 **Acad.PGP** file has an extensive list of sample aliases for the most commonly used AutoCAD commands.

Use **Reinit** to reinitialize the **Acad.PGP** file if you edit it and want to activate those changes in the current drawing session.

See Also   System Variable: Re-init

Ai_molc

Ai_molc sets the layer of the object you select as the current layer.

To Set a Layer Current

Command Line: **Ai_molc**

Object Properties Toolbar: Make Object's Layer Current

Select object whose layer will become current: Select an object on a layer you wish to set as current.

Ai_propchk

Ai_propchk lets you change an object's property.

To Modify One or More Objects

Command Line: **Ai_propchk**

Object Properties Toolbar: Properties

Ddmodify is executed if a single object is selected, otherwise, selecting multiple objects invokes **Ddchprop**. See *Ddmodify* and *Ddchprop*.

Align

Align moves, rotates, and/or scales objects in two or three dimensions using source points on the original object and destination points on the reference object.

To Align Objects

Command Line: **Align**

Menu: Modify ➤ 3D Operation ➤ Align

1. **Select objects:** Pick objects to move, rotate, and/or scale, then respond to steps 2-5 to align an object in only two dimensions or continue to step 7 to move, rotate and scale objects in 3D space.

2. **Specify 1st source point:** Select first source point on object you wish to align.

3. **Specify 1st destination point:** Select new position of first destination point where object is to be realigned.

4. **Specify 2nd source point:** Select second source point on object you wish to align.

5. **Specify 2nd destination point:** Select second destination point where object is to be realigned.

6. **Specify 3rd source point or <continue>:** To relocate the object in three dimensions specify the next pair of points or press Enter for 2D alignment options.

7. **Scale objects to alignment points? [Yes/No] <No>:** Enter **No** to rotate the object from the source point to the destination point and **Yes** to rotate and scale the object directly from the source point to the destination point.

Ameconvert

*See **Solid Modeling***

Aperture

Aperture sets the size of the Osnap (object snap) target box to your preference. The equivalent dialog box command is **Ddosnap**.

To Set the Size of the Osnap Target Box

Command Line: **Aperture** (or **'Aperture**, to use transparently)

Menu: Tools ➤ Object Snap Settings

Object Snap Toolbar: Object Snap Settings

Choosing either method will bring up a dialog box. Enter the desired size of osnap target in pixels. Default settings may vary depending on your display.

Object snap target height (1-50 pixels) <10>: Using the Osnap Settings dialog box allows you to use the **Aperture** size slider bar to visually set the Osnap box size.

See Also Ddosnap, Ddselect, Gripsize, Osnap, Pickbox; *System Variables:* Aperture

Appload

Appload displays a dialog box for loading AutoLISP files or loading and unloading ADS and ARX applications.

To Load AutoLISP Applications

Command Line: **Appload**

Menu: Tools ➤ Load Application

Options

File Opens the Select AutoLISP, ADS, or ARX File dialog box and allows you to search for files to add.

Remove Deletes files from list box.

Load Loads one or more selected file(s) from list box using Shift or Ctrl key combinations with the mouse pick button.

Unload Removes ADS, AutoLISP, or ARX applications.

Save List Saves applications shown in list box to the Appload.dfs file in the current directory.

Exit Saves changes to Save List and exits the dialog box.

NOTE File types listed are AutoLISP (.LSP), AutoCAD Development System (.EXE), and Rendering (.ARX) file extensions.

See Also AutoLISP, Arx

Arc

Arc allows you to draw an arc using a variety of methods. The system prompts shown below will vary with the options chosen.

To Draw an Arc

Command Line: **Arc**

Menu: Draw ➤Arc ➤ Preset Options

Draw Toolbar: Arc

1. **Center/<Start point>:** Use the mouse to pick the start point of the arc or select **C** for more options.

2. **Center/End/<Second point>:** Pick the second point of the arc or select **C** for *Angle/Length of Chord/End point:* options or **E** for *Angle/Direction/Radius/<Center point>* options.

Depending on the option selected, prompt 3 or 4 will appear:

3. **Angle/Length of Chord/End point:** Pick the end point of the arc.

4. **Angle/Direction/Radius/<Center point>:** Pick the end point of the arc or specify a value for selected option.

Options

Angle   Enters an arc in terms of degrees or current angular units. The "Included angle:" prompt appears. You can enter an angle value or use the cursor to select angle points on the screen.

Center   Enters the location of an arc's center point. At the prompt "Center:", enter a coordinate or pick a point with your cursor.

Direction   Enters a tangent direction from the start point of an arc. At the prompt "Direction from start point:", either enter a relative coordinate or pick a point with your cursor.

End   Enters the end point of an arc. At the prompt "End point:", enter a coordinate or pick a point with your cursor.

Length   Enters the length of an arc's chord. At the prompt "Length of chord:", enter a length or drag and pick a length with your cursor.

Radius   Enters an arc's radius. At the prompt "Radius:", enter a radius or pick a point that defines a radius length.

Start point Enters the beginning point of an arc.

If you press ↵ at the first prompt of the **Arc** command, AutoCAD uses the most recent point entered for a line or arc as the first point of the new arc. It then prompts you for a new end point. An arc is drawn at a tangent to the last line or arc drawn.

If you select **Arc** from the pull-down menu, the Arc Cascading menu appears, with ten preset arc options. For example, *S,E,D* allows you to select the start point, the end point, and the direction of the arc. Figure 1 illustrates how these options draw arcs.

You can convert arcs to light weight polyline arcs with the **Pedit** or **Bpoly** command. You can also lengthen existing arcs using the **Lengthen** command.

See Also Change, Elev, Ellipse, Lengthen, UCS

FIGURE 1: The Arc menu options and their meanings

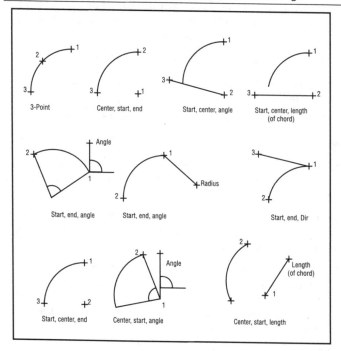

Area

Area carries out an area calculation based on dimensions that you specify by defining line segments, by selecting lines and polylines, or by doing both.

To Calculate an Area

Command Line: **Area**

Menu: Tools ➤ Inquiry ➤ Area

Standard Toolbar: ⊞Distance Flyout ⊞Area

Inquiry Toolbar: ⊞Area

1. **<First point>/Object/Add/Subtract:** Pick first point or enter option.

2. **Next Point:** Pick the next point. Continue picking points until you have defined the area, then press ⏎ to display the calculated area and perimeter in the following format:

   Area = <Calculated area>, **Perimeter = <Perimeter>**

   The option for Object displays the calculated area and length in the following format:

   Area = <Calculated area>, Length = <Length>

Options

Next point   Continues selecting points until you have defined the area to be calculated. Once you have defined the area, press ⏎ at the "Next Point:" prompt.

Object   Selects a circle or polyline for area calculation. If you pick an open polyline, AutoCAD will calculate the area of the polyline as if its two end points were closed.

Add   Keeps a running count of areas. Normally, **Area** returns you to the command prompt as soon as an area has been calculated. If you enter the Add mode, you are returned to the **Area** command prompt once an area has been calculated, and you can continue to add area values to the current area.

Subtract   Subtracts areas from a running count of areas.

Return   Exits the command.

   Area does not calculate areas for arcs. To find the area of a shape that includes arcs, you must convert the arc areas into polylines (see **Pedit**) before you issue the **Area** command. Then issue the command, select the *Object* option, and pick the polyline—**Area** will calculate the area of the polyline. Add all the polyline areas to rectangular areas to arrive at the total area. You can also obtain areas for ellipses, splines, polygons, regions or solids. Use Bpoly to create a closed polyline automatically. **Area** only calculates areas in a plane parallel to the current user coordinate system.

See Also   Bhatch, Bpoly, Dblist, List, Pedit, Perimeter; *System Variables:* Area

Array/Array 3D

Array makes multiple copies of an object or group of objects in a row-and-column matrix, a single row or column, or a circular array (to form such objects as teeth in a gear or the numbers on a circular clock).

To Create Object Arrays

Command Line: **Array**

Menu: Modify ➤ Array

Menu: Modify ➤ 3D Operation ➤ 3D Array

Modify Toolbar: 🔡 Array

1. **Select objects:** Pick objects to array.

2. **Rectangular or Polar array (<R>/P):** Enter desired array type.

   If you select the **Rectangular** option or enter **R** at the prompt "Rectangular or Polar array:", you are given the following series of prompts:

   Center point of array: Pick the center of rotation.

   Number of rows (—-) <1>: Enter the number of rows.

   Number of columns (|||) <1>: Enter the number of columns.

   Unit cell or distance between rows (--): Enter the numeric distance between rows or depth of cell (see *Unit cell* option below).

   Distance between columns (|||): Enter the numeric distance between columns.

   If you select the **Polar** option or enter **P** at the prompt "Rectangular or Polar array:", you are asked for the following information:

   Base/<Specify center point of array>: Pick a center point for the polar array or enter **B** for options to set a new base point at the prompt "Specify base point of objects:", then "Specify center point of array:".

- **Number of items:** Enter number of items in the array, including the originally selected objects.

- **Angle to fill <360>:** Enter the angle the array is to occupy. Use a negative value to indicate a clockwise array.

- **Rotate objects as they are copied? <Y>:** Enter **N** if the arrayed objects are to maintain their current orientation.

Options

Rectangular Copies the selected objects in an array of rows and columns. You are then prompted for the number of rows and columns and the distance between them.

Polar Copies the selected objects in a circular array. You are prompted first for the center point of the array and then for the number of items in the array. You are asked whether you want to rotate the objects as they are copied. If you press ↵ without entering a value at the "Number of items:" prompt, you will be prompted for the angle between items.

Unit cell Enter the size of the rectangular unit cell by picking two points dynamically or with an Osnap mode. After picking the first point, you are given the "Other corner:" prompt. Select the other corner of the unit cell.

Usually, row-and-column arrays are aligned with the X and Y axes of your current user coordinate system. A positive distance number copies objects to the right and/or upward, a negative number copies objects to the left and/or downward. To create an array at an angle, set the **Snap** command's *Rotate* option to the desired angle. Rectangular arrays will be rotated by the snap angle. The *Snapang* system variable also allows you to set the cursor rotation angle. The order in which you select the two points for the *Unit cell* option determines the direction of the array.

See Also Minsert, Select, Snap/Rotate; *System Variables:* Snapang, 3D array

ARX

Loads, unloads and furnishes information relating to **ARX** applications, such as third-party CAD software programs or internal applications, such as Render or ASE.

To load or unload ARX applications

Command Line: **Arx**

?/Load/Unload/Commands/Options: Specify an option.

Options

?   Lists the **ARX** applications that are loaded in current drawing.

Load   Displays prompt "Load ARX file:". Enter the **ARX** file name. A tilde (~) can be used to open and choose a file from the Select **ARX** File dialog box.

Unload   Displays prompt "Unload ARX file:" Enter name of ARX file to unload at the prompt.

Command   AutoCAD lists the commands registered by extension programs.

Options   Depending on the option selected, the "Group/Classes/Services" prompt appears. Group prompts for the "Command Group Name:, Classes" lists hierarchy for specific **ARX** applications and "Services" displays the names of services entered into the ARX service dictionary.

ASE

ASE is an application that links AutoCAD to external database files. You can modify database files from within AutoCAD and link AutoCAD objects to database records. Use ASE to access dBASE III, Microsoft ODBC, and Oracle 7.

To Use the ASE Application

Command Line: **Ase**

Menu Tools ➤ External Database Options

Toolbar: External Databases ➤ ▦Administration ▦Rows ▦Links ▦Select Objects ▦Export Links ▦SQL Editor

Options

The following options appear in the External Database menu and toolbar. The command-line equivalent of each menu or toolbar options is shown in parenthesis.

Administration   Allows you to set the ASE environment. First, specify the type of database (*Database Object*) to connect to, and define the path to the actual database table (*Catalog/Schema/Table*). Set a *User Name* and *Password*, and select an *Isolation level* to determine whether data in different transactions by different users is interleaved or isolated. Once the database object has been defined, use the *Set by* option to define a *Link Path Name* by selecting key columns in the database, and to select AutoCAD (*Graphical*) objects for linking (**Aseadmin** command).

ASE

Rows Displays the current Database Object Settings and allows you to *Select Objects* and view and edit rows in the database via the *Edit Rows* subdialog box. This command option is also used to edit and delete links to selected rows in the database, and create selection sets and displayable attributes (**Aserows** command).

Links Allows you to select AutoCAD objects and edit or delete their database links. You may delete specific links or all links (**Aselinks** command).

Select Objects Allows you to create a selection set based on a combination of graphic and nongraphic data. Define search criteria based on database information via the *Select* option by entering a selection statement in the Condition field. Then select AutoCAD (*Graphical*) objects and compare the selection sets using the Union/Intersect/Subtract A-B/Subtract B-A logical operators. Depending on the logical operation selected, the final selection set will contain all objects that belong in each selection set—only those that meet both sets of selection parameters, or a set based on subtraction of one set from the other (**Aseselect** command).

Export Links Allows you to select AutoCAD objects and their linked database information, and export this information into a text file in a variety of formats. Available export formats are space-delimited (SDF), comma-delimited (CDF), and native database formats. These export tables can be used to generate reports using the appropriate report-writing software. A separate table is generated for each *Link Path Name* (**Aseexport** command).

SQL Editor Allows you to interact with the external database via SQL statements. This method allows you to generate more complex queries and edits than are available via the AutoCAD external database commands. You may enter SQL statements directly into the SQL Editor dialog box, or load and run saved SQL statements (**Asesqled** command).

Attachurl

Attachurl attaches a URL to objects or areas in your drawing. A URL can be attached as xdata (extended data) to one or more objects. Use the object method if geometry is scattered throughout the drawing. Attaching a URL by area places a rectangle around the specified area on the layer urllayer. Use area if there is no geometry.

To Attach a URL

Command Line: **Attachurl**

Internet Utilities Toolbar ➤ Attach URL

URL by (Area/<Objects>): Specify an option

12

Options

Area   Pick *First corner:* and *Other corner:* using window selection methods, then specify a name at the "Enter URL:" prompt.

Object   First *Select objects:* to be attached, then specify a name at the "Enter URL:" prompt.

WARNING   Deleting, freezing, locking or changing the visibility of the layer urllayer can destroy the hyperlink information in your drawing. Modifying the rectangles on urllayer or attaching URL's to them can create problematic results. If you turn the urllayer Off, turn it On prior to using the **Dwfout** command.

See Also   Detachurl, Gotourl, Listurl, Selecturl, Openurl, Inserturl, Saveurl, Inetcfg, Inethelp

---

Attdef

Attdef creates an attribute definition that allows you to store textual and numeric data with a block. When you insert a block containing an attribute definition into a drawing, you are prompted for the data that is to be stored with the block. Use **Attdef** to work from the command line and **Ddattdef** to work from the Attribute Definition dialog box. The **Ddattdef** command provides the added feature of aligning your new attribute definition below the previous one. Later you can use **Ddatte** to view the data and edit attributes. The **Attext** or **Ddattext** command extracts attribute data into an ASCII text file. You can control the format of the extracted file for easy importation to a database manager, spreadsheet, or word processing program.

To Create an Attribute Definition with Attdef

Command Line: **Attdef**

1. **Attribute modes—Invisible: N Constant:N Verify:N Preset:N Enter (ICVP) to change, or press ENTER when done:** Enter **I**, **C**, **V**, or **P** to toggle an option on or off, or press ⏎ to go to the next prompt.

2. **Attribute tag:** Enter the attribute name.

3. **Attribute prompt:** Enter the prompt to be displayed for attribute input.

4. **Default attribute value:** Enter the default value for attribute input.

5. Justify/Style/<Start point>: Enter coordinates or pick with the cursor to indicate the location of attribute text, or select an option to determine orientation or style of the attribute text.

6. Height (0.2000): Enter the attribute text height. This prompt appears only if the current text style height is set to 0.

7. Rotation angle <0>: Enter the angle of the attribute text.

Options

Invisible Makes the attribute invisible when inserted.

Constant Gives the attribute a value that you cannot change.

Verify Allows review of the attribute value after insertion.

Preset Automatically inputs the default attribute value on insertion. Unlike the Constant option, it lets you change the input value of a pre-set attribute by using the **Ddatte** or **Attedit** commands. See **Text** for **Attdef** options related to location, style, and orientation of attributes. Use **Change, Ddmodify** or **Ddedit** to edit the attribute definition before making the attribute into a block.

TIP When inserting a block with attributes, the prompt sequence is determined by the order selected during creation of the block.

See Also Attedit, Attdisp, Attext, Attredef, Block, Change, Chprop, Ddatte, Ddattext, Ddedit, Insert, Text, Xdata/Xdlist; *System Variables:* Aflags, Attdia, Attreq, Attmode

Attdisp

Attdisp allows you to control the display and plotting of all attributes in a drawing. You can force attributes to be visible or invisible according to their display mode.

To Set Attribute Display Using Attdisp

Command Line: **Attdisp** (or '**Attdisp**, to use transparently)

Menu: View ➤ Display ➤ Attribute Display ➤ Options

Normal/ON/OFF <Normal>: Enter **ON**, **OFF**, or ↵ for your selection.

Options

Normal Hides attributes that are set to be invisible. All other attributes are displayed.

ON Displays all attributes, including those set to be invisible.

OFF Hides all attributes, whether or not they are set to be invisible.

If automatic regeneration is on (see **Regenauto**), your drawing will regenerate when you complete the command, and the display of attributes will reflect the option you select. If automatic regeneration is off, the drawing will not regenerate until you issue **Regen**.

See Also Attdef, Regen, Regenauto, *System Variables:* Aflags, Attmode

Attedit

Attedit edits attribute values after you have inserted them in a drawing. You can edit attributes individually or globally.

To Edit Attribute Values with Attedit

Command Line: **Attedit**

Menu: Modify ➤Object ➤ Attribute ➤ Global

1. **Edit attributes one at a time? <Y>:** Enter **Y** for individual or **N** for global attribute editing. Depending on your response, you may see one or more additional prompts before the prompt "Block name:". These prompts are self-explanatory; respond to them to move on to the following.

2. **Block name specification <*>:** Press ↵, or enter a block name to restrict the attribute edits to a specific block, or enter a wildcard filter list to limit it to a group of blocks.

3. **Attribute tag specification <*>:** Press ↵, or enter an attribute tag to restrict attribute edits to a specific attribute, or enter a wildcard filter list.

4. **Attribute value specification <*>:** Press ↵, or enter a value to restrict attribute edits to a specific attribute value, or enter a wildcard to filter a list.

5. **Select Attributes:** Pick the attributes you want to edit. If you elected in Step 1 to edit the attributes one at a time, an *X* appears on the first attribute to be edited, and you will see the following prompt:

    Value/Position/Height/Angle/Style/Layer/Color/
    Next/<N>: The options in this prompt are discussed below.

Options

Y (at first prompt)   Allows you to edit attribute values one at a time, and change an attribute's position, height, angle, text style, layer, and color.

N (at first prompt)   Allows you to modify attribute values globally. If you select this option, you are asked whether you want to edit only visible attributes.

Value   Changes the value of the currently marked attribute(s).

Position   Moves an attribute.

Height   Changes the height of attribute text.

Angle   Changes the attribute angle.

Style   Changes the attribute text style.

Layer   Changes the layer that the attribute is on.

Color   Changes the attribute color. Colors are specified by numeric code or by name. See **Color/Colour**.

Next   Displays the next sequential attribute.

If you choose to edit attributes individually and answer all of the prompts (you select *Y* at the first prompt), you are prompted to select attributes. After you have made your selection, an *X* marks the first attribute to edit. The default option, *Next,* will move the marking *X* to the next attribute.

By entering **V** at the "Value/Position/Height" prompt, you can either change or replace the attribute value. If you choose *Replace,* the default option, you are prompted for a new attribute value. The new attribute value replaces the previous one and you return to the "Value/Position/ Height" prompt. If you choose *Change,* you are prompted for a specific string of characters to change and for a new string to replace the old. This allows you to change portions of an attribute's value without having to enter the entire attribute value. Clicking on an attribute's grip also allows you to change its position using the *Stretch* edit option.

If you choose to edit only visible attributes (after entering **N** at the first prompt), you are prompted to select attributes. You can then visually pick the attributes to edit. You are next prompted for the string to change the replacement string. Once you have answered the prompts, AutoCAD changes all the selected attributes. If you enter **N** at the prompt "Visible attribute:", you won't be prompted to select attributes. Instead, AutoCAD assumes you want to edit all the attributes in the drawing, regardless of whether they are visible. The "Select attribute" prompt is skipped and you are sent directly to the prompt "Change string:".

When answering the attribute specification prompts, you can use wildcard characters (the question mark, the asterisk, and a few others—see Wildcard Characters) to "filter" a group of attribute blocks, tags, or values. To restrict attribute edits to attributes that have a null value, enter \ (a backslash) at the "Attribute value specification <*>:" prompt. The Ddatte Attribute dialog box limits editing to attribute values only.

See Also   Attext, Ddattdef, Ddatte, Ddattext, Select, Wildcards

---

Attext

Attext converts attribute information into external ASCII text files. You can then bring these files into database or spreadsheet programs for analysis. **Attext** allows you to choose from three standard database and spreadsheet file formats.

To Do an Attext Conversion

Command Line: **Attext**

1. **CDF, SDF or DXF Attribute extract (or Objects)? <C>:** Enter format of extracted file or **O** for objects to select specific attributes for extraction.

2. If the *Filedia* system variable is set to 1, the Select Template File dialog list box will appear to pick a template file, and the Create extract file dialog list box will then open to name the extract file.

If the *Filedia* system variable is set to 0, the command-line prompts are as follows:

> **CDF, SDF or DXF Attribute extract (or Objects)? <C>:** Enter format of extracted file or type **O** to select specific attributes for extraction from objects.

> **Template file <filename.txt>:** Enter the name of the external template file

> **Extract file name <drawing name>:** Enter the name of the file to hold the extracted information.

Options

CDF **(comma-delimited file)**   Creates an ASCII file using commas to delimit fields. Each attribute is treated as a field of a record, and all the attributes in a block are treated as one record. Character fields are enclosed in quotes. Some database programs such as dBASE III, III Plus, and IV can read this format without any alteration.

ATTEXT

SDF **(space-delimited format)**   Creates an ASCII file using spaces to delimit fields. Each attribute is treated as a field of a record, and all attributes in a block are treated as one record. The field values are given a fixed width, and character fields are not given special treatment. If you open this file using a word processor, the attribute values appear as rows and columns (the rows are the records and the columns are the fields).

DXF **(data-exchange format)**   Creates an abbreviated AutoCAD DXF file that contains only the block reference, attribute, and end-of-sequence objects. Objects prompts you to select objects. You can then select specific attributes to extract. Once you are done with the selection, the "Attribute extract:" prompt reappears.

Before you can extract attribute values with Attext, you need to create a *template file*, an external ASCII file containing a list of attribute tags you wish to extract. Template files, which have the extension TXT, also contain a code describing the characteristics of the attributes associated with each tag. The code denotes character and numeric values as well as the number of characters for string values or the number of placeholders for numeric values. For example, if you expect the value entered for a numeric attribute whose tag is *cost* to be five characters long with two decimal places, include the following line in the template file:

    cost N005002

The *N* indicates that this attribute is a numeric value. The next three characters indicate the number of digits the value will hold. The last three characters indicate the number of decimal places the number will require. If you want to extract a character attribute, you might include the following line in the template file:

    name C030000

The C denotes a character value. The next three characters indicate the number of characters you expect for the attribute value. The last three characters in character attributes are always zeros, because character values have no decimal places.

Follow the last line in the template file by a ↵, or you will receive an error message when you try to use the template file.

You can also extract information about the block that contains the attributes. Table 1 shows the format you use in the template file to extract block information. A template file containing these codes must also contain at least one attribute tag, because AutoCAD must know which attribute it is extracting before it can tell what block the attribute is associated with.

TABLE 1: Template Tags and Codes for Extracting Information about Blocks

Tag	Code	Description
BL:LEVEL	N*xxx*000	Level of nesting for block
BL:NAME	C*xxx*000	Block name
BL:X	N*xxxxxx*	X value for block insertion point
BL:Y	N*xxxxxx*	Y value for block insertion point
BL:Z	N*xxxxxx*	Z value for block insertion point
BL:NUMBER	N*xxx*000	Block counter
BL:HANDLE	C*xxx*000	Block handle
BL:LAYER	C*xxx*000	Name of layer block is on
BL:ORIENT	N*xxxxxx*	Block rotation angle
BL:XSCALE	N*xxxxxx*	Block X scale
BL:YSCALE	N*xxxxxx*	Block Y scale
BL:ZSCALE	N*xxxxxx*	Block Z scale
BL:XEXTRUDE	N*xxxxxx*	X value for block extrusion direction
BL:YEXTRUDE	N*xxxxxx*	Y value for block extrusion direction
BL:ZEXTRUDE	N*xxxxxx*	Z value for block extrusion direction

Note: Italicized zeros indicate adjustable numeric variables.

See Also Attdef, Attedit, Ddattdef, Ddattext; *System Variables:* Filedia

ATTREDEF

Attredef allows you to redefine an existing block and delete and/or update the associated attributes.

To Redefine Block Attributes

Command Line: **Attredef**

1. **Name of Block you wish to redefine:** Enter the block name.

2. **Select objects:** Select objects and attribute definition.

3. **Insertion base point of new Block:** Pick a new insertion point for block.

ATTREDEF

When you assign new attributes to an existing block reference, they are given default values; existing attributes keep their old values. If an old attribute is not included in the new block definition, it will be deleted from the block reference.

TIP To avoid unpredictable results, it is important to redefine the attribute using the same insertion point. Drawing a circle and inserting the attribute as an exploded object at the circle's center point provides you with the blocks same insertion point when the prompt "Insertion base point of new Block:" appears.

See Also Attedit, Ddate, Ddattdef

Audit

Use **Audit** to check a drawing file for errors or corrupted data. If errors are detected, you can choose to have them corrected.

To Use Audit

Command Line: **Audit**

Fix any errors detected? <N>: Enter **Y** to correct any errors found. Selecting N reports errors but will not fix them. If no errors are detected, a screen display like the following will be appear:

```
4 Blocks audited
Pass 1 4 objects audited
Pass 2 4 objects audited
total errors found 0 fixed 0
```

Audit creates a ASCII file that contains a report of the audit and any action taken. The file has the extension ADT. The information presented by the **Audit** command may not be important to most users. However, it may help your AutoCAD dealer or Autodesk's product support department to diagnose a problem with a file.

See Also Recover, *System Variables:* Auditctl

AutoLISP

AutoLISP is a programming language embedded in AutoCAD. It allows you to automate repetitive tasks and add custom commands to AutoCAD. AutoLISP enables you to link applications written in C to AutoCAD.

Several AutoLISP programs are provided with AutoCAD, and others can be obtained from computer bulletin boards such as the Autodesk forum on Compuserve.

To Use AutoLISP

1. Enter your AutoLISP program code directly through the command prompt, or write your code with a word processor and store it as an ASCII file with the file name extension .LSP.

2. If you save your program code as a file on disk, use the **AutoLISP** *Load* function to load your program while in the AutoCAD drawing editor or issue the **Appload** command. The following example shows the syntax for the Load function at the command line:

   (load "drive/directory/file name") ↵

   You can leave off the drive and directory information if the Acad environment variable points to the directory that holds the AutoLISP programs.

3. You can also open the Appload dialog box and save the LISP file in the list box, then activate it by selecting *Load*.

4. Once a program file is loaded, you can use it by entering its name through the keyboard, just like a standard AutoCAD program. You don't have to load the file again while in the current editing session.

You can combine your favorite AutoLISP programs into a single file called Acad.LSP. Place this file in your AutoCAD directory. It will be loaded automatically every time you open a drawing file. AutoCAD routines do not need reloading and now remain "persistent" throughout the duration of drawing file initialization. AutoLISP code can also be embedded in the AutoCAD menu system.

See Also Appload

Base

Base sets the drawing's *base point,* a point of reference for insertion when you insert one drawing into another. Select the base point in relation to the world coordinate system (WCS). The default base point for all drawings is the WCS origin point at coordinate 0,0,0.

To Set a Base Point

Command Line: **Base** (or **'Base**, to use transparently)

Menu: Draw ➤ Block ➤ Base

Base point <0.0000,0.0000,0.0000>: Enter the coordinates of a point or pick a point.

See Also Block, Bmake, Ddinsert, Insert, Select, Wblock; *System Variables:* Insbase

Batchplt

Batchplt is a utility that opens the AutoCAD Batch Plot Utility dialog box allowing you to plot multiple AutoCAD drawings to a single or multiple devices.

To Run Batch Plotting

Windows NT 3.51: In the Autodesk R14 program group, double-click the **Batch Plot Utility** icon. On NT 4.0 this utility starts a new session of AutoCAD R14 and then starts the batchplot utility.

Batch Plot Utility

Assuming you have installed AutoCAD Release 14 in the default folder for Windows 95 or NT 4.0: From the Start menu ➤ Programs ➤ AutoCAD R14 ➤ Batch Plot Utility.

Options

The AutoCAD Batch Plot Utility dialog box contains pick boxes to select drawing files and previously saved plot configurations for batch plotting. The list box division headings identify the Drawing File and PCP/PC2 File.

Add Drawing Opens Add Drawing file subdialog box to search drives, directories, and files, allowing you to select drawing files using standard Windows methods for a batch list. Selected files are displayed in a list box.

Associate PCP/PC2 Opens the Associate PCP/PCP2 File dialog box to save one or more drawing files with a .PC2 or .PCP extension for the duration of a batch plot. Plot configuration parameters (.PCP) files contain information such as pen assignments, plot area, scale, paper size, and orientation. Complete plot configuration (.PC2) files store device-specific information (usually defined in the acad.CFG file) as well as .PCP file information.

Delete Entry   Pick box to delete drawings from list box.

Save List As   Opens the Save Batch Plot List File dialog box to select a drive and path for saving current batch list and associated configurations as a Batch Plot List (.BPL) file.

Open List   Displays the Open Batch Plot List File dialog box to select a drive and path to load a .BPL file, replacing the contents of the current list box.

Append List   Opens the Append Batch Plot List File dialog box to load a BPL file, appending its contents to the list box.

Plot   Plot drawings displayed in list box.

Close   Exits the dialog box and does not retain the current list of drawings and configurations unless previously saved to a .BPL file.

Drawings, plotted views, or existing device configurations cannot be edited with the Batch Plot utility. Prepare drawings prior to plotting by reviewing their completeness, saving plotted views, and checking default plotter configurations. For multiple configurations of a single device, save configurations as .PCP files in AutoCAD prior to batch plotting. For multiple devices, check device configurations and save them as .PC2 files.

NOTE   To terminate a batch plot in progress, pick *Cancel Remaining Drawings* in the Batch Plot Progress dialog box and all remaining plots will be cancelled. Otherwise, pick Cancel to discontinue plotting of the current drawing.

Bhatch

Bhatch opens a dialog box with hatching options, enabling you to fill an enclosed boundary defined by lines, arcs, circles, and polylines with a predefined pattern, a simple hatch pattern, or solid fill by pointing to it. The pattern can also be previewed from an image box or a hatch pattern pallette dialog box before being applied. Use -Hatch to display all the prompts at the command line.

To Use the Bhatch Dialog Box

Command Line: **Bhatch**

Menu: Draw ➤ Hatch

Draw Toolbar: ▨ Hatch

Pick the appropriate options from the Bhatch dialog box.

Options

Pattern Type   Allows you to set hatch patterns using *Predefined* stored patterns from the Acad.PAT file, *User-defined* single line patterns, or *Custom* patterns. An onscreen graphic allows you to cycle through the predefined patterns by simply clicking the graphic. *Pattern...* opens the Hatch pattern pallette subdialog box and displays a slide or icon of each pattern. Select the pattern by double-clicking the icon to close the dialog box and display it in the image box. The first pattern is named *Solid*, a new feature in Release 14, which provides a new solid fill capability.

Pattern Properties   Allows you to change the pattern *Scale*, *Angle*, and *Spacing*. You may optionally Double (cross-hatch) the hatch pattern or Explode it. If an ISO hatch pattern has been selected, you may select an ISO Pen Width to produce ISO-related scaling. The greyed Double hatch box becomes active when the User-defined is selected, allowing you to draw lines at 90 degrees. The Custom Pattern edit box is active when Custom is selected as the pattern type.

Boundary   Controls aspects of boundary definition. *Pick Points* prompts you to pick a point within the bounded area, including blocks. If Island Detection (below) is enabled, objects within the boundary are defined as "islands" and are not hatched. Text contained within the bounded area is considered an island. An imaginary rectangle is created around it and the text is not hatched. *Select Objects* allows you to select objects or use **Osnap** modes to define the area to be hatched. *Remove Islands* removes from the boundary set "islands" defined by the *Pick Points* option. *View Selections* highlights boundaries and objects selected for the hatching area, then returns you to the dialog box.

Inherit Properties   Allows you to select an existing associative hatch object and apply its properties to the current hatch pattern.

Preview Hatch   Displays a preview of the hatch pattern, then returns you to the dialog box.

Advanced Options   Allows you to control the method AutoCAD uses to define the boundary to *Make New Boundary Set*. Pick boxes allow you to select set *From Everything on Screen* or *From Existing Boundary Set*. *Style* allows you to set boundary options by selecting from a list box, or visually by clicking an onscreen icon. You can also *Retain Boundaries* as a polyline or region; if you don't choose this option, it is erased after the hatch pattern is created. *Island Detection* allows you to specify whether objects within the outermost boundary are to be hatched or to be treated as "islands."

Associativity   Associates the hatch pattern with the hatch boundary object, so that it will adjust its shape when the object boundary is changed.

Apply   Applies the selected pattern to the bounded area.

You cannot copy a hatch pattern created with a version of AutoCAD earlier than Release 12. Hatch boundaries can be defined by a line, arc, circle, 2D or 3D polyline, 3D face, or viewport objects. Areas in nested blocks can also be hatched. The fillmode system variable globally controls the visibility of solid fills and hatches.

See also   Blipmode, Hatch; *System Variables:* Hpang, Hpbound, Hpdouble, Hpname, Hpscale, Hpspace, Fillmode

Blipmode

When you draw with AutoCAD, tiny crosses called *blips* appear wherever you select points. These blips are not part of your drawing; they merely help you locate the points that you have selected. You can use **Blipmode** to suppress these blips if you don't want them. Use the Redraw, Regen, Zoom, or Pan commands to remove blips.

To Reset Blipmode

Command line: **Blipmode** (or **'Blipmode**, to use transparently)

ON/OFF <current setting>: Enter ON or OFF.

Options

ON   Displays blips when you enter points.

OFF   Suppresses blips when you enter points.

See also   Ddrmodes; *System Variables:* Blipmode

Block

Block groups a set of drawing objects together to act as a single object. You can then insert, copy, mirror, move, rotate, scale, or save the block as an external file. The dialog box equivalent is **Bmake**.

To Create a Block

Command line: **Block**

Toolbar: Block

1. **Block name (or ?):** Enter the name for the block. Enter a question mark to list existing blocks. A *Block name:* edit box allows you to enter a name in the dialog box. Clicking *List Block Names...* opens the Block Names In This Drawing subdialog box to specify a *Pattern* using wildcards to filter block names or pick a block name from the list box with your cursor.

2. **Insertion base point:** Enter a coordinate value or pick a point to set the base point of the block. A Base Point can be selected by clicking *Select Point<* or specified from *X, Y* and *Z* edit boxes in the dialog box.

3. **Select objects:** Pick objects to include in the block. The objects you select will disappear, but you can restore them as individual objects by using the **Oops** command or checking *Retain Objects* in the Block Definition dialog box. If your block includes attributes, select each one in the order you wish them to appear in the dialog box. If you use the dialog box, clicking *Select Objects<* temporarily exists the dialog box to pick objects on the screen.

Blocks exist only within the drawing in which they are created. However, you can convert them into drawing files with the **Wblock** command. Blocks can contain other nested blocks. You can include attributes in blocks to allow the input and storage of information with the block; see **Attdef**.

If you attempt to create a block that has the same name as an existing block, you will see the prompt:

Block <name> already exists. Redefine it? <N>

To redefine the existing block, enter **Y**. The Block command proceeds as usual and replaces the existing block with the new one. If the existing block has been inserted into the drawing, the new block appears in its place. If **Regenauto** has been turned off, the new block will not appear until you issue a **Regen** command.

If you make a block containing a nested block with the same name, AutoCAD displays the prompt:

Block <block name> references itself

To correct the problem, open the drawing, explode the block, and purge the duplicate nested block name. To insert an exploded block into a drawing, preface the block name with an asterisk.

See also Attedit, Attdisp, Attext, Attredef, Ddatte, Ddinsert, Insert, Regen, Regenauto, Wblock, Wildcards, Xref, Xbind

Bmake

Bmake is the same as **Block,** except instead it displays the Block Definition dialog box. You can then insert, copy, mirror, move, rotate, scale, or save the block as an external file.

To Create a Block Using a Dialog Box

Command line: **Bmake**

Menu: Draw ➤ Block ➤ Make

Draw Toolbar: ⬚ Enter information in the dialog box.

Options

Block Name   Enter a name for the block in the edit box.

Select Objects   Clicking the box temporarily closes it so you can select objects in your drawing. Use any selection method at the *Select objects:* prompt to pick objects to include in the block. Pressing ↵ returns you to the dialog box.

Base Point   Clicking *Select Point>* returns you to the drawing, allowing you to specify an *Insertion base point:*, then reopens the dialog box.

List Block Names   Opens the Block Names In This Drawing dialog box to view existing blocks in your drawing.

Retain Objects   If checked, AutoCAD will retain the original entities after creating the block. Otherwise, the objects will be deleted.

See also   Block, Wblock

BMPOUT

*See **Import/Export***

Boundary/Bpoly

Boundary works like the **Pedit** command and makes a region or polyline boundary from overlapping objects. It displays a dialog box to automatically create a polyline boundary from enclosed objects by picking a point within the area. To display prompts at the command line, use **-Boundary**.

To Create an Enclosed Polyline or Region

Command Line: **Boundary** or **Bpoly**

Menu: Draw ➤ Boundary

1. Specify the object type (polyline or region), and define the boundary set and other parameters.

2. Click the *Pick Points* button in the Boundary Creation dialog box and pick a point within the connected objects. This highlights the boundary, then joins the objects into a polyline or region.

Boundary uses the same options and parameters as the **Bhatch** command. Refer to **Bhatch** for further details. Use **3Dpoly** to draw a 3D polyline with straight line segments. The **Pedit** command edits 3D polylines. **Bpoly** has been renamed to **Boundary**.

TIP Use the Esc key to cancel the command completely.

See also Area, Bhatch, Pedit, Polygon, Psfill, Region

-Boundary

-Boundary creates a region or polyline boundary from overlapping objects. The equivalent dialog box commands are **Boundary** and **Bpoly.**

To Create an Enclosed Polyline or Region at the Command Line

Command Line: **-Boundary**

1. **Advanced options/<Internal point>:** Pick a point within the area you wish to create an enclosed polyline or region, enter **u** to undo a selection, enter **A** for Advanced options or press ↵ to end your point selection.

2. If you entered A, the prompt **Boundary set/Island detection/ Object type/<eXit>:** appears with additional options:

   • Entering **B**, displays the "Specify candidate set for boundary, New/<Everything>:". prompt. If you enter **N,** you are prompted to "Select objects" to define the boundary set, otherwise, entering **E** reports "Selecting everything visible..." and returns you to step 1.

   • Entering **I**, then **Y** at the prompt "Do you want island detection? <Y>" treats objects within the outermost boundary as "islands." If you enter N, the prompt "Specify ray:, Nearest/+X/-X/+Y/-Y/Angle <Nearest>: " allowing you to set controls for AutoCAD to define the boundary object.

   • Entering **O**, then **R** to create the boundary as a region or **P** to define the boundary as polyline at the prompt "Region/Polyline/<current>:". Pressing ↵ specifies the current default and returns you to step 1.

   • Press ↵ to exit the command after setting one or more of the above options.

See Also Bhatch, Boundary, Hatch, Hatchedit; *System Variables:* Hpbound

Box

*See **Solid Modeling***

Break

Break erases a line, trace, circle, or arc, or a 2D polyline between two points.

To Use Break

Command line: **Break**

Menu: Modify ➤ Break

Modify Toolbar: Break

1. **Select object:** Pick an object to be broken.

2. **Enter second point (or F for first point):** Pick second point of break or enter **F** to specify first and second points.

Options

1 Point Breaks an object in one place, at the point of selection.

1 Point/Select Allows you to select the object first, and then specify the break point.

2 Points Allows you to break an object in two places. The *first* break is at the point of selection.

2 Points/Select Allows you select the object, and then specify the *first* break point.

If you use the cursor to pick the object, the "pick" point becomes the first point of the break. Pick the second point of the break or enter **F** to specify a different first break point. If you selected the object using a window, crossing window, wpolygon, cpolygon, fence, or a last or previous option, you are automatically prompted for a first and second point.

Break does not work on blocks, solids, text, shapes, 3D faces, or 3D polylines. You can now break objects that do not lie in a plane parallel to the current user coordinate system (UCS). Also, if you are not viewing the current UCS in plan, you may get the wrong result. Use the **Plan** command to view the current UCS in plan. When breaking circles, you must use the proper break-point selection sequence:

- In the case of a circle, a counterclockwise pick sequence causes the break to occur between the two break points.

BREAK

- A clockwise pick sequence causes the segment between the two points to remain and the rest of the circle to disappear.

You can break a line at a distance from a specified base point if you use tracking. After selecting the object, use the *F for first point* option, then Shift+click to open the cursor menu and pick *Tracking*. Once tracking is started, specify an object snap point, enter a distance, then press ↵ to end tracking. When the "Enter second point" prompt appears, specify the break distance.

See also   Change, Trim, UCS

Browser

Browser launches your installed Web browser.

To Access the Internet

Command line: **Browser**

Standard Toolbar: Launch Browser

Location <http://www.autodesk.com/acaduser>: Press ↵ or specify another location for your connection.

To use the Browser command, you must have 3.0 or later versions of Netscape Navigator 3.0 or Microsoft Internet Explorer 3.0 software installed on your computer.

Cal

Cal is an on-line calculator. It stores calculated values as variables that can be recalled any time during the current editing session. It can be used transparently to supply values in response to command prompts. **Cal** also allows you to translate between World and UCS coordinates.

To Use the Calculator

Command Line: **Cal** (or **'Cal**, to use transparently)

>>Expression: Enter the desired mathematical expression.

Cal evaluates vector (point), real, or integer expressions. The expressions can access existing geometry using the object snap functions such as Cen, End, and Ins. You may insert AutoLISP variables into the arithmetic expression and assign the value of the expression back to an AutoLISP variable. You may use these arithmetic and vector expressions in any AutoCAD command that expects points, vectors, or numbers.

Catalog/Dir

Catalog displays a list of files in a specified drive or directory folder.

To View a Catalog or Directory in a DOS Window

Command line: **Catalog**

Command line: **Dir**

File specification: Enter any drive letter, directory name, or wildcard character, as you would in DOS. If you give no specifications, **Catalog** displays the list for the current drive.

Both commands are stored in the Acad.pgp file. **Catalog** is assigned to the external DOS command **dir/w** and displays the directory in a DOS window with the DOS switch for wide. Dir invokes the DOS **dir** command and scrolls the directory in a DOS window as a list of filenames.

See also Acad.PGP

Chamfer

Chamfer joins two nonparallel lines with an intermediate line or bevel, or adds intermediate lines between the line segments of a 2D polyline. You can chamfer a spline, ellipse, 3D polyline, ray, xline, segments of polylines, polyline arcs as well as Lines and Polylines.

To Use Chamfer

Command line: **Chamfer**

Menu: Modify ➤ Chamfer

Modify Toolbar: [icon] Chamfer

1. **Polyline/Distance/Angle/Trim/Method<select first line>:** Pick first line or enter an option.

2. **Select second line:** Pick second line.

If the object is a 3D solid, the following prompts appear for step 3:

3. **Select base surface:**

   Next/<OK>: Enter N to select an adjacent surface, or ↵ to accept the surface as the base surface.

4. Specify the two edges of the base surface to chamfer.

Enter base surface distance <0.2500>: ↵ or, Enter a distance value.

Enter other surface distance <0.2500>: ↵ or, Enter another distance value.

5. Select individual or all edges to chamfer.

Loop/<Select edge>: Enter **L**, select an edge or press ↵ to select all edges. Loop switches to loop mode and prompts to select an *Edge* or *Select edge loop*.

Options

Polyline   Allows you to chamfer all line segments within a polyline. This option prompts you to select a two-dimensional polyline. All the joining polyline segments are then chamfered.

Distance   Allows you to specify the length of the chamfer. This option prompts you for the first and second chamfer distance, then sets the values as defaults. These are the distances measured from the intersection point of the two lines to the beginning of the chamfer.

Angle   Allows you to specify the angle of the chamfer from a selected point on the line segment. The prompts are:

Enter chamfer length on the first line <1.0000>:

Enter chamfer angle from the first line <0>:

Trim   Allows you to toggle the trim option *ON* or *OFF*, and set it as a default. Turning Trim *OFF* allows you to add a chamfer while retaining the original line segments.

Method   Allows you to establish a default method of chamfering, either by distance or angle.

You can chamfer objects that do not lie on the current user coordinate system (UCS). The two lines meet when the chamfer distances are set to 0 (the default value). If selected objects are not on the same layer, the chamfer line assumes all the properties of the current layer.

See also   Fillet; *System Variables:* Chamfera, Chamferb

Change

Change can alter several properties of an object. You can change all the properties of lines. Move line end points by selecting a point at the first prompt. If you select several lines, all of the end points closest to the selected point are moved to the new point. If the Ortho mode is on, the lines become parallel and their end points align with the selected point.

You can change the color, elevation, layer, line type, line type scale or thickness of arcs, circles, lines and polylines. You can also change the rotation angle, insertion point or layer assignment of a block.

To Change the Properties of an Object

Command line: **Change**

1. **Select objects:** Select objects to be changed.

2. **Properties/<Change point>:** Enter **P** to change the property of the selected object(s), or select a line and change its end point.

3. **Change what property (Color/Elev/LAyer/LType/LtScale/ Thickness) ?):** Enter the desired option.

4. Depending on what you have selected to change, some or all of the following prompts will appear:

   Enter text insertion point: Pick new location for text.

   Enter block insertion point: Pick new location for block.

   New style or press ENTER for no change: Enter style for text. The style must have previously been created using the **Style** command.

   New height <height>: Enter new height.

   New rotation angle <0>: Enter new rotation angle.

   New text <text>: Enter new text.

   New tag <tag name>: Enter new attribute tag name.

   New prompt <prompt>: Enter new attribute prompt.

   New default value <value>: Enter new attribute value.

Options

Properties   Changes the color, elevation, layer, line type, or thickness of an object.

Color   Prompts you for color to change selected objects to.

Elev   Prompts you for a new elevation in the objects Z axis.

LAyer   Prompts you for a new layer.

LType   Prompts you for a new line type.

LtScale   Prompts you for a new ltScale value for the selected object(s).

Thickness   Prompts you for a new Thickness in the object's Z axis.

The *Thickness* option will extrude a 2D line, arc, circle, or polyline into the Z axis. This option does not work on blocks, however. *Elev* changes an object's location in the Z axis. This option does not work on objects that are not in a plane parallel to the current UCS.

When you change an object's color, the object no longer has the color of the layer on which it resides. This can be confusing in complex drawings. To make an object the same color as its layer, enter **Bylayer** at the *Color* prompt.

See also   Chprop, Color, Ddmodify, Select, UCS

Chprop

Chprop works like the **Change** command except that **Chprop** allows you to change the properties of all object types regardless of their 3D orientation. However, the *Elev* option is not offered—use the **Move** command instead. The equivalent dialog box command is **Ddchprop**.

To Change an Object's Properties

Command line: **Chprop**

1.   **Select objects:** Select objects whose properties you wish to modify.

2.   **Change what property (Color/LAyer/LType/ltScale/ Thickness)?:** Enter the option.

Options

Color   Prompts you for a color to which selected objects will be changed.

LAyer   Prompts you for a new layer.

LType   Prompts you for a new line type.

LtScale   Prompts you for a new ltScale value for the selected object(s).

Thickness   Prompts you for new Thickness in the object's Z axis.

See also   Change, Color, Ddchprop, Elev, Select, UCS

Circle

Circle offers several methods for drawing circles, the default being to choose a center point and enter or pick a diameter or radius.

To Draw a Circle

Command line: **Circle**

Menu: Draw ➤ Circle ➤ Preset Options

Draw Toolbar: 🔘 Circle

1. **3P/2P/TTR/<Center point>:** Pick a center point or enter an option.

2. **Diameter/<Radius> <current default>:** Depending on the current default, provide a diameter or radius by dynamically dragging, entering the letter **D** or **R**, or enter a value.

   Selecting **TTR** prompts appear to enter two tangent osnap points and a radius.

1. **Enter Tangent spec:** Pick first osnap point

2. **Enter second Tangent spec:** Pick second osnap point

3. **Radius <current value>:** Specify a radius.

   The Draw ➤ Circle ➤ Tan, Tan, Tan pulldown menu option offers a method similar to the three point, allowing you to draw a circle by specifying three tangent points and automatically displaying Deferred Tangent autosnap points. Prompts for *First point:* , *Second point:* and *Third point:* appear to set the circle's size.

Options

3P **(3 Point)**   Allows you to define a circle based on three points. Once you select this option, you are prompted for a first, second, and third point. The circle will be drawn to pass through these points.

2P **(2 Point)**   Allows you to define a circle's diameter based on two points. Once you select this option, you are prompted to select the first and second point. The two points will be the opposite ends of the diameter.

TTR **(Tangent, Tangent, Radius)**   Allows you to define a circle based on two tangent points and a radius. The tangent points can be on lines, arcs or circles.

Color/Colour

Color/Colour sets the color of objects being drawn. Once you select a color, all objects will be given the selected color regardless of their layers, unless you specify *Bylayer* or *Byblock* as the color. Objects you drew before using the **Color** command are not affected. The dialog box equivalent is **Ddcolor**.

To Set the Color of Objects

Command line: **Color** or **Colour** (or **'Color** or **'Colour**, to use transparently).

New object color <current default>: Specify a color name, color number or option.

Options

Bylayer   Gives objects the color of the layer on which they are placed. It is the default color setting.

Byblock   Works on objects used in blocks. If such an object is assigned the Byblock color, it will take on the color of the layer in which the block is placed. Table 2 shows the color names that AutoCAD recognizes, and their number codes. You can enter any of these names or numbers—in fact, you can enter any number from 1 to 255. The color that is displayed depends on your display adapter and monitor, but the first seven colors are the same for most display systems.

TABLE 2:   Color Names Recognized by AutoCAD

Color Name	Color Number
Red	1
Yellow	2
Green	3
Cyan	4
Blue	5
Magenta	6
White	7
Bylayer	Color of the layer on which the object is located
Byblock	Color of the layer on which the block is located

Assign colors carefully, especially if you use them to distinguish different layers. A color control pop-up list is accessible through the Object Properties toolbar. Choosing *Other...* opens the Select Color dialog box.

See also   Change, Chprop, Ddcolor, Layer

Command-Line Editing

You can repeat previous commands line entries using the up and down arrow keys. AutoCAD has adapted standard Windows editing methods allowing the use of the insert, backspace, overwrite, end, home, delete, page up and page down keys at the command line. If you highlight a previously entered command and right click the mouse, a menu appears offering the *Paste to Cmdline* option. Selecting this option pastes the text at the command line.

Right clicking the mouse over the command line displays a pop-up menu to select the **Paste to Cmdline**, **Copy**, **Copy Hist**, **Paste** and **Preferences...** commands.

See also   Copy, Copy, Copy Hist, Paste, Preferences

Compile

To create your own text fonts and shapes, compile a shape/font description file. This file is an ASCII file that uses a special system of codes to describe your fonts or shapes. **Compile** displays a dialog box listing ASCII files with .SHB or .PFB extensions for converting into a form that lets AutoCAD read the descriptions and include them in a drawing.

To Compile Your Own Text Fonts

Command line: **Compile**

- When the *Filedia* system variable is set to 1, Compile opens the Select Shape or Font File dialog box, displaying .SHP extensions for Shape files or .PFB extensions for PostScript files. Enter a Shape/Font file name into the *Filename:* box to compile into a .SHX extension.

- When *Filedia* is set to 0 and Compile is entered at the command line, the following prompt appears:

Enter NAME of shape file: Enter the shape or font file name.

Load inserts compiled files into a drawing. Compiled PostScript font .PFB files load quicker in drawings.

Cone

See Solid Modeling

Convert

Convert converts 2D polylines and associative hatches, optimizing them as AutoCAD Release 14 objects.

Command line: **Convert**

1. **Hatch/Polyline/<All>:** Press ↵ to specify both hatch and polyine objects, enter **H** for hatch or **P** for polylines.

2. **Select/<All>:** Depending on what you enter for item 1, you can press ↵ to convert all hatches or polylines in the drawing, or enter an **S** to select specific objects.

NOTE Generally, polylines are converted automatically by the PLINETYPE system variable when drawings are saved in AutoCAD release 14.

System Variables: Plinetype

Config

See **Preferences, Command-line editing**

Copy

Copy copies a single object or a set of objects.

To Copy

Command line: **Copy**

Menu: Modify ➤ Copy

Modify Toolbar: Copy

1. **Select objects:** Select objects to be copied.

2. **<Base point or displacement>/Multiple:** Pick the reference or "base" point for copy or enter **M** for multiple copies. The **M** option instructs AutoCAD that you wish to make several copies and prompts you for the base point again.

3. **Second point of displacement:** Pick the copy distance and direction in relation to the base point or enter the displacement value.

Options

Multiple Allows you to make several copies of the selected objects. The second point is repeated until you press ↵ or Esc.

AutoCAD assumes you want to make copies within the current user coordinate system (UCS). However, you can make copies in 3D space by entering **0,0,0** as the base point and the desired X,Y,Z coordinates as the second point, or by using the **Osnap** overrides to pick objects in 3D space.

If you press ↵ at the "Second point:" prompt without entering a point value, the selected objects may be copied to an area that is off your current drawing. To recover, use the **Undo** command or **Zoom** entents. For multiple copying using grips, see **Move**.

See also   Array, Grips, Move, Multiple, Select

Copyclip

Copyclip uses the Windows Clipboard to copy objects from AutoCAD to other windows applications.

To Copy Objects to other Applications

Command line: **Copyclip**

Menu: Edit ➤ Copy

Standard Toolbar: 🗐Copy to Clipboard

Select objects: Select the object(s) you wish to Copy.

Right click or use Ctrl+C to copy highlighted text from the command line or AutoCAD text window or selected objects in the graphics area to the clipboard. When only text is selected, copyclip stores it in ASCII format.

See also   Copyhist, Copylink

Copyhist

Copyhist copies all text from the command line or history window to the Clipboard. The text can then be placed into other windows applications by choosing *Paste* from most standard windows pulldown menus or pressing Ctrl+V.

To Copy the AutoCAD Command Line History

Command line: **Copyhist**

All the text in the history window is copied to the clipboard.

Press the F2 function key to display the AutoCAD text window, then use your pick button to hightlight the text you wish to copy. Once highlighted, click the right mouse button to display the cursor menu and pick *Copy* or *Copy History*.

See also   Copyclip, Copylink, Command-line editing

Cutclip

Cutclip allows you to export vector and bitmap graphics from AutoCAD to other programs that accept graphics from the Clipboard. It also lets you exchange graphics between multiple AutoCAD sessions, or to import text to AutoCAD from a text-based application.

To Cut Objects

Command line: **Cutclip**

Menu: Edit ➤ Cut

Standard Toolbar: Cut to Clipboard

Select objects: Select the object(s) you wish to Cut.

Cutclip moves selected objects to the Windows Clipboard. Cutting deletes the selected objects from the current drawing and stores them on the Clipboard for pasting into another drawing or applicaiton. The **Cut** command can also be activated by using the control key sequence Ctrl+X.

See Also   Copyhist, Copylink, Pastclip, Pastespec

Copylink

Copylink copies the current graphics screen to the Windows Clipboard for linking to other OLE applications.

To Copylink Objects

Command line: **Copylink**

Menu: Edit ➤ Copylink

Once invoked, all objects displayed on the graphics screen are copied to the clipboard, then command prompt returns.

Pastespec allows you to paste and link the copied view into another document. Views of AutoCAD drawings in both modelspace and paperspace can be linked to and updated in other OLE applications. AutoCAD uses the current view when a single viewport is selected.

See also Pastespec, OLE

Cylinder
See Solid Modeling

Dblist

Dblist lists the properties of all objects in a drawing.

To Display Drawing Information
Command Line: **Dblist**

When you invoke **Dblist**, the screen switches to Text mode and the list of objects pauses at each screen of text. Press Escape to cancel the listing. **Dblist** is similar to the **List** command.

See Also ID, List

Ddattdef

Ddattdef opens the Attribute Definition dialog box that lets you create attribute definitions that can store textual and numeric data with a block.

To Use the Attribute Definition Dialog Box
Command Line: **Ddattdef**

Menu: Draw ➢ Block ➢ Define Attributes

Provide information as needed in the dialog box(es).

Options
Mode   Sets Invisible, Constant, Verify, and Preset modes.

Attribute   Sets Tag name, input Prompt, and default Value.

DDATTDEF

Insertion Point   Allows you to Pick Point or enter the XYZ coordinates.

Text Options   Sets text Justification, Text Style, Height, or Rotation.

Align below previous attribute   Locates an attribute tag below a previously defined attribute.

> **NOTE** Use **Change, Ddmodify,** or **Ddedit** to edit the attribute definition. The Properties icon (**Ai_propchk**) in the Object Properties Toolbar can also be used to edit attribute definitions. Attribute tags are always displayed in uppercase. AutoCAD replaces the tag name with the attribute value once the attribute definitions are inserted as a block.

See Also   Attdef, Change, Ddedit

Ddatte

Ddatte displays the Edit Attributes dialog box that lets you view and edit the attribute values of a single block. The equivalent command-line prompt is **Attedit**.

To Edit Attribute Values

Command Line: **Ddatte**

Menu: Modify ➤ Object ➤ Attribute ➤ Single

Modify II Toolbar: [icon] Edit Attribute

Select block: Pick the block containing the attribute(s) to edit. The Edit attributes dialog box appears containing the attribute prompts and values. Enter new attribute text or edit the existing attribute text by positioning the cursor at the appropriate location, deleting text, and typing your correction.

See Also   Attdef, Attedit, Attext, Ddattdef, Ddattext, Ddselect, Multiple

Ddattext

Ddattext displays an Attribute Extraction dialog box allowing you to convert attributes into external ASCII text files. These files can then be imported into database or spreadsheet programs. The equivalent command-line prompt is **Attext**.

To Convert Attributes to ASCII

Command Line: **Ddattext**

1. **File Format:** Pick CDF, SDF, or DXF format for the extracted file. (See **Attext** for descriptions of the file formats).

2. **Select Objects:** Temporarily exits the dialog box, allowing you to select the attribute entities.

3. **Template File...:** Opens the Template File dialog box, displaying a list box showing all .TXT files from which to make a selection for the corresponding edit box. A template file must have previously been created. A .TXT file extension is automatically assigned to the file name in the edit box if you don't enter an extension.

4. **Output File...:** Opens the Output File subdialog box, displaying a list box showing all .TXT files from which to make a selection for the corresponding edit box. When an output file name is selected, the current drawing file name is automatically assigned to the file name in the edit box but with a .TXT extension.

NOTE The Template File... button is disabled when the .DXF format is active.

See Also   Attdef, Attedit, Attext, Ddattdef, Multiple

Ddchprop

Ddchprop opens the Change Properties dialog box that lets you change properties of all object types. The equivalent command-line prompt is **Chprop.**

To Change an Object's Properties

Command Line: **Ddchprop**

Select objects: Select the object(s) whose properties you wish to modify.

Options

Color   Opens the Select Color dialog box to set object colors. (See **Color/Colour/Ddcolor**.)

Layer   Opens the Select Layer dialog box, displaying a list of layer names to make selection.

Linetype   Opens the Select Linetype dialog box, displaying *Bylayer*, *Byblock*, and a list of linetypes to make selection.

Linetype Scale   Edit box to change selected object's linetype scale value.

Thickness   Edit box to change an object's 3D thickness.

See Also   Ai_propchk, Change, Chprop, Color, Ddlmodes, Layer, Linetype, Thickness

Ddcolor

Ddcolor opens the Select Color dialog box and allows you to set the color for new objects. Once you select a color, all objects will be given the selected color regardless of their layers, unless you specify *Bylayer* as the color. The equivalent command-line prompt is **Color** or **Colour.**

To Set the Object Color

Command Line: **Ddcolor**

Menu: Format ➤ Color...

Object Properties Toolbar: Color Control pop-up list, Other...

Options

Bylayer   Gives objects the color of the layer on which they are placed. It is the default color setting.

Byblock   Works on objects used in blocks. If such an object is assigned the Byblock color, it will take on the color of the layer in which the block is placed.

See Also   Color, Layer

Ddedit

Ddedit changes annotation (text) or attribute definition by displaying a line of text. **Ddedit** displays a line of text in a dialog box for editing and viewing. You can position a cursor to delete single characters, make corrections, or add to the text. The equivalent command-line prompt is **Change.**

To Edit Text Objects

Command Line: **Ddedit**

Menu: Modify ➤ Object ➤ Text

Modify II Toolbar: Edit Text

<Select an annotation object>/Undo: Pick the line of text or attribute definition to edit. Depending upon your object selection, the Edit Text dialog box will open (with a Text edit box) or the Edit Attribute Definition dialog box will open (with the Tag, Prompt, and Default edit boxes).

> **NOTE** If an attribute has not yet been made into a block, you can edit the tag name, attribute prompt, or default value.

Options

Annotation   Edit box for revising text.

Tag   Edit box to change the tag name.

Prompt   Edit box to change the attribute prompt.

Default   Edit box to change the attribute value.

> **NOTE** Every time you finish editing one line of text, AutoCAD prompts you to select another text or Attdef object rather than returning you to the command prompt. To exit the **Ddedit** command, press ↵ (do not enter any text at the last "Text:" or "Attdef:" prompt), or the Escape key.

See Also   Attdef, AutoLISP, Chtext, Change, Ddattdef, Mtext

Ddgrips

Ddgrips displays the Grips dialog box for enabling or disabling grips, also to change color and size. **Grips** allows fast editing of objects on the screen. The equivalent command line prompt is **Grips.**

To Open the Grips Dialog Box

Command Line: **Ddgrips** (or **'Ddgrips**, to use transparently)

Menu: Tools ➤ Grips…

Provide information as needed in the dialog box(es).

Options

Select Settings   Lets you *Enable Grips* to pick objects for editing using a grip box. *Enable Grips Within Blocks* determines whether one grip appears for the block or multiple grips appear for the entities in the block.

Grip Colors   Opens the Select Color dialog box to define a color for *Unselected* grips that are not filled in or for *Selected* solid grips.

Grip Size   Controls grip size using a slider bar and adjacent tile box.

Grips can be set with their specific system variables and are associated with specific AutoCAD commands, including **Stretch**, **Move** (multiple copy), **Rotate**, **Scale**, and **Mirror**.

See Also   Grips; *System Variables:* Gripblock, Gripcolor, Griphot, Grips, Gripsize

Ddim

Ddim opens the Dimension Styles dialog box and allows you to set and visually control dimension and extension line settings, arrow type and size, text location and format, measurement units, dimension text appearance, and colors. Dimension styles can now have "families" of different settings. From a parent style, you can specify different settings for each member of the family.

To Control and Modify Dimension Styles

Command Line: **Ddim** (or **'Ddim**, to use transparently)

Menu: Format ➤ Dimension Style...

Dimension Toolbar: Dimension Style

The Dimension Styles list box contains the names of all the dimension styles that were created for the current drawing. To activate a style, pick it from the list box with your cursor and the style will appear in the Name edit box. The Family settings allow you to specify variations in the style for each of the related dimension types: *Linear, Radial, Angular, Diameter, Ordinate,* or *Leader*. Once you have selected the appropriate dimension style, use the Geometry, Format, and Annotation sub-dialog boxes to make changes to the Dimension Style.

Options

Geometry   The Geometry sub-dialog box allows you to manipulate the appearance of the geometry and overall scale of the dimension. All Geometry settings are stored as *Dimension Variables*.

Dimension Line: Controls the appearance of the dimension line. You can *Suppress* the display of dimension lines when they are outside the extension lines; *1st suppresses* the first dimension line and stores the value in the variable *Dimsd1*; *2nd suppresses* the second

D DGRIPS

dimension line and stores the value in the variable *Dimsd2*. When you are using oblique strokes (ticks) rather than arrows on the dimension line, the *Extension* option allows you to specify the distance that the dimension line is to extend beyond the extension line (*Dimdle* variable). The *Spacing* option allows you to enter a distance for the spacing between the dimension lines of a baseline dimension (*Dimdli* variable). The *Color* option allows you to set the color for a dimension line via the Select Color dialog box, or by entering a color value in the text box (*Dimclrd* variable).

Extension Line: Controls the appearance of the extension lines. The *Suppress* option suppresses the display of extension lines; *1st* suppresses the first extension line and stores the value in the variable *Dimse1*; *2nd* suppresses the second extension line and stores the value in the variable *Dimse2*. The *Extension* option allows you to specify a distance to extend the extension line above the dimension line (*Dimexe* variable). The *Origin Offset* allows you to specify a distance for the offset between the extension lines and the origin points (*Dimexo* variable). The *Color* option allows you to display and set the color for an extension line, via the Select Color dialog box or by entering a color value in the text box (*Dimclre* variable).

Arrowheads: Controls the appearance of the arrowheads. By default the second arrowhead is set the same as the first selected and the value is stored in the *Dimblk* variable. You may also specify different arrowheads by picking the image box or from the popup list for the first and second arrowheads; in that case, the values are stored in the *Dimblk1* and *Dimblk2* variables. The *Size* option displays and sets the size of arrowheads (*Dimasz* variable). To change the size, enter a value in the text box. Selecting *User Arrow...* from the preset options shown in the 1st and 2nd Arrowhead drop boxes, opens the User Arrow dialog box and allows you to load a user-defined arrowhead (*Dimsah* variable). Several new arrowheads, including an Architectural Tick, have been added to the list.

Center: Controls the appearance of center marks and lines for the diameter and radial dimensions used by the **Dimcenter**, **Dimdiameter**, and **Dimradius** commands. When you are using **Dimdiameter** or **Dimradius**, the center mark will be drawn only if you position the dimension line outside the circle or the arc. The *Mark* option creates a center mark; the *Line* option creates a center line; the *None* option creates no center mark or line; and the *Size* option displays and sets the size of the center mark or line. All of these values are stored in the *Dimcen* variable: a center mark is stored as a positive value; a center line is stored as a negative value; None is stored as a zero; and the size is stored as an actual value.

DDIM

Overall Scale: Sets the overall scale factor of your drawing by specifying size, distances, or offsets and storing it in the *Dimscale* variable.

Scale to Paper Space: AutoCAD calculates the scale factor based on scaling between the current model-space viewport and paper space. Selecting Scale to Paper Space deactivates Feature Scaling and converts the *Dimscale* value to 0.0.

Format The Format sub-dialog box allows you to set the location of dimension text, arrowheads, leader lines, and the dimension line. All Format settings are stored as *Dimension Variables*.

User Defined: Allows you to pick a location for dimension text by specifying a position at the *Dimension line* location prompt (*Dimupt* variable). If this option is not selected, AutoCAD determines the location of dimension text using the *Horizontal Justification* settings.

Force Line Inside: Draws dimension lines between extension lines even when arrowheads are placed outside the extension lines (*Dimtofl* variable).

Fit: Controls the placement of text and arrowheads inside or outside the extension lines based on the available space between the extension lines (*Dimfit* variable).

Horizontal Justification: Controls the horizontal justification of text along dimension and extension lines (*Dimjust* variable) by picking from the pop-up list or clicking on the image box. The *Centered* option centers the text between the extension lines; *1st Extension Line* left-justifies the text along the dimension line, near the first extension line; *2nd Extension Line* right-justifies the text along the dimension line, near the second extension line; *Over 1st Extension Line* positions the text parallel to the first extension line; *Over 2nd Extension Line* positions the text parallel to the second extension line.

Text: Determines the position of dimension text inside and outside the extension lines. *Inside:* when this is selected, text inside the extension lines will always be horizontal, rather than aligned with the dimension line (*Dimtih* variable). *Outside:* when this is selected, text outside the extension lines will always be horizontal (*Dimtoh* variable). Pick one or more of the check boxes or click on the image box.

Vertical Justification: Controls the vertical justification of dimension text along the dimension line (*Dimtad* variable) by picking from the popup list or clicking on the image box. *Centered* centers the text between the extension lines; *Above* positions the text above the dimension line, at a distance determined by the *Annotation: Gap* option; *Outside* positions the text on the side of the dimension line farthest away from the defining points; and *JIS* sets the text position to conform to Japanese Industrial Standards.

Annotation   The Annotation sub-dialog box allows you to specify the measurement units for dimensions, alternate measurement units, tolerances for dimension text, dimension text style variables, and linear and paper space scale factors. All Annotation settings are stored as *Dimension Variables*.

Primary Units: Controls the display of primary measurement units and also lets you add a *Text Prefix* or *Text Suffix* to the default dimension text by entering labels in each edit box (*Dimpost* variable). The Units button opens the Primary Units dialog box and allows you to set all the measurement variables. The Units section lets you select the unit format, Decimal, Scientific, Engineering, Architectural (stacked), Fractional (stacked), Architectural, Fractional or Windows Desktop (*Dimunit* variable). The *Angles* section lets you select the angle format, Decimal degrees, Degrees/Minutes/Seconds, Grads, Radians, and Surveyor. In the Dimension and Tolerance sections you can specify the *Precision* or number of decimal places to be used in measurements (*Dimdec*) and also the *Zero Suppression* setting (*Dimzin*). The Zero Suppression setting contains check boxes for setting the appearance of *Feet* and *Inches* as well as suppressing *Leading* and *Trailing* zeros in dimension text. In the *Scale* section, the *Linear* option sets a length scale variable, which specifies a global scale factor for dimension length (*Dimlfac* variable). Checking the *Paper Space Only* box allows you to dimension accurately in paper space using model space units. AutoCAD stores the length scale for paper space as negative value in the *Dimlfac* variable.

Alternate Units: This option allows you to set alternate unit dimensioning. The variables are identical to those in the Primary Units, including labels for alternate dimension text *Prefix* and *Suffix*. The *Dimaltd, Dimaltf, Dimalttd, Dimalttz, Dimaltu, Dimaltz*, and *Dimaunit* variables are all manipulated in this option.

Tolerance: This option allows you to append dimension tolerances, with a choice of *None, Unilateral* (a plus/minus expression of tolerance in one direction), *Bilateral* (a plus/minus expression in both directions), *Limits* (a limit expression with the maximum value over the minimum value), and *Basic*. The Basic option creates dimension text with a box drawn to its full extents. Depending upon the choice selected, you will need to specify *Upper* and/or *Lower* Value, and *Text Justification* (Top/Middle/Bottom) and *Height* for the tolerance text. The variables *Dimtol*, *Dimlim*, *Dimtm Dimtp*, and *Dimtfac* are used to store the tolerance values.

Text: This option allows you to manipulate text style, height, text gap, and text color. The *Style* list box allows you to display and set the current style for dimension text (*Dimtxsty* variable). Use the **Style** command if you need to modify a style for dimension text. *Height* allows you to set the current dimension text height. If text style height is set to 0, you can enter a dimension text *Height*, which will be stored in the *Dimtxt* variable. The *Gap* option specifies the text gap (*Dimgap* variable), which determines a number of dimension text positioning variables: the distance around dimension text at the dimension line break; the distance of dimension text above a dimension line; and the position of the box drawn around tolerance text (*Tolerance Option: Basic Method*). The *Color* option allows you to set the color for dimension text (*Dimclrt* variable), via the Select Color dialog box, or by entering a color value in the text box. The selected color is shown in the color box.

Round Off: This option controls the rounding off of all dimension measurements (*Dimrnd* variable). A value of 0.25 will round all measurements to the nearest 0.25 unit; a value of 1.0 rounds all measurements to the nearest unit. The rounding value is not applied to angular dimensions.

Ddinsert

Ddinsert opens the Insert dialog box for inserting a block into your drawing. You can preset the block's insertion point, scale, and rotation angle, or insert the block as an exploded block. The equivalent command line prompt is **Insert**.

To Insert a Block

Command Line: **Ddinsert**

Menu: Insert ➤ Insert Block

Draw Toolbar: 🔲 Insert Block

Insert Toolbar: 🔲 Insert Block

Provide information as needed in the dialog box(es).

Options

Block   Opens the Defined Blocks in this Drawing subdialog box offering an alphabetical list of the blocks that have been defined in your drawing. Select from this list for a block to insert. The *Pattern* edit box can be used as a query with wildcards to filter block names. Picking a block name from the list with your cursor duplicates the block name in the *Selection* edit box.

File   Opens the Select Drawing File subdialog box showing a list of *Directories* and drawing *Files*. An image tile box displays selected drawings. Queries can be made using the *Pattern* edit box, with the results displayed in the *File* edit box. During the process the *Type it* and *Default* buttons are disabled. Use the *Find File* button to open the Browse/Search dialog box if you need to search for files.

Specify Parameters on Screen   Allows you to specify the block's insertion point from the command line or by picking a point on the screen. When enabled, you can avoid prompts by preselecting *Insertion Point*, *Scale*, and *Rotation* by recording that information in their appropriate edit boxes. When the *Attdia* variable value is 1, an Attribute Edit dialog box appears during block insertion.

Explode   Inserts an exploded version of the block into your drawing. The equivalent command-line procedure requires an asterisk before the block name:

    Block name (or ?): *blockname

See Also   Base, Ddatte, Insert; *System Variables:* Attdia, Attreq, Insbase

Ddlmodes/Ddltype

Ddlmodes, **Ddltype**, **Layer** and **Linetype** commands all display the Layer & Linetype Properties dialog box for control of layers and linetypes properties. Use the **Layer** and **Ddltype** commands to activate their appropriate tabbed sections of the dialog box. Use -**Layer** and -**Linetype** to display prompts at the command line.

To Invoke Ddlmodes Layer Control

Command Line: **Ddlmodes** (or '**Ddlmodes**, to use transparently), **Ddltype** (or '**Ddltype**, to use transparently), **Layer** or **Linetype**

Menu: Format ➤ Layer

Menu: Format ➤ Linetype

Object Properties Toolbar: Layer

Object Properties Toolbar: | —— ByLayer | Linetype Control

DDLMODES/DDLTYPE

The dialog box contains two tabbed sections: *Layer* and *Linetype*. Each tab contains a *Details<<* button that expands the dialog box and displays edit boxes, check boxes and pop-up lists specific to its section. Based on the columns function, clicking on a heading sorts layers or linetypes in descending or ascending order. Column widths are drag divisions that can be resized by pressing the pick button on your cursor over the vertical line to the right of the column until an anchor symbol appears. Drag the column heading to expand or shrink its size. Double click the vertical line to restore the column's default width. Use the right click menu in their appropriate tabs to *Select All* and *Clear All* layers or linetypes. You can also select single or groups of names by holding the Shift key or Control key. Triple click a layer name in the list box and a box appears around it, allowing you to move your cursor over any character to rename an exiting layer.

Provide information as needed in the dialog box(es).

Options

Layer Tab   The layer list box contains the following eight drag division headings: *On, Freeze in All Viewports, Freeze in Current Viewport, Freeze in New Viewports, Lock, Color* and *Linetype*. Depending on the particular layer icon, clicking the graphic image will set the layers status as On or Off, Frozen or Thawed, Locked or Unlocked, open the Set Color dialog box or display the Select Linetype dialog box.

Current   Sets and identifies the current layer.

Show   Click the drop-down list to select from pre-defined layer filters which may or may not be xref dependent and are frozen in current or new viewports. Choose Set Filter dialog to set layer groups or filters using wildcards based on name, state, color, layer and/or linetype. A check box offers the option to *Appy this filter to the layer control on the Object Properties toolbar*. Pick the *Reset* button to restore all filters to their default values.

New   Creates new editable default layer names Layer1, Layer2, and so forth. Once a new default layer is created in the list box, press ↵ immediately if you wish to add default sequential layer names. Additional layers can also be created within a newly selected layer edit box if separated with commas. If a layer in the list box is highlighted, new layers automatically inherit their properties.

Delete   Purges any unused layers.

Details   Expands the Layer tabbed section providing an alternate method to create new layer names and set layer status. New or less experienced users can click *Details<<* to access the more conventional edit and check boxes to manage layers.

Name   Click new for a default Layer name, which can be renamed or edit an existing layer name.

Color   Click the pop-up list to select a layers assigned color or pick *Other...* to open the standard Select Color dialog box.

Linetype   Click the pop-up list to select from pre-loaded linetype.

On   Displays On/Off status of layers.

Freeze in All Viewports   Displays Freeze/Thaw status of layers in all viewports.

Freeze in Current Viewports   Displays Freeze/Thaw status of layers in current viewports.

Freeze in New Viewports   Displays Freeze/Thaw status of layers for new viewports.

Lock   Displays Lock/Unlock status of layers. Clicking the *Retain changes to xref-dependent layers* check box toggles the *Visretain* system variable on and off.

Linetype Tab   The linetype list box contains the following three drag division headings: *Linetype, Appearance* and *Description*. The appearance column provides a graphic replica for each linetype.

Current   Sets and identifies the current linetype.

Show   Allows you to set the same filters as described for the layer tab.

Load   Opens the Load & Reload Linetypes dialog to view and select predefined linetypes stored in the Acad.LIN file. The right click mouse menu allows you to *Select All* or *Clear All* linetypes.

File   Open the Select Linetype File dialog box for user-defined linetypes stored in alternate .LIN files.

List box   Click the drag division to sort by Linetype or Description in the list box.

Delete   Purges any highlighted unused linetypes.

Details   Expands the *Linetype* tab with *Name* and *Description* edit boxes to edit names and linetype descriptions, as well as set a linetypes *Global Scale Factor (Ltscale), Current Object Scale (Celtscale)* and *ISO pen width.* When you select a pen width from the ISO linetypes list, the linetype scale is updated to conform to the ISO Standard for that width. Clicking the *Use paper space units for scaling* toggles the *Psltscale* system variable On and Off.

See Also   Color, Ddcolor, Layer, Linetype, Mspace, Mview, Pspace, Rename; *System Variables:* Tilemode, Viewports, Vplayer, Celscale, Psltscale, Visretain

Ddmodify

Ddmodify opens a dialog box specific to the type of object selected, including 3dfaces, arc, associative hatch, attribute definitions, body, block, circle, dimension, ellipse, external reference, leader, line, mtext, point, polyline, ray, region, shape, solid, spline, trace, text, viewport or xline. The upper portion of each dialog box contains a Properties section to modify color, linetype, layer name, thickness, and handle number.

To Modify an Object

Command Line: **Ddmodify**

Object PropertiesToolbar: ▦ Properties (For single object selection only, otherwise runs **Ddchprop**)

Select one object to modify: Pick the object you wish to change. Provide information as needed in the dialog box(es).

Options

The following controls are common to all the Modify dialog boxes:

Color   Picking this button or its adjacent color swatch displays the Select Color subdialog box to change an object's color. (See **Color/Colour**, **Ddcolor**.)

Layer   Opens the Select Layer subdialog box to change an object's layer by highlighting it in the *Current Layer* list box or entering it in the *Set Layer Name* edit box.

Linetype   Opens the Select Linetype subdialog box to view and change linetype for selected objects from a list or edit box. (See **Ddlmodes/Ddltype** for loading layers.)

Handle   Displays the AutoCAD "handle" or unique identifier associated with the object selected. The Handle identifier is not editable; however, if the *Handles* system variable is entered as Off at the command, the Handle: label is None.

Thickness   An edit box to enter an object's thickness value.

Linetype Scale   An edit box to change an object's Ltscale value.

Other Options

The control options presented vary depending upon the type of object selected, including a 3D face, 3D solid, arc, attribute definition, block insertion, body, circle, dimension, ellipse, external reference, hatch, image, leader, line, mtext, multiline, point, polyline, ray, region, shape, solid, spline, text, tolerance, trace, viewport and xline. The following controls are found in one or more of the Modify dialog boxes:

Center   Edit boxes to change the radius value then display its Diameter, Circumference and Area.

X,Y,Z   Edit boxes for relocating an object's initial coordinates.

Pick Point   If you are using the current UCS (user coordinate system), you can temporarily exit the dialog box to pick a new point on the screen, using your cursor or entering coordinates from the command line.

Scale and Rotation   Edit boxes to update the object's XYZ scale and rotation.

Justify   Opens a pop-up list of text justifications.

Style   Opens a pop-up list of text styles currently defined in your drawing by the **Style** command. Additional check boxes are included to toggle *Text* as Right Side Up/Upside Down or Forward/Backward, and to select *Mode* as Invisible, Constant, Verify, and/or Preset.

Radius and Angle   Edit boxes to change an arc angle's *Radius*, *Start Angle*, and *End Angle* while displaying Total Angle and Arc Length.

Tag   Edit box to change an attribute's tag value.

Prompt   Edit box to modify an attribute's prompt label.

Default   Edit box to alter an attribute's default assignment.

Height, Rotation, Width Factor, and Obliquing   Edit boxes to change each property.

Size, Rotation, Width Factor and Obliquing   Edit boxes to change each property using the current UCS to define angles and points.

Columns and Rows   Edit boxes to create a rectangular array of a block.

Col Spacing and Row Spacing   Edit boxes to set the columns and row spacing for a rectangular array of a block. This feature duplicates the **Minsert** command and works on a single block as well as Minsert blocks.

Radius   Edit box lets you enter a new radius while displaying the Diameter, Circumference, and Area of a circle.

Columns and Rows   Edit boxes to create a rectangular array of an external reference (xref).

Vertex Listing   Lists successive vertices of coordinate X, Y, and Z values for polylines.

Fit/Smooth   Offers option buttons for changing the type of line or surface curve fitting from None to Quadratic, Cubic, Bezier, or Curve Fit.

Mesh   Provides toggles to set Closed or Open mesh in the M or N direction for polylines. Also provides boxes accepting a range between 2 and 200 to control the accuracy of surface approximation in the M and N directions when using surface fit for a 3D polyline mesh. The edit boxes store the system variables *Surfu* and *Surfv*.

Polyline   Displays check boxes to confirm a Closed polyline and to establish an Ltgen (linetype generation) pattern.

Visibility   Toggles to make a 3Dface's edges invisible. Assigning the system variable *Splframe* to 1 makes all edges visible regardless of the visibility settings.

NOTE The Properties tool icon runs the **Ddmodify** command when selecting a single object, otherwise, AutoCAD uses the **Ddchprop** command.

See Also   Arc, Attdef, Block, Circle, Ddattdef, Dimensioning Commands, Dtext, Layer, Line, Pline, Point, Shape, Solid, Text, 3D Face, Trace, Viewport, Xref

Ddosnap

Ddosnap displays the Osnap Settings dialog box with tabbed sections for Running Osnap and AutoSnap. The Running Osnap tab allows you to have multiple object snap modes active while picking specific geometric points on an object and to set the target box size for your graphic's cursor crosshairs. To override a running osnap, enter the specific osnap at the command line. The AutoSnap tab offers you choices to set graphic methods for selecting points. You can set controls for a marker, magnet, and snap tip.The equivalent command-line commands are **-Osnap, Aperture, Autosnap**.

To Invoke the Ddosnap Osnaps

Command Line: **Ddosnap** (or **'Ddosnap**, to use transparently)

Menu: Tools ➤ Object Snap Settings...

Standard Toolbar: [icon] Object Snap Flyout   [icon] Object Snap Settings

Object Snap Toolbar: [icon] Object Snap Settings

Select settings as appropriate in the dialog box.

Options

Running Osnap Tab   Activating one or more pick boxes in the Select Settings section lets your pick location determine the osnap modes applied. For example, if both the Endpoint and Midpoint boxes are checked, AutoCAD automatically selects the mode based on which point is closer to the target box. Position your cursor over the object, then use the TAB key to cycle through checked snap settings. Depending on the settings, when an object snap box is checked, an associated marker and snap tip appears. Each mode can be overridden at the command line by entering the uppercase letters shown:

ENDpoint	Picks the end point of objects.
MIDpoint	Picks the midpoints of lines and arcs.
CENter	Picks the center of circles and arcs.
NODe	Picks a point object. (See **Ddptype.**)
QUAdrant	Picks a main point on an arc or circle.
INTersection	Picks the intersection of objects.
INSertion	Picks the insertion point of blocks and text.
PERpendicular	Picks the point on an object perpendicular to the last point.
TANgent	Picks a tangent point on a circle or arc.
NEArest	Picks the point on an object nearest to the cursor.
APParent Intersection	Picks the apparent intersection of two dimensionally separated lines.
QUIck	Shortens the time it takes AutoCAD to find an object snap point by stopping as soon as it finds one object. Quick does not work in conjunction with INTersect.

Aperture Size   This section lets you adjust the aperture box size by moving the slider bar and viewing it in the adjacent tile box.

Clear All   Turns off all checked osnap settings .

DDOSNAP

Automatic Snap Tab   One or more automatic snap values can be set as active at the command line using the *Autosnap* system variable. See *System Variables* for a list of autosnap values.

Select Settings   Controls method and appearance of active object snap settings.

Marker   Toggles on and off the display of a unique geometric shape for each object snap mode when your aperture box is placed over a snap point.

Magnet   Toggles on and off the locking feature for selected object snaps at their snap point.

Snap Tip   Toggles on and off the tooltip or identification for the specified snap location.

Marker Size   This section lets you adjust the marker size by moving the slider bar and viewing it in the adjacent tile box.

Marker Color   Pick from the pop-up list to changes the markers color.

NOTE Entering **Osnap** at the command line and pressing ↵ at the Object snap modes: prompt will also cancel all osnap modes.

See Also   Aperture, Osnap, Point Filters, *System Variables:* Aperture, Osmode, Autosnap

Ddptype

Ddptype opens the Point Style dialog box to select and control the appearances of points and to place point objects in your drawing, using the Node Osnap override. Points also appear as markers for the **Divide** and **Measure** commands.

To Set a Point Style

Command Line: **Ddptype** (or **'Ddptype**, to use transparently)

Menu: Format ➤ Point Style...

Select a point style, and define the point size.

Options

The dialog box offers 16-point mode image tiles. Pick the desired tile, then use the *Point Size* edit box to adjust point size.

Point Size   Edit box for setting point size. Selecting an option button changes the size specifications from Relative to Absolute as described below.

Set Size Relative to Screen   Option button to set point size as percentage of screen size.

Set Size in Absolute Units   Option button to set actual point size based on absolute units.

> **NOTE**   Each point style has an associated integer value or pdmode. For example, the node number for a cross is 2, a circle is 33 and its combined shape is 34. Different node types can also be set at the command line with the pdmode system variable by entering the sum of the active modes.

See Also   Point; *System Variables:* Pdmode, Pdsize

Ddrename

Ddrename opens the Rename dialog box to change the name of a block, dimension style, layer, linetype, text style, user coordinate system, named view, or viewport configuration.

To Activate the Rename Dialog Box

Command Line: **Ddrename**

Menu: Format ➤ Rename...

Select the appropriate object from the Named Objects list box.

Options

Selecting the object from the *Named Objects* list box registers associated names in the *Items* list box. Pick the item to be renamed and it will appear in the *Old Name* edit box.

Old Name   Enter item to be renamed or pick from *Items* list box. Use wildcards for renaming groups of objects with common characters. For example, hold the Shift or Ctrl key to select multiple layers (layer1, layer2, layer3), then enter a portion of the modified name (new*) in the Rename To edit box.

Rename To: Enter new name of item(s) shown in the *Old Name* edit box, using wildcards for groups of objects with common characters, then pick the *Rename To* box. The renamed objects will appear in the Items list box.

> **TIP**   You can also use **Ddrename** to find out which objects are in use in a current drawing.

See Also   Rename, Wildcard Characters

Ddrmodes

Ddrmodes opens the Drawing Aids dialog box to change several mode settings by accessing the functions for **Ortho**, **Fill** (Solid Fill), **QText**, **Blipmode**, **Groups**, **Snap**, **Grid**, **Isoplane**, and the system variable *Highlight*.

To Open the Ddrmodes Dialog Box

Command Line: **Ddrmodes** (or **'Ddrmodes**, to use transparently)

Menu: Tools ➤ Drawing Aids...

Select the desired function from the dialog box.

Options

When you issue **Ddrmodes**, the following options appear as check-boxes in which you can either select an option or enter a distance value.

Modes Pick boxes to toggle *Ortho* mode, *Solid Fill*, *Quick Text*, *Blips*, *Hatch* and *Highlight*. Ortho mode forces lines to be drawn vertically or horizontally following the orientation of the crosshairs. The *Fill* command or Fillmode system variable makes areas of solid fill, filled or not for solids, traces and polylines. Quick Text toggles the **Qtext** command or Qtextmode system variable to temporarily replace text with rectangles to reduce drawing regeneration. Blips are toggled on or off with the *Blipmode* system variable, placing tiny crosses on the screen when you select points. *Hatch* determines which object will be selected when you use associative hatching. When toggled on, selection includes the associative hatch and its boundary objects. The *Highlight* system variable controls the ghosting appearance of objects when selected. *Groups* toggles automatic group selection on or off.

Snap Picking *On* sets the Snap mode, while the *X Spacing*, *Y Spacing*, and *Snap Angle* edit boxes let you adjust the spacing and angle of the X and Y axis. *X Base* and *Y Base* edit boxes let you enter a Snap basepoint's X and Y coordinates. The F9 function key or the Ctrl+B combination performs the same toggle function as the Snap pick box. *Snap Angle* values determine the orientation of crosshairs on the screen.

Grid Picking *On* toggles Grid mode on and off, to display a series of reference dots on the screen. Edit boxes for *X Spacing* and *Y Spacing* allow you to set the same intervals for your Grid and Snap distances.

Isometric Snap/Grid Picking *On* switches your drawing to an isometric mode. Option buttons set the cursor orientation for *Left*, *Top*, and *Right* drawing planes. These isoplanes can also be toggeled through by using Crtl +E, when the isometric snap/grid is on.

See Also   Blipmode, Dtext, Fill, Grid, Isoplane, Ortho, Qtext, Snap; *System Variables:* Gridmode, Gridunit, Orthomode, Pickstyle, Snapang, Snapbase, Snapisopair, Snapmode, Snapstyl, Snapunit, Hpang, Hpbound, Hpdouble, Hpname, Hpscale, and Hpspace

---

Ddselect

Ddselect opens the Object Selection Settings dialog box to define your method for selecting objects.

To Set Object Modes

Command Line: **Ddselect** (or **'Ddselect**, to use transparently)

Menu: Tools ➤ Selection...

Provide information as needed in the dialog box(es).

Options

Selection Modes   Multiple settings can be configured from this section. *Noun/Verb Selection:* adds a target box to the graphics cursor for selecting objects prior to issuing specific commands, thus permitting the cursor to function as a pickbox or drag a window. Table 3 shows the commands that support noun/verb selections.

TABLE 3:   Commands Allowing You to Use the Cursor as a Pick Box

Array	Dview	Move
Block	Erase	Rotate
Change	Explode	Scale
Chprop	Hatch	Stretch
Copy	List	Wblock
Ddchprop	Mirror	

The Selection Modes section also offers the following combinations for object selection methods: *Use Shift to Add:*, which allows you to select objects. Once a selection set is defined you must hold the shift key to add more objects to the set. If shift is not held down, the original selection set is discarded and a new one is started for *Noun/Verb Selection* sets; *Press and Drag:,* which permits you to hold down the pick button, drag, then release, for creating a selection window; *Implied Windowing:,* which enables you to use a selection window by picking from left to right, or use a crossing window by picking from right to left at the *Select objects:* prompt; *Object Grouping,* which toggles object grouping on or off; *Associative Hatch,* controls object selection for associative hatched objects; *Default:,* which returns the Selection Mode settings to their original Noun/Verb Selection and Implied Windowing.

Pickbox Size   This section furnishes a slider bar with an image tile to dynamically alter your pickbox size.

Object Sort Method   This section opens the Object Sort Method subdialog box and lets you rearrange the following sort methods for entities in your database. In most cases, you will not want to edit the sort order for object snaps or regens. However, you may want to use Object Selection to control which of two overlapping lines are selected when you pick them. Plotting and Postscript allow you to determine the overlay of screened or hatched areas.

* Object Selection
* Object Snap
* Redraws
* Regens
* Plotting
* PostScript Output

See Also   Ddgrips, Grips; *System Variables:* Noun/Verb Selection-Pickfirst, Use Shift to Add-Pickadd, Press and Drag-Pickdrag, Implied Windowing-Pickauto, Pickbox Size-Pickbox, Object Grouping-Pickstyle

Ddstyle/Style

Ddstyle and **Style** both open the Text Styles dialog box and allow you to create new text styles and modify existing styles for the Text, Dtext and Mtext commands. Use -**Style** to display all prompts at the command line.

To Create or Modify a Text Style

Command Line: **Ddstyle** or **Style**

Menu: Format ➤ Text Style

Options

Style Name The Style Name section contains pick buttons to open a dialog box to allow you to create *New...* text styles, *Rename...* exiting styles and *Delete* unused styles. Click the list box to locate and set a text style as current.

New Opens the New Text Style dialog box. New styles appear in the Style Name edit box with editable sequentially numbered default names, such as Style1, Style2, and so forth.

Rename Opens the Rename Text Style dialog box displaying the name of the text style that appears in the pop-up list. Enter a new name.

Delete Click the button to delete the unused style's name appearing in the list box.

Font Name The Font Name section contains pop-up boxes to create a font name and font style: set text height or use big fonts.

- **Height:** edit box.

- **Font Name:** Pick a font file from the *Font Name* list box. The list box contains the font family name for all registered TrueType fonts and all AutoCAD compiled shape (SHX) fonts stored in the AutoCAD Fonts directory. You can define multiple styles for the same font.

- **Font Style:** Depending on the font selected, the *Font Style* list box and *Use Big Font* check box ungreys. Font styles define the available font character formats, such as italic, bold, regular, light and medium for the selected font.

- **Use Big fonts:** Check this box to specify an Asian-language Big Font file. Fonts with the extension .SHX are valid file types for creating Big Fonts.

- **Height:** Use the *Height* edit box to set a fixed height for the style. Setting the height at 0 prompts for the text height each time you enter text using that style. A 0 height will also make changes in dimscale take effect on dimension text.

Effects The Effects section has check boxes to toggle font settings for *Backwards; Upside-Down; Vertical;* and edit boxes to set the text style's *Width Factor* and *Oblique Angle*.

Preview The Preview section contains an image tile box to view the text style. You can modify the sample text displayed by picking the box below the character preview image and editing its contents. Clicking the *Preview* button updates the image tile box.

Apply   Applies any text changes to the style listed in the Style Name pop-up list.

Close   Cancel is replaced by Close after a modification is made to any of the options under Style Name and it is Applied to the text style.

See Also   Change, Style, Ddrename, Ddlmodes, Layer

Dducs

Dducs opens the UCS (user coordinate system) Control dialog box to rename, restore, list, or delete any existing UCS.

To Open the Dducs Dialog Box

Command Line: **Dducs**

Menu: Tools: ➤ Named UCS...

Standard Toolbar: [icon]UCS Flyout ➤ [icon]Named UCS

UCS Toolbar: [icon]Named UCS

View or provide information as needed in the dialog box.

Options

Current   Select the UCS to be made current from the UCS Names list box.

Delete   Deletes a highlighted UCS from the list box.

List   Opens the UCS dialog box to display origin point and direction of X, Y, and Z axis relative to current UCS.

Rename To: Highlight *name* in list box for editing in the edit box, then pick *Rename To:* to confirm new UCS name in the list box.

The list box always contains the *World* Coordinate System name. Entries for *Previous* and *No Name* may also appear.

See Also   Ddrename, Dview, Elev, Plan, Rename, Vpoint, UCS; *System Variables:* Ucsfollow, Ucsicon, Ucsname, Ucsorg, Ucsxdir, Ucsydir, Worlducs; Thickness

Dducsp

Dducsp opens the UCS Orientation dialog box. It displays image tiles of preset UCS (User Coordinate System) views, and allows you select one and change the current UCS setting.

To Invoke the Dducsp Dialog Box

Command Line: **Dducsp**

Menu: Tools ➤ UCS ➤ Preset UCS...

Standard Toolbar: UCS Flyout

UCS Toolbar: Preset UCS

Select preset image tile and set it *Relative to Current UCS* or *Absolute to WCS*.

Options

(Image tiles)   For the following UCS orientations: World, Top, Back, Left, Front, Right, Current View, Bottom, and Previous.

Relative to Current UCS   Option button to change current UCS based on an associated image tile.

Absolute to WCS   Option button to change UCS based on an associated image tile.

See Also   Dducs, Dview, Plan, UCS, View, Vpoint; *System Variables:* Ucsfollow, Ucsicon, Ucsname, Ucsorg, Ucsxdir, Ucsydir, Worlducs; Ucsicon

Ddunits

Ddunits opens the Units Control dialog box to set up the drawing's units of measure, angle measurement and direction, and precision. Use **Units** to display all the prompts at the command line.

To Display the Ddunits Dialog Box

Command Line: **Ddunits** (or **'Ddunits**, to use transparently)

Menu: Format ➤ Units...

Provide information as needed in the dialog box(es).

Options

Units   This section includes the following option buttons for setting units of measure: Scientific, Decimal, Engineering, Architectural, and Fractional.

Angles   This section provides the following option buttons to set angle measurement: Decimal Degrees, Deg/Min/Sec, Grads, Radians, and Surveyor.

Precision   A list box displays default accuracy levels for measurement units and angles.

Direction   This option opens a *Direction Control* subdialog box with buttons to indicate the direction of angles: East, North, West, and South indicate the location for 0. An *Other* option button enables a *Pick* button and *Angle* edit box as options. Radio buttons for clockwise and counterclockwise set the direction of positive and negative angles.

See Also   Units

Ddview

Ddview opens the View Control dialog box to make, delete, and restore views. The equivalent command line prompt is **View.**

To Invoke the Ddviews Dialog Box

Command Line: **Ddview**

Menu: View ➤ Named Views...

Standard Toolbar: 🔲 Viewport Flyout

Viewpoint Toolbar: 🔲 Named Views

Provide information as needed in the dialog box(es).

Options

Views   Displays view names with Pspace or Mspace.

Restore   Pick button to restore view by highlighting view name from the list box.

New   Opens the Define New View subdialog box for saving a new view. Option buttons allow you to save the *Current Display* as a view or to *Define Window*. Assign a *New Name* in the edit box, then use the *Window* button to temporarily exit dialog box for creating the view. Pick the *Save View* button to exit. Display boxes identify X and Y coordinates for the *First Corner* and *Other Corner*.

Delete   Pick button to delete view by highlighting view name from the list box.

Description   Opens the View Description subdialog box specifying data on the highlighted view.

See Also   Mspace, Pspace; View *System Variable:* Tilemode

Ddvpoint

Ddvpoint opens the Viewpoint Presets dialog box for establishing a 3D view by dynamically picking an angle from the X axis in the XY plane and an angle from the XY plane. The equivalent command-line prompt is **Vpoint**.

To Set a 3D View

Command Line: **Ddvpoint**

Menu: View ➤ 3D Viewpoint ➤ Select…

Provide information as needed in the dialog box.

Options

The Viewpoint Presets dialog box provides pick buttons to *Set Viewing Angles* Absolute to WCS or Relative to UCS. An image tile box rotates a white arm to preset viewing angles with your cursor when picking outside the circle and to specific angles when picking within the circle. The designated angle then appears in the edit box for X Axis and XY Plane. The image on the left indicates the angle in the XY plane. The image on the right indicates the angle above or below the XY plane. Picking *Set to Plan View* shifts the view to plan view relative to the selected coordinate system.

See Also   Plan, View, Vpoint

Delay

Delay lets you set a designated time period for viewing a slide in a script file.

To Delay a Slide

Command Line: **Delay** (or **'Delay**, to use transparently)

Delay time in milliseconds: Enter the desired number (maximum 32767 ms).

See Also   Mslide, Rscript, Script, Vslide

Detachurl

Detachurl lets you detach the URL from an object in a drawing to remove the hyperlink to a web site.

To Detach a URL

Command Line: **Detachurl**

Internet Utilites Toolbar: Detach URLs

Use any selection method to detach the URL from a drawing. AutoCAD removes the object's xdata or the rectangle and its xdata that represents the area. The urllayer created during attachment of the URL can be purged from the drawing. To update the drawing and its associated `.DWG` file, save the drawing as a `.DWG` and a `.DWF` file.

See Also   Attachurl, Gotourl, Listurl, Selecturl, Openurl, Inserturl, Saveurl, Inetcfg, Inethelp

Dimensioning Commands

In earlier releases of AutoCAD, dimensioning was accomplished by first using the **Dim** command to put the command line in dimensioning mode (Dim: mode), then issuing a dimensioning subcommand. To maintain compatibility with previous versions of AutoCAD, all of the existing Dimensioning mode subcommands are still available and may be used in the same way.

AutoCAD generally uses the same types of dimensions and dimension label components as standard drafting. Figure 2 gives examples of the five types of dimensions possible in AutoCAD drawings: linear, angular, diametric, radial, and ordinate. Dimension labels consist of the elements illustrated in Figure 3.

FIGURE 2: Types of dimensions

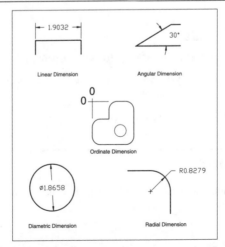

FIGURE 3: Components of dimension labels

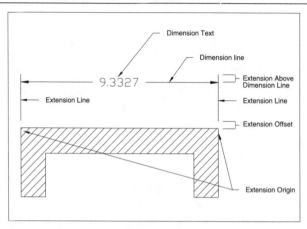

Variables for Controlling Dimensions

Table 4 describes variables that control the way AutoCAD draws dimensions. These variables control extension line and text location, tolerance specifications, arrow styles and sizes, and much more.

TABLE 4: The Dimension Variables

Variable	Description
Dimalt	When on, dimension texts for two measurement systems are inserted simultaneously (**alt**ernate). Dimaltf and Dimaltd must also be set appropriately. The alternate dimension is placed within brackets. Angular dimensions are not affected. This variable is commonly used when inches and metric units must be displayed at the same time in a dimension. The default setting is off.
Dimaltd	When Dimalt is on, Dimaltd controls the number of decimal places the alternate dimension will have (**alt**ernate **d**ecimal places). The default value is 2.
Dimaltf	When Dimalt is on, Dimaltf controls the multiplication factor for the alternate dimension (**alt**ernate **f**actor). The value held by Dimaltf will be multiplied by the standard dimension value to determine the alternate dimension. The default value is 25.4, the number required to display metric units.

TABLE 4: The Dimension Variables (continued)

Variable	Description
Dimapost	When Dimalt is on, you can use Dimapost to append text to the alternate dimension (**a**lternate **post**). For example, if Dimapost is given the value "mm," the alternate dimension will appear as va⎺luemm instead of just va⎺lue. The default value is null. To change a previously set value to null, enter a period for the Dimapost new value.
Dimaso	When on, dimensions will be associative (**asso**ciative). When off, dimensions will consist of separate drawing entities with none of the associative dimension properties. The default is on.
Dimasz	Sets the size of dimension arrows or Dimblks (**a**rrow **s**ize). If set to 0, a tick is drawn in place of an arrow. (See Dimblk.) The default value is .18 units.
Dimblk	You can replace the standard AutoCAD dimension arrow with one of your own design by creating a drawing of your symbol and making it a **bl**ock. You then give Dimblk the name of your symbol block. This block must be drawn corresponding to a one-by-one unit area and must be oriented as the right side arrow. The default value is null.
Dimblk1	With Dimsah set to on, you can replace the standard AutoCAD dimension arrows with two different arrows using Dimblk1 and Dimblk2. Dimblk1 holds the name of the block defining the first dimension arrow, while Dimblk2 holds the name of the second dimension arrow **bl**ock.
Dimblk2	See Dimblk1.
Dimcen	Sets the size of **cen**ter marks used during the Center, Diameter, and Radius dimension subcommands. A negative value draws center lines instead of the center mark cross, while a 0 value draws nothing. The default value is 0.09 units.
Dimclrd	Lets you specify **col**ors for **d**imension lines, arrowheads, and dimension leader lines.
Dimclre	Sets **col**or for dimension **e**xtension lines.
Dimclrt	Sets **col**or for dimension **t**ext.
Dimdle	With Dimtsz given a value greater than 0, dimension lines can extend past the extension lines by the amount specified in Dimdle (**d**imension **l**ine **e**xtension). This amount is not adjusted by Dimscale. The default value is 0.
Dimdli	Sets the distance at which dimension lines are offset when you use the Baseline or Continue dimension subcommands (**d**imension **l**ine **i**ncrement). The default is 0.38 units.

TABLE 4: The Dimension Variables (continued)

Variable	Description
Dimexe	Sets the distance the extension lines are drawn past the dimension lines (**ex**tension line **e**xtension). The default value is 0.18 units.
Dimexo	Sets the distance between the beginning of the extension line and the actual point selected at the "Extension line origin:" prompt (**ex**tension line **o**ffset). The default value is 0.0625 units.
Dimgap	Sets the distance or **gap** between the text and the dimension line and lets you enclose text within a box by assigning it a negative value. The default value is 0.09.
Dimlfac	Sets the global scale factor for dimension values (**l**ength **fac**tor). Linear distances will be multiplied by the value held by Dimlfac. This multiple will be entered as the dimension text. The default value is 1.0. This can be useful when drawings are not drawn to scale.
Dimlim	When set to on, dimension text is entered as two values representing a dimension range rather than a single value. The range is determined by the values given to Dimtp (**p**lus tolerance) and Dimtm (**m**inus tolerance). The default value is off.
Dimpost	Automatically appends text strings to dimension text. For example, if Dimpost is given the value "inches," dimension text will appear as value inches instead of just value. The default value is null. To change a previously set value to null, enter a period for the Dimpost new value. If you use Dimpost in conjunction with appended dimension text, the Dimpost value is included as part of the default dimension text.
Dimrnd	Sets the amount to which all dimensions are **round**ed. For example, if you set Dimrnd to 1, all dimensions will be integer values. The number of decimal places affected depends on the precision value set by the Units command. The default is 0.
Dimsah	When set to on, allows the separate arrow blocks Dimblk1 and Dimblk2 to replace the standard AutoCAD arrows (**s**eparate **a**rrow **h**eads). If Dimtsz is set to a value greater than 0, Dimsah has no effect.
Dimscale	Sets the **scale** factor for dimension variables that control dimension lines and arrows and text size (unless current text style has a fixed height). If your drawing is not full scale, you should set this variable to reflect the drawing scale. For example, for a drawing whose scale is ~q~" equals 1~', you should set Dimscale to 48. The default value is 1.0.

TABLE 4: The Dimension Variables (continued)

Variable	Description
Dimse1	When set to on, the first dimension line extension is not drawn (**s**uppress **e**xtension **1**). The default is off.
Dimse2	When set to on, the second dimension line extension is not drawn (**s**uppress **e**xtension **2**). The default is off.
Dimsho	When set to on, dimension text in associative dimensions will dynamically change to reflect the location of a dimension point as it is being moved (**sho**w dimension). The default is off.
Dimsoxd	When set to on, dimension lines do not appear outside of the extension lines (**s**uppress **o**utside e**x**tension **d**imension lines). If Dimtix is also set to on and the space between the extension lines prohibits the display of a dimension line, no dimension line is drawn. The default is off.
Dimstyle	Identifies the current dimension **style**. Use the Save and Restore dimensioning commands for alternate Dimstyles. The default is *UNNAMED.
Dimtad	When set to on and Dimtih is off, dimension text in linear dimensions will be placed above the dimension line (**t**ext **a**bove **d**imension line). When off, the dimension line will be split in two and text will be placed in line with the dimension line. The default value is off.
Dimtdec	Controls **t**olerance value **dec**imal place for primary units dimension. Values can be selected from the Precision popup list under Primary Units in the Annotation dialog box.
Dimtfac	Sets **t**ext scale **fac**tor for text height of tolerance values based on Dimtxt, the dimension text height variable. Use Dimtfac to display the plus and minus characters when Dimtol is on and Dimtm does not equal Dimtp, or when Dimlim is on. The default is 1.0.
Dimtih	When set to on, dimension text placed between extension lines will always be horizontal (**t**ext **i**nside **h**orizontal). When set to off, text will be aligned with the dimension line. The default value is on.
Dimtix	When set to on, dimension text will always be placed between extension lines (**t**ext **i**nside e**x**tension). The default value is off.
Dimtm	When Dimtol or Dimlin is on, Dimtm determines the minus tolerance value of the dimension text (**t**olerance **m**inus).

TABLE 4: The Dimension Variables (continued)

Variable	Description
Dimtofl	With Dimtofl on, a dimension line is always drawn between extension lines even when text is drawn outside (**t**ext **o**utside— **f**orced **l**ine). The default is off.
Dimtoh	With Dimtoh on, dimension text placed outside extension lines will always be horizontal (**t**ext **o**utside—**h**orizontal). When set to off, text outside extension lines will be aligned with dimension line. The default is on.
Dimtol	With Dimtol on, tolerance values set by Dimtp and Dimtm are appended to the dimension text (**tol**erance). The default is off.
Dimtp	When Dimtol or Dimlim is on, Dimtp determines the plus tolerance value of the dimension text (**t**olerance **p**lus).
Dimtsz	Sets the size of tick marks drawn in place of the standard AutoCAD arrows (**t**ick **s**ize). When set to 0, the standard arrow is drawn. When greater than 0, tick marks are drawn and take precedence over Dimblk1 and Dimblk2. The default value is 0.
Dimtvp	When Dimtad is off, Dimtvp allows you to specify the location of the dimension text in relation to the dimension line (**t**ext **v**ertical **p**osition). A positive value places the text above the dimension line, while a negative value places the text below the dimension line. The dimension line will split to accommodate the text unless the Dimtvp value is greater than 1.
Dimtxt	Sets the height of dimension **text** when the current text style height is set to 0. The default value is 0.18.
Dimzin	Determines the display of inches when Architectural units are used. When set to 0, zero feet or **z**ero **in**ches will not be displayed. When set to 1, zero feet and zero inches will be displayed. When set to 2, zero inches will not be displayed. When set to 3, zero feet will not be displayed.

Dimensioning and Drawing Scales

Take care when dimensioning drawings at a scale other than one-to-one. If the *Dimscale* dimension variable is not set properly, arrows and text will appear too small or too large. In extreme cases, they may not appear at all. If you enter a dimension and arrows or text do not appear, check the Dimscale setting and make sure it is a value equal to the drawing scale. For instance, a drawing at 1 to 1 that is going to be plotted at _" =1' the dimscale should be set to 48.

Starting the Dimensioning Process

Depending upon your system configuration or your preferences, you may access the dimensioning commands in a number of different ways.

- **Toolbar** From the Dimensioning toolbar, click on the appropriate Dimensioning button.

- **Pull-down menu** From the Dimensioning Menu, select the appropriate command on the menu.

- **Command line directly** Each dimensioning mode command has an equivalent AutoCAD command that can be invoked directly at the command prompt; for example, **Dimaligned.**

- **Command line with Dim/Dim1** All of the dimensioning sub-commands from previous releases of AutoCAD are still available for compatibility purposes. To use them, enter **Dim** or **Dim1** at the command prompt. At this point, the prompt changes to "Dim:" and you can enter any dimensioning subcommand. These and the trans-parent commands (see **Transparent**) are the only AutoCAD com-mands you can enter while in the dimensioning mode. When you have finished entering dimensions under the Dim command, issue the **Exit** command or press Escape to return to the standard com-mand prompt. If you want to enter only a single dimension, use **Dim1**. The 1 tells AutoCAD to return you automatically to the com-mand prompt after you complete one dimension. You can invoke any dimension command by entering just its first three letters. For example, you can enter **Dia** instead of **Diameter**. Alternative short command forms are shown with each subcommand as appropriate.

Dimaligned

Dimaligned aligns a dimension with two points or an object. The dimension text appears in the current style. Figure 4 illustrates the dif-ference between aligned and rotated dimensions. Dimension settings are modified with the Ddim dialog box. The Dimensioning mode equiv-alent is **Dimaligned/Al**.

To Align a Dimension

Command Line: **Dimaligned**

Menu: Dimension ➤ Aligned

Dimension Toolbar: Aligned Dimension

FIGURE 4: Aligned and rotated dimensions

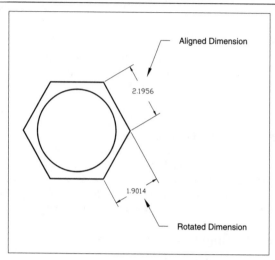

1. **First extension line origin or press ENTER to select:** Pick one end of object to be dimensioned. If you entered coordinates for an extension line, you will be prompted for the following:

   Second extension line origin: Pick the other end of the object.

2. **Dimension line location (Mtext/Text/Angle):** If you wish to modify the text or text angle, enter an option (**M, T , A**). To position the dimension line dynamically, drag your cursor and pick a point; or enter a coordinate for the location of the dimension line.

3. **Dimension text <default dimension>:** Press ⏎ to accept the default dimension, or enter dimension value.

Options

Mtext Enter (**M**) to open the Multiline Text Editor dialog box and display the text as angle brackets <>. Accept the default and pick OK, or enter a new dimension text. Additional text can be placed before or after the angle brackets as described in the Text option.

Text This option (**T**) allows you to edit and customize the dimension. AutoCAD displays the dimension measurement at the command prompt **Dimension text <measured length>:** and allows you to modify it. If you wish to enter a different value, enter it at the command prompt and press ⏎. If you wish to insert additional text before the dimension measurement, or append text after it, place angle bracket signs (<>) to represent the default dimension value and add the desired text before or after. For example, if you wish to add "inches" *after* the value, type <> **inches** at the "Dimension text:" prompt.

Angle   This option (**A**) allows you to change the default angle of the text. Text will be placed horizontally (0 degrees) unless you specify a dimension text orientation to the "Enter text angle:" prompt.

Dimangular

Dimangular creates a dimension label showing the angle described by an arc, circle, or two lines, or by a set of three points. An arc with dimension arrows at each end is drawn and the angle value is placed using current text style. Dimension settings can be modified with the Ddim dialog box, or by selecting each individual Dim variable. The Dimensioning mode equivalent is **Dim ⌐ Angular/An** .

To Create an Angle Dimension Label

Command Line: **Dimangular**

Menu: Dimension ➤ Angular

Dimension Toolbar: ⬛Angular Dimension

1. **Select arc, circle, line, press ENTER:** Pick an object as indicated by the prompt or press ⌐ to indicate angles using your cursor.

   • If you selected an arc, or a circle, continue with Step 2.

   • If you selected a line, you will be prompted **Second Line:.** Select another line, and then continue with step 2.

   • If you pressed ⌐ , you may specify the desired angle by giving three points: the **Angle vertex:**, the **First angle endpoint:**, and **the Second angle endpoint:.** Then continue with step 2.

2. **Dimension arc line location (Mtext/Text/Angle):** If you wish to modify the text or text angle, enter an option (**M, T, A**). Otherwise, drag your cursor and pick a point, or enter a coordinate for the location of the dimension line as the extension line with text appears.

Options

For a description of the *Mtext*, *Text* and *Angle* options, see the **Dimaligned** command**.**

Dimbaseline

Dimbaseline continues a dimension string using the first extension line of the most recently inserted dimension as its first extension line. You are prompted only for the second extension line origin. Each new dimension is offset by an increment set in the *Dimdli* system variable from the previous dimension line. Prompts vary depending on the type of dimension that was last created. The Dimensioning mode equivalent is **Dim ⏎ Baseline/B**.

To Continue a Dimension from the Baseline

Command Line: **Dimbaseline**

Menu: Dimension ➤ Baseline

Dimension Toolbar: ⊞ Baseline Dimension

1. **Specify a second extension line origin or (<select>/Undo):**
   Pressing ⏎ prompts to **Select base dimension:** if you wish to pick a new dimension for the start point. Otherwise, select as many points as you wish along the measured object. AutoCAD responds **Dimension text =default dimension** and draws a series of dimensions, each starting from the second point extension of the last dimension in the chain. To end the command, press ⏎ or use the Escape key.

   - If no dimensions exist in the current session, the prompt appears: **Select base dimension:, Linear, Ordinate, or Angular associative dimension required.**

   - If the previous dimension was linear, the prompt in step 1 appears. Otherwise, previous angular or ordinate dimensions display the prompt: **Specify a point on an object or (<select>/Undo):**. Pick a point, use an object snap mode option to select, or press ⏎ to select a base dimension.

Option

Undo Removes the last dimension string. AutoCAD allows you to repeat the *U* option until all dimension strings are undone, then displays the prompt to *Select base dimension*.

See Also Dimension Variable: Dimdli

Dimcenter

Dimcenter places a cross at the center point of a selected arc or circle. To choose center lines instead of center marks, and to change the size of the center mark, use the *Dimcen* dimension variable or reset them in the

Geometry dialog box of the **Ddim** command. The Dimensioning mode equivalent is **Dim ⏎ Center/Ce**.

To Mark the Center of an Arc or Circle

Command Line: **Dimcenter**

Menu: Dimension ➤ Center Mark

Dimension Toolbar: ⊕ Center Mark

Select arc or circle: Pick an arc or circle and the mark will appear.

Dimcontinue

Dimcontinue draws a series, or "chain," of related dimensions by using the second extension line of the most recently inserted dimension as its first extension line. All of the "chained" dimension measurements add up to a total measurement of the object. You are prompted only for the second extension line origin. If the original dimension is linear, the related dimensions are placed in line with, and parallel to, this dimension. The *Dimfit* system variable controls the positioning of the dimension lines and text between the selected points. The Dimensioning mode equivalent is **Dim ⏎ Continue/Co**.

To Continue a Dimension

Command Line: **Dimcontinue**

Menu: Dimension ➤ Continue

Dimension Toolbar: ⊢⊢⊣ Continue Dimension

> **Specify a second extension line origin or (<select>/Undo):**
> Select as many points as you wish along the measured object.
> AutoCAD responds with **Dimension text=default dimension**
> and draws a series of dimensions, each starting from the second
> extension line of the last dimension in the chain.

> **NOTE** Pressing ⏎ displays the prompt "Select continued dimen-
> sion:". Pick a new dimension for the start point or ⏎ to exit
> Dimcontinue.

Option

Undo Removes the last dimension string. AutoCAD allows you to repeat the *U* option until all dimension strings are undone, then displays the prompt to "Specify a second extension line origin or (<select>/Undo):".

Dimdiameter

Dimdiameter draws different types of diameter dimensions depending upon the size of the arc or circle and upon the dimension settings created in **Ddim** Format dialog box, and stored in the dimensioning system variables as a *dim* style. The Dimensioning mode equivalent is **Dim ⌐ Diameter/Di**.

To Dimension an Arc or Circle Diameter

Command Line: **Dimdiameter**

Menu: Dimension ➤ Diameter

Dimension Toolbar: Diameter Dimension

1. **Select arc or circle:** Pick the arc or circle as appropriate.

2. **Dimension line location<Mtext/Text/Angle>:** As the leader line extends in a dragging mode from the arc or circle, pick a point that indicates the location of the text or enter an option (**M,T, A**). AutoCAD displays the value with **Dimension text =default dimension.** The direction of the leader is toward the center point. A center mark is also placed at the center of the arc or circle.

Options

For a description of the *Mtext, Text* and *Angle* options, see the **Dimaligned** command.

> **NOTE** Unless you modify the text, the dimension value will be preceded by a diameter symbol. The point at which you pick the arc or circle determines one end of the dimension arrow. If you want the dimension to be in a horizontal or vertical orientation, use the **Quadrant Osnap** override. Pick the left or right quadrant for a horizontal dimension; pick the top or bottom quadrant for a vertical dimension. If the *Dimtix* dimension variable is set to on, the dimension is placed inside the circle starting at your pick point. A center mark is also placed at the center of the arc or circle.

See Also   Dimension Variables: Dimcen, Dimtix.

Dimedit

Dimedit allows you to change and manipulate selected text and extension lines. **Dimedit** can be used to change the same elements on several dimension objects at once. Using this command, you can Rotate text; shift it back to its original "home" position; and edit dimension text. The *Oblique* option allows you to skew existing dimension extension lines to an angle other than 90 degrees to the dimension line. This is used for iso-metrics. The **Dimedit** command combines the dimensioning subcommands Dim: Hometext, Dim: Newtext, Dim: Trotate, and Dim: Oblique.

To Edit Dimension Text

Command Line: **Dimedit**

Menu: Dimension ➤ Oblique

Dimension Toolbar: ⊞ Dimension Edit

1. **Dimension Edit (Home/New/Rotate/Oblique) <Current>:** Select an option or press ↵.

2. **Select Objects:** Select dimensions and dimension text to edit.

Options

Home   Repositions all selected dimension text objects in their default positions. This has the same effect as the **Dim: Home** dimensioning subcommand.

New   Opens the Multiline Text Editor, allowing you to replace associative dimension text on several dimensions at once. Replace the angle brackets with new dimension text, then pick OK. Entering text outside the brackets appends it to the existing dimension string. All associative dimensions selected will be changed to the new text. This has the same effect as the **Dim: Newtext** dimensioning subcommand.

Rotate   Allows you to rotate dimension text to a specified angle. At the prompt *Enter text angle,* enter the required angle. This has the same effect as the **Dim: Trotate** dimensioning subcommand.

Oblique   Allows you to change all selected extension lines to a specified angle. At the prompt "Enter obliquing angle (press ENTER for none):", enter the required angle. This has the same effect as the **Dim: Oblique** dimensioning subcommand.

Dimlinear

Creates a linear dimension. **Dimlinear** allows you to position linear dimensions in either a horizontal or a vertical direction, as well as allowing you to rotate the dimension line and text to a specified angle. This command combines the dimensioning subcommands Dim: Horizontal, Dim: Vertical, and Dim: Rotate.

To Create Linear Dimensions

Command Line: **Dimlinear**

Menu: Dimension ➤ Linear

Dimension Toolbar: ⊢⊣ Linear Dimension

1. **First extension line origin or press ENTER to select:** Pick a point on the object to be dimensioned or press ↵.

2. **Second extension line origin:** Pick a second point on the object.

   • If you pressed ↵, you will be prompted to **Select object to dimension:**. When you select an object, AutoCAD automatically locates the origin points for the extension lines.

3. **Dimension line location (Mtext/Text/Angle/Horizontal/ Vertical/Rotated):** Enter an option, pick a location or enter a coordinate for the location of the dimension line as the extension line with mtext or text appears.

Options

For a description of the *Mtext, Text* and *Angle* options, see the **Dimaligned** command.

Horizontal Allows you to specify a horizontal dimension at "the Dimension line location (Mtext/Text/Angle):" prompt, or enter an option. You may also do this dynamically. If you drag your cursor up or down the screen, the horizontal dimension will appear.

Vertical Allows you to specify a vertical dimension at "the Dimension line location (Mtext/Text/Angle):" prompt, or enter an option. You may also do this dynamically. If you drag your cursor to the left or right across the screen, the vertical dimension will appear.

Rotated Allows you to create rotated dimensions. If you enter R to select the Rotated option, you will be prompted "Dimension line angle <default angle>:". Enter an angle of rotation for the dimension line.

> **NOTE** If you select a line or an arc, its end points are used as origins for the dimension lines; if you select a circle, the diameter end points are used as the origin points. Selecting polylines and other explodable objects only dimensions the individual line or arc segments. Objects in a non-uniformly scaled block reference are not selectable.

Dimordinate

Dimordinate creates an ordinate dimension string based on a datum or origin point. The Dimensioning mode equivalent is **Dim ↵ Ordinate/Or**. To set the origin point use the UCS command and specify an origin point for the part, i.e., the lower left corner of the part.

DIMENSIONING COMMANDS

To Create Ordinate Dimensioning

Command Line: **Dimordinate**

Menu: Dimension ➤ Ordinate

Dimension Toolbar: Ordinate Dimension

1. **Select Feature:** Pick the location of the feature to be dimensioned.

2. **Leader endpoint (Xdatum/Ydatum/Mtext/Text):** Specify an endpoint for the leader. AutoCAD will determine automatically whether to measure the X or Y coordinate. Alternatively, you may enter **X** or **Y** to specify the axis along which the dimension is to be taken. Enter **T** or **M** if you wish to modify the dimension text. Then press ↵ to display the value.

> **Dimension text = <dimension default >**

Options

For a description of the *Mtext* and *Text* options, see the **Dimaligned** command.

> **NOTE** If you pick a point at the first Leader endpoint: prompt, then AutoCAD selects the dimension axis based on the angle defined by the points you pick during the *Select Feature:* and *Leader endpoint:* prompts.

See Also UCS

Dimoverride

Dimoverride changes an individual dimension's properties, such as its arrow style, colors, scale, text orientation, etc. It allows you to override current dimension variable settings for selected objects only, without changing the current Dimension Style. The Dimensioning mode equivalent is **Dim ↵ Override/Ove**.

To Override Dimension Variable Settings

Command Line: **Dimoverride**

Menu: Dimension ➤ Override

1. **Dimension variable to override (or Clear to remove overrides):** Enter the name of a dimension variable, or type **C** to clear.

2. **Current value <(variables value)> New value:** Enter new value or setting for the dimension variable.

3. **Dimension variable to override:** Enter another dimension variable name and repeat the process or press ↵ to continue.

4. **Select objects:** Select dimension object(s) to change.

Options

Clear Allows you to clear any dimension variable overrides. AutoCAD clears any overrides and the dimension object reverts to the setting defined by its dimension style

See Also Dimstyle, Restore, Ddmodify

Dimradius

Dimradius adds a radius dimension to arcs and circles in essentially the same way that **Dimdiameter** adds diameter dimensions. The Dimensioning mode equivalent is **Dim ↵ Radius/Ra**.

To Add a Radius Dimension

Command Line: **Dimradius**

Menu: Dimension ➤ Radius

Dimension Toolbar: Radius Dimension

1. **Select arc or circle:** Pick the arc or circle. The point at which you pick the arc or circle determines one end of the dimension arrow.

2. **Dimension line location (Mtext/Text/Angle):** If you wish to modify the mtext, text or text angle, enter an option (**M, T, A**). Or drag the cursor to position the mtext or text (and leader). The **Dimension text = default radius** value is displayed above the prompt.

Options

For a description of the *Mtext, Text* and *Angle* options, see the **Dimaligned** command.

NOTE Unless you modify the mtext or text, the dimension value will be preceded by the letter R. If a dimensioned circle or arc is large enough, the radius dimension will be positioned within it. Otherwise it is positioned outside the circle or arc, with a leader line pointing to the center. A center mark is also placed at the center of the arc or circle. To drag the dimension text outside the circle or arc turn on *dimupt* or *use Ddim* and click *User defined in Format* . In *Ddim* it is in *Format...*, user defined.

Dimstyle

Dimstyle allows you to create and modify dimension styles at the command line. The Ddim dialog boxes offer a more detailed and graphical approach to creating dimension styles, but **Dimstyle** allows a quick method of saving and creating dimension styles on the fly. The Dimensioning mode equivalent is **Dim ⌐ Dimstyle**.

To Create/Modify a Dimension Style

Command Line: **Dimstyle**

Menu: Dimension ➤ Dimstyle

Dimension Toolbar: 🔲 Dimension Style

1. **Dimension Style Edit (Save/Restore/STatus/Variables/ Apply/?) <Restore>:** Type **?** to list the dimension styles in the current drawing, or select an option. AutoCAD also reports the current dimension style along the prompt.

2. Depending upon the option chosen, the prompts will vary. Enter the required information.

Options

Save   Displays the prompt *?/Name for new dimension style*: when you type **S**. Enter a name to save the current dimension variable settings as a dimension style that can later be restored using the Restore option. You can save multiple dimension styles. You can also redefine an existing style by saving it back as the same name. This updates all the dims that have that style.

Restore   Typing **R** returns the prompt "?/Enter dimension style name or press ENTER" to select dimension: Enter a name to makes an existing dimension style the current default style. You can either name a specific style or select an object that uses the style. *Restore* immediately changes the current dimension style to reflect any differences.

Status   Select this option by entering **Sta** to display the current dimension variable settings and descriptions. Once the dimension variables have been listed, **Dimstyle** ends.

Variables   To list the dimension variable settings of a dimension style, enter **V**, then press ⌐. You can either name a specific style or select an object that uses the style at the "Select dimension:" prompt. Once the dimension variables have been listed, **Dimstyle** ends.

Apply   Typing **A** displays the "Select objects:" prompt allowing you to update selected dimension objects with the current dimension style, including any overrides.

? Lists the named dimension styles in the current drawing. Pressing ↵ displays the "Dimension style(s) to list <*>:" prompt and reports the *Named dimension styles:* that are stored in the current drawing.

See Also Restore, Save, Ddim

Dimtedit

Modifies the placement, justification, and rotation angle of a single dimension text object. The Dimensioning mode equivalent is **Dim** ↵ **Dimtedit**.

To Modify Dimension Text

Command Line: **Dim** ↵ **Tedit/Te**

Menu: Dimension ➤ Align Text ➤ Home/Angle/Center/Right

Dimension Toolbar: Dimension Text Edit

1. **Select dimension:** Pick a single dimension.

2. **Enter text location (Left/Right/Home/Angle):** Enter an option or pick a new location for the dimension text. You can drag the text to the next location with the cursor. If you move the text to a position in line with the dimension line, the dimension will automatically join to become a continuous line.

Options

Left Justifies text to the left within the extension lines on linear, radius, and diameter dimensions.

Right Justifies text to the right within the extension lines on linear, radius, and diameter dimensions.

Home Places text in its default dimension. This has the same effect as the **Hometext** subcommand.

Angle Changes the angle for text. At the prompt "Text angle:", enter an angle value, or indicate an angle by picking two points.

> **NOTE** When **Tedit** is used on a dimension, the style is updated to the current dimension style setting. If no style is associated with the dimension, then current dimension variable settings are used

See Also Dim:, Hometext; *System Variables:* Dimaso, Dimsho

Dimensioning Mode Subcommands

Most of the dimensioning commands are still available as subcommands in Dimensioning mode (**Dim: mode**). **Dim: mode** equivalents, where available, are identified with each command reviewed above. A number of dimensioning variables remain as Dim subcommands only.

TABLE 5: The DIM Subcommands and the Dimensioning Commands

DIM subcommand	Dimensioning Commands
Dim: Aligned/AL	DIMALIGNED
Dim: Angular/AN	DIMANGULAR
Dim: Baseline/B	DIMBASELINE
Dim: Center/CE	DIMCENTER
Dim: Continue/CO	DIMCONTINUE
Dim: Diameter/D	DIMDIAMETER
Dim: Hometext/HOM	DIMEDIT Home
Dim: Horizontal/HOR	DIMLINEAR Horizontal
Dim: Leader/L	LEADER
Dim: Newtext/N	DIMEDIT New
Dim: Oblique/OB	DIMEDIT Oblique
Dim: Ordinate/OR	DIMORDINATE
Dim: Override/OV	DIMOVERRIDE
Dim: Radius/RA	DIMRADIUS
Dim: Restore/RES	DIMSTYLE Restore
Dim: Rotated/RO	DIMLINEAR Rotated
Dim: Save/SA	DIMSTYLE Save
Dim: Status/STA	DIMSTYLE Status
Dim: Tedit/TE	DIMTEDIT
Dim: Trotate/TR	DIMEDIT Angle
Dim: Variables/VA	DIMSTYLE Variables
Dim: Tedit/TE	DIMTEDIT
Dim: Vertical/VE	DIMLINEAR Vertical

TABLE 5: The DIM Subcommands and the Dimensioning Commands (continued)

DIM subcomand	Dimensioning Commands
Remaining Subcommands	
Dim: Exit/E	Exits Dim mode and returns to command mode
Dim: Redraw/RED	Redraws the display
Dim: Style/STY	Switches to a new text style
Dim: Undo/U	Erases the most recent dimension objects
Dim: Update/UP	Redraws dimensions to match the current settings

Dim: Exit/E

This command exits the **Dim** command and returns you to the standard command prompt.

To Exit Dim

Command Line: **Dim** ↵ **Exit/E**

You can press the Escape key or type **E** in place of Exit. If you entered **Dim1** to begin dimensioning, Exit is not needed.

Dim: Leader/L

Dim: Leader adds leadered dimensions to drawings based on the current dimension style. You can replace the default dimension text with a single line of text.

To Add Dimensions/Text with Leaders

Command Line: **Dim** ↵ **Leader/L**

1. **Leader start:** Pick a point to start the leader. This is the point where the arrow will be placed.

2. **To point:** Pick the next point along the leader line or continue to pick points as you would in drawing a line. When you are finished, press ↵. You can enter **U** to Undo the last drawn line segment.

3. **Dimension text <default dimension>:** Press ↵ to accept the default, enter new dimension text or a single line of text.

The distance between the Leader start point and the next point must be at least twice the length of the arrow; otherwise an arrow will not be placed. If the last line segment of the leader is not horizontal, a horizontal line segment is added.

Leadered text does not take on the properties of associative dimensioning. You can append text to the default dimension value. The default value is usually the last dimension entered.

See Also   Dimstyle, Leader, Mtext, Tolerance, Spline

Dim: Oblique/Ob

Dim: Oblique skews existing dimension extension lines to an angle other than 90 degrees to the dimension line.

To Skew Extension Lines

Command Line: **Dim** ↵ **Oblique/Ob**

Menu: Dimension ➤ Oblique

1. **Select objects:** Pick the dimensions to be edited.

2. **Enter obliquing angle (press ENTER for none):** Enter the desired angle for extension lines.

If the dimension being edited has a dimension style setting, then this setting is maintained. If no style is associated with the dimension, the current dimension variable settings are used to update the obliqued dimension.

See Also   Dimedit, Dimstyle

Dim: Redraw/Red

Redraw behaves like a transparent command and allows you to refresh the screen in the current viewport.

To Refresh the Screen

Command Line: **Dim** ↵ **Redraw/Red**

See Also   Redraw

Dim: Restore/Res

Makes an existing dimension style the current default style.

To Use Restore

Command Line: **Dim** ↵ **Restore/Res**

?/Enter dimension style name or press ENTER to select dimension: Enter **?** to list available dimension styles, enter the name of a known dimension style (wildcard characters are accepted), or press ⏎ to pick a dimension whose dimension style you want to make current.

To select a dimension style, either pick an associative dimension that is associated with the desired style, or enter the name of the style. The tilde (~) can also be used to compare styles. To find the differences between the current dimension style and another style, enter a dimension style name preceded by a tilde (~) at the prompt "Dimension style(s) to list <*>:". Differences are displayed in a list of dimension variable settings.

See Also   Dimoverride, Dim: Save

Dim: Save/Sav

Dim: Save saves the current dimension variable settings as a dimension style that can later be restored using the **Dim: Restore** subcommand. You can save multiple dimension styles.

To Save Dimension Settings

Command Line: **Dim** ⏎ **Save/Sa**

?/Name for new dimension style: Enter a new dimension style name. If you enter **?**, the following prompt appears:

> **Dimension style(s) to list <*>:** ⏎ or enter a name specification using wildcards.

> **NOTE** The tilde (~) can also be used to compare styles. To find the differences between the current dimension style and another style, enter a dimension style name preceded by a tilde (~) at the prompt "Dimension style(s) to list <*>:". Differences are displayed in a list of dimension variable settings.

See Also   Ddim, Dimoverride, Restore

Dim: Status/Sta

Dim: Status displays the current dimension variable settings and descriptions.

To Display Dimension Settings

Command Line: **Dim** ⏎ **Status/Sta**

The text screen appears listing dimension settings, their status or values and a brief description.

Dim: Style/Sty

Dim: Style specifies a text style for the dimension text. Once the text style is changed, any subsequent dimensions will contain text in the new style. Existing dimension text is not affected.

To Specify a Text Style

Command Line: **Dim:** ↵ **Style/Sty**

1. **New text style <current style nane>:** Press ↵ to accept the current style, or enter another previously created style name to set as the current text style.

    • If you enter the name of a style that does not exist, you receive the message *No such text style: Use the main STYLE command to create it.*

See Also   Ddstyle, Style

Dim: Undo/U

Undo rescinds a dimension you decide you do not want, as long as you are still in the dimension mode.

To Undo a Dimension

Command Line: **Dim** ↵ **Undo/U**

NOTE If you issue Undo during the **Leader** command, the last leader line segment drawn will be undone.

Dim: Update/Up

Update changes old dimensions to new dimension variable settings. Update works only on associative dimensions that have not been exploded.

Command Line: **Dim** ↵ **Update/Up**

Menu: Dimension ➤ Update

Dimension Toolbar: ▨Update

Select objects: Pick dimension string to update.

Dim: Variables/Va

Variables lists the dimension variable settings of a dimension style.

To List the Dimension Variable Settings

Command Line: **Dim** ↵ **Variables/Va**

?/Enter dimension style name or press ENTER to select dimension: Enter **?** to view available dimension styles, enter the name of a known dimension style (wildcards are accepted), or press ↵ to pick a dimension whose dimension style you wish to list.

The tilde (~) can also be used to compare styles. To find the differences between the current dimension style and another style, enter a dimension style name preceded by a tilde (~) at the prompt "Dimension style(s) to list <*>:". Differences are displayed in a list of dimension variable settings.

See Also   Ddim

Additional Dimensioning Options

The two processes described below can be used in conjunction with both Dimensioning commands as well as in Dim: mode.

At the "Dimension text:" prompt, you can append text to the default dimension text.

To Append Dimension Text

Start the required dimensioning command, then provide the following information:

Dimension text <default text>: Place <> signs where you want the text to appear, then enter the text.

At the "First extension line origin or press ENTER to select:" prompt or the "Select arc, circle, line, or press ENTER:" prompt, you can let AutoCAD dimension a line, arc, or circle automatically.

To Use Automatic Dimensioning

Start the required dimensioning command, then provide the following information:

1. **First extension line or press ENTER to select:** Press ↵.

2. **Select arc, circle, line, or press ENTER:** Pick the object to be dimensioned.

NOTE After selecting a line, circle, or arc, you may drag your cursor and the dimension text and then pick a location point.

DIST

Dist gives the distance between two points in 2D or 3D space. It also gives the angle in the current XY plane, the angle *from* the current XY

DIST

plane, and the distance in X, Y, and Z coordinate values. It also gives you the change in X, Y, and Z. This is the *Delta* X, Y, and Z information.

To Find the Distance between Two Points

Command Line: **Dist** (or **'Dist**, to use transparently)

Menu: Tools ➤ Inquiry ➤ Distance

Inquiry Toolbar: ▥Distance

1. **First point:** Pick the beginning point of the distance.

2. **Second point:** Pick the end point of the distance.

DIVIDE

Divide marks an object into equal divisions. You specify the number of divisions, and AutoCAD marks the object into equal parts.

To Divide an Object

Command Line: **Divide**

Menu: Draw ➤ Point ➤ Divide.

1. **Select object to divide:** Pick a single object.

2. **<Number of segments>/Block:** Enter the number of segments to be marked or enter the name of the block to use for marking.

Options

Number of segments   A marker or point is located at specified intervals using the *Pdmode* and *Pdsize* variables for point size and type.

Block   Allows you to use an existing block as a marking device. You receive the prompt "Block name to insert:" and are asked whether you want to align the block with the object. If you respond **Y** to the "Align block with object:" prompt, the block will be aligned either along the axis of a line or tangent to a selected polyline, circle, or arc. The *Block* option is useful for drawing a series of objects that are equally spaced along a curved path.

By default, Divide uses a point object as a marker. Often, a point is difficult to see when placed over a line or arc. You can set the *Pdmode* system variable using the **'Ddptype** command transparently to change the appearance of the points, or you can use the *Block* option. The point marker can be picked with the **Node** object snap mode.

See Also   Block, Ddptype, Measure, Point; *System Variables:* Pdmode, Pdsize

Donut/Doughnut

Donut draws a circle whose line thickness you specify by entering its inside and outside diameters (see Figure 5). To create a solid dot, enter **0** at the *Inside diameter:* prompt. The most recent diameters entered are the default values for the inside and outside diameter. Once you issue the **Donut** command and answer the prompts, you can place as many donuts as you like. Press ⏎ to terminate the command.

FIGURE 5: Inside and outside diameters of a donut

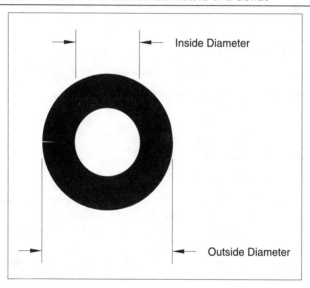

To Create a Donut

Command Line: **Donut** or **Doughnut**

Menu: Draw ➤ Donut

1. **Inside diameter <current default>:** Enter the inside diameter of the donut or pick a point, for which a prompt appears to specify a "Second point:".

2. **Outside diameter <current default>:** Enter the outside diameter of the donut or pick two points.

3. **Center of donut:** Pick a point for the center of the donut, then press ⏎ to exit the command or continue selecting center points.

NOTE Because donuts are actually polylines, you can edit them with the **Pedit** command.

See Also Fill, Pedit; *System Variables:* Fillmode

Dragmode

Dragmode controls when the drag facility is used. The default, Auto, lets you temporarily reposition selected objects by moving them with your cursor.

To Drag an Object

Command Line: **Dragmode** (or **'Dragmode** to use transparently)

ON/OFF/Auto <current setting>: Enter the setting.

Options

ON   Enables the Drag mode, so that objects will be dragged whenever you issue the Drag command modifier.

OFF   Disables the Drag mode, so that no dragging can occur.

Auto   Causes all commands that allow dragging to automatically drag objects, whether you issue the **Drag** command modifier or not.

   When you are editing large sets of objects, the Drag function can slow you down. It takes time for AutoCAD to refresh a temporary image, especially a complex one. If you set **Dragmode** on, you can use the Drag function when appropriate by entering **Drag** as a subcommand while performing a operation, and dispense with it when editing large groups of objects.

See Also *System Variables:* Dragmode

Draworder

Draworder prioritizes the display of objects and hard copy output when two or more objects overlay each other.

To Set the Display of Objects

Command Line: **Draworder**

1. **Select objects:** Select one or more objects to arrange their display and plotted output, by picking or using any selection set method.

2. **Above object/Under object/Front/<Back>:** Select an option.

Options

Above object   Moves object above or on the top of other objects.

Under object   Moves object below or under other objects.

Front   Selected object is reassigned to the top of the drawing order.

Back   Selected object is reassigned to the bottom of the drawing order.

The **Draworder** command toggles all object sort method options on. Sorting is enabled only for plotting and PostScript output. Specifying the appropriate value at the command line for the sortents system variable will also set an object sort method. You can also toggle grouping on and off by using Crtl+A.

Dsviewer

Dsviewer opens the Aerial View dialog box as a navigation tool that lets you see an entire drawing in a separate window, locate the area you want, and move to it quickly. The dialog box contains a View, Mode, Options and Help pulldown menus.

To Open the Aerial View Window

Command Line: **Dsviewer**

Menu: View ➤ Aerial View

Standard Toolbar: Aerial View

The entire drawing is displayed in the Aerial view window.

Menus

View   *Zoom In* increases and *Zoom Out* descreases drawing magnification by a factor of 2. *Global* displays the entire drawing and the current view.

Mode   Allows you to switch between *Pan* and *Zoom* modes.

Options   Toggle Auto Viewport to automatically display the model space view of the active viewport, Dynamic Update to update the aerial view while the drawing is being edited and RealTime Zoom to turn real time zoom on or off.

Dtext/Text

Dtext allows you to enter several lines of text at once. This command also displays the text on the drawing area as you type. At the first prompt, you can set the justification or set the current text style. Using either the *Fit* or *Align* options, you can tell AutoCAD to fit the text between two points.

To Enter Text

Command Line: **Dtext**

Menu: Draw ➤ Text ➤ Single Line Text

1. **Justify/Style/<Start point>:** Enter the desired options or pick a start point for your text.

2. If you pick a point to indicate the beginning location of your text, you get the following prompts:

    Height <default height>: Enter the desired text height, or press ↵ to accept the default. This prompt only appears if the current style has its height set to 0.

    Rotation angle <default angle>: Enter a rotation angle, or press ↵ to accept the default.

    Text: Enter the desired text.

   These prompts also appear after you have selected a style or set the justification option.

Options

Start point   Lets you indicate the location of your text. The text is automatically left-justified.

Justify   Specifies the justification of text. The prompt is:

   Align/Fit/Center/Middle/Right/TL/TC/TR/ML/MC/MR/ BL/BC/BR:

The two-letter options in this prompt set the justification based on the combination of top, middle, or bottom, and left, center, or right. For example, TL stands for "top left" and MC stands for "middle center." If you know the option, it can be entered directly at the "Justify" prompt.

Align   Forces proportional resizing of text to fit between two points. You are prompted to select the two points. The text height is scaled in proportion to its width in the current text style.

Center   Centers text on the start point, which also defines the baseline of the text.

Fit   Forces text to fit between two points. Unlike *Align, Fit* keeps the default height and either stretches or compresses the text to fit.

Middle   Centers text at the start point. The start point is in the middle of the text height.

Right   Right-justifies the text. The start point is on the right side of the text.

Style   Allows a new text style. The style you enter becomes the current style.

↵   If no option has been selected at the first prompt, pressing ↵ highlights the most recently entered line of text and displays the prompt "Text:", allowing you to continue to add text just below that line. The current text style and angle are assumed, as is the justification setting of the most recently entered text.

If you use **Dtext**, a box appears showing the approximate size of the text. The text appears on your drawing as you type and the box moves along as a cursor. When you press ↵, the box moves down one line. You can also pick a point anywhere on the screen for the next line of text and still backspace all the way to the beginning line to make corrections. If you choose a justification option other than Left, the effects will not be seen until you finish entering the text.

The **Text** command works much like **Dtext**; however, it does not display the text on your drawing as you type. The text you enter appears only in the command-prompt area. Further, once you press ↵, the text appears on the drawing and you are returned to the command prompt. You must press ↵ twice to enter multiple lines of text. Dtext does not work with script files. Control codes such as %%d can be entered before or after your text to add diameter, underscores, tolerance symbols, and so on to your text.

See Also   AutoLISP, Chtext, Mtext Ptext, Change, Color, Ddedit, Ddrename, Ddstyle, Rename, Qtext; *System Variables:* Texteval, Textsize, Textstyle, Style

Dview

Dview displays your drawing in perspective and enables you to clip a portion of a view. Unlike the standard **Zoom** and **Pan** commands, **Dview** allows you to perform zooms and pans on perspective views.

DVIEW

To Display a Drawing with DView

Command Line: **Dview**

Menu: View ➤ 3D Dynamic View

1. **Select object:** Pick the objects that will help set up your perspective view.

2. **CAmera/TArget/Distance/Points/PAn/Zoom/TWist/ CLip/Hide/Off/Undo/< eXit>:** Pick a point or select an option from the menu or enter the capitalized letter(s) of the desired option.

   • If you pick a point you will be prompted to **Enter direction and magnitude angles:** BEFORE you select an option, enter the direction (+ or -) and the desired angle, separated by a comma.

   The prompts you receive next depend on the option selected in the preceding step.

Options

CAmera   Allows you to move the camera location as if you were moving a camera around, while continually aiming at the target point. CAmera prompts you for the two angles of rotation: *Enter angle from XY plane:* and *Enter angle in XY plane from X-axis.* At each prompt, you can either enter a value or select the view by using the cursor. If you enter a value, it will be interpreted in relation to the current UCS. See Figure 6.

FIGURE 6:   The CAmera option controls the camera location relative to the target.

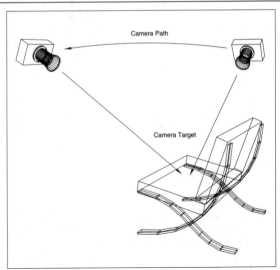

Camera Path

Camera Target

TArget Allows you to move the target location, as if you were pointing a camera in different directions while keeping the camera location the same. TArget prompts you for two angles of rotation, *Enter angle from XY plane:* and *Enter angle in XY plane from X-axis:*. At each prompt, you can either enter a value or select the view by using the cursor. See Figure 7.

FIGURE 7: The TArget option controls the target location relative to the camera.

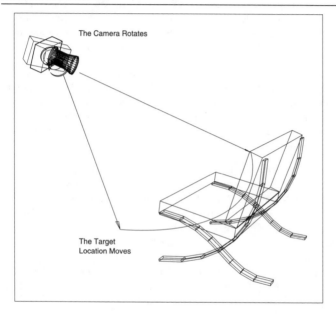

The Camera Rotates

The Target
Location Moves

Distance Turns on the Perspective mode and allows you to set the distance from the target to the camera, as if you were moving a camera toward or away from the target point. At the prompt, enter a new distance or move the slide bar at the top of the screen to drag the 3D image into the desired position.

Points Sets the target and camera points at the same time. The points you pick are in relation to the current UCS. At the prompt, pick a point for the target first, and then pick one for your camera location.

PAn Moves your camera and target point together, as if you were pointing a camera out the side window of a moving car. You cannot use the standard Pan command while viewing a drawing in perspective. See **Pan** for more information.

Zoom Zooms in and out when you are viewing a drawing in parallel projection. Provides the lens focal length when you are viewing a drawing in perspective. You cannot use the standard **Zoom** command while viewing a drawing in perspective.

If your 3D view is a parallel projection, enter a new scale factor or use the slide bar at the top of the screen to visually adjust the scale factor at the **Dview/Zoom** prompt. If your 3D view is a perspective, enter a new lens length value or use the slide bar at the top of the screen to determine the new lens length at the "Dview/Zoom" prompt. If you use the slide bar to adjust the focal length, the coordinate readout on the status line will dynamically display the focal length value.

TWist Rotates the camera about the camera's line of sight, as if you were rotating the view in a camera frame. At the "Dview/Twist" prompt, enter an angle or use the cursor to visually twist the camera view. If you use the cursor, the coordinate readout on the status line dynamically displays the camera twist angle. Use the *Twist* option if you wish to rotate your paperspace veiwpoints.

CLip Hides portions of a three-dimensional view. For example, it removes foreground objects that may interfere with a view of the background (see Figure 8). CLip displays the prompt "Back/Front/<Off>:". Enter **B** to set Back Clip Plane, **F** to set Front Clip Plane, or **O** or ⏎ to turn off the Clip Plane function. If you select Back or Front, a prompt allows you to either turn the selected clip plane on or off or to set a distance to the clip plane. You can use the slide bar at the top of the screen to visually determine the location of the clip plane, or enter a distance value. A positive value places the clip plane in front of the target point; a negative number places it behind the target point.

FIGURE 8: The CLip option allows you to hide foreground or background portions of your drawing.

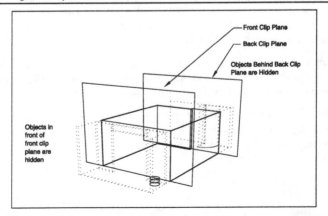

Hide Removes hidden lines from the objects displayed, turning a wire-frame view into a planar view.

eXit Returns you to the AutoCAD command prompt. Any operation you performed while in the **Dview** command prompt will affect the entire drawing, not just the selected objects.

> **NOTE** Because a large drawing slows down the drag function, you are prompted to select objects for dragging at the beginning of the Dview command. This limits the number of objects to be dragged. You should select objects that give the general outline of your drawing and sufficient detail to indicate the drawing's orientation. If you do not pick any objects, a default 3D house image appears to help you select a view. You can create your own block image and use that as the default. The block should be named *Dviewblock*.

See Also UCS; *System Variables:* Backz, Frontz, Lenslength, Target, Viewctr, Viewdir, Viewmode, Viewsize, Viewtwist

Dwfout

Dwfout displays the create .DWF File dialog box to create an external drawing web format (.DWF) file.

To Export a *.DWF* Drawing

Command Line: **Dwfout**

If the *Filedia* system variable is set to 0, the following prompts appear at the command line:

1. **Enter file name <current drawing name>:** Enter a name to export as a .DWF file.

2. **Enter precision (Low/High/<Medium>):** Set the level of decimal precision as low, medium or high.

3. **Compress file? (No/<Yes>):** Specify if the .DWF file should be exported using file compression.

If the *Filedia* system variable is set to 1, the create .DWF File dialog box opens to enter a drive/path and name for the .DWF file.

Options

Options Click the *Options...* button to set buttons for *Low*, *Medium* or *High* precision. Check *Use File Compress* box if wish the file to be exported using compression.

> **NOTE** Drawings created in paperspace (Tilemode = 0) do not have drawing web format support. Only the geometry in the current view is written to the .DWF file. Values set for the system variables *Viewres*, *Facetres*, *Dispsilh* and *Hide* determine output quality of the .DWF file. Named view are saved with the .DWF file; and a view called Initial is automatically created of the current drawings view when the command is invoked. Clicking the right mouse button restores named views of .DWF files if you are using the WHIP! menu. The .DWF file contains the same background color as the AutoCAD graphics window. To reduce file size, use a black or white background.

Dxbin

See Import/Export

Dxfin

See Import/Export

Dxfout

See Import/Export

Edge

Edge turns the visibility of 3D face edges on or off.

Command Line: **Edge**

Menu: Draw ➤ Surfaces ➤ Edge

Surfaces Toolbar: Edge

To Change the Visibility of a 3D Edge

Display/<Select edge>: Type **D** or select an edge to make invisible. The prompt is repeated, allowing you to select different edges until you press ⏎.

If you select the Display option by typing **D**, you will be prompted "Select /<All>:". Select an edge, or type **A** to highlight all edges. Then select the edge(s) to unhide. Use ⏎ to complete the command.

Options

Select edge Allows you to select individual edges, and then hides the selected edges.

Display Highlights invisible edges, either selected edges or all invisible edges.

See Also Edgesurf; *System Variables:* Splframe, 3DFace

Edgesurf

Edgesurf draws a 3D surface polygon mesh from four adjoining edges. These edges can be lines, arcs, polylines, or 3D polylines, but they must join exactly end-to-end.

To Create a 3D Surface Using Edgesurf

Command Line: **Edgesurf**

Menu: Draw ➤ Surfaces ➤ Edge Surface

Surfaces Toolbar: Edge Surface

1. **Select edge 1:** Pick the first object defining an edge.

2. **Select edge 2:** Pick the second object defining an edge.

3. **Select edge 3:** Pick the third object defining an edge.

4. **Select edge 4:** Pick the fourth object defining an edge.

The type of surface drawn by **Edgesurf** is called a *Coons surface patch* (see Figure 10). The first edge selected defines the M direction of the mesh, and the edges adjoining the first define the N direction. The endpoint closest to the point selected becomes the origin of the M and N directions.

FIGURE 10: A Coons surface patch

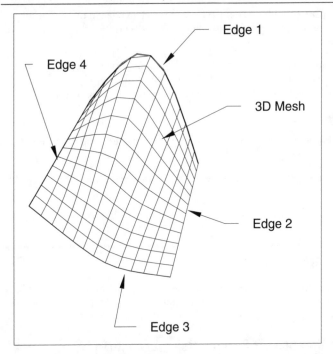

The *Surftab1* and *Surftab2* system variables control the number of facets in the M and N directions, respectively. Increasing the number of facets gives a smoother mesh, but increases the file size of the drawing. This increases file-opening, redrawing, and regeneration times. Increasing the values of *Surftab1* and *Surftab2* after creating the edgesurf will not smooth the 3D surface. Only edgesurfs created after, with the new values, will reflect the changes. See **System Variables** for details.

See Also   Pedit, Pface, 3DFace; *System Variables:* Splframe, Surftab1, Surftab2

Elev

Elev allows you to set the default Z-axis elevation and thickness of objects being drawn. Normally, objects will be placed at a zero elevation. Once you enter an elevation or thickness with **Elev**, all objects drawn afterwards will be given the new Z-axis value; objects you drew before using the **Elev** command are not affected. You can also change the elevation of an existing object with the **Move** command.

To Set Elevation and Thickness

Command Line: **Elev**

1. **New current elevation <current default>:** Set a new default starting plane elevation in the Z-axis.

2. **New current thickness <current default>:** Set a new default extrusion thickness in the Z-axis.

> **NOTE** 3D polylines, faces, and meshes, as well as viewports and dimensions, ignore the **Elev** setting of thickness. They do so because these entities cannot have thickness. Text and attribute definition entities are always given a zero thickness, regardless of the **Elev** values used during initial creation.

See Also Dducs, Move; *System Variables:* Elevation

Ellipse

Ellipse draws an ellipse for which you specify the major and minor axes, a center point, and two axis points; or the center point and the radius or diameter of an isometric circle. It also allows you to define a second projection of a 3D circle by using the *Rotation* option.

To Draw an Ellipse

Command Line: **Ellipse**

Menu: Draw ➤ Ellipse ➤ Center/Axis, End/Arc.

Draw Toolbar: Ellipse

The following prompts vary depending upon the preset options selected, and the isometric snap mode.

1. The isometric option under **Snap** is On or Off.

If your isometric snap mode is active, the following prompt appears:

Arc/Center/Isocircle/<Axis endpoint 1>: Enter **I**, then pick a point defining one end of the ellipse, **A** for arc or **C** to enter a center point.

If your isometric Snap mode is not active, the prompt is:

Arc/Center/<Axis endpoint 1>: Pick a point defining one end of the ellipse or type **C** to enter the center point.

2. For either of the above, the following prompts appear if you select the default option by picking a point:

> **Axis endpoint 2:** Pick a point defining the opposite end of the ellipse.

> **<Other axis distance>/Rotation:** Pick a point defining the other axis of the ellipse or enter **R** to enter a rotation value.

Options

Axis endpoint Allows you to enter the endpoint of one of the ellipse's axes (see Figure 11).

FIGURE 11: Axis endpoints and other axis distance

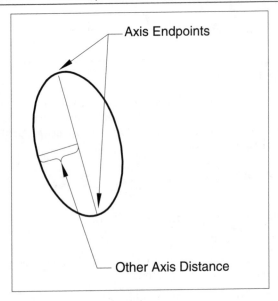

Axis Endpoints

Other Axis Distance

Center Allows you to pick the ellipse center point.

Arc Creates an elliptical arc. The angle of the first axis determines the angle of the arc.

Other axis distance Appears after you have already defined one of the ellipse's axes. Enter the distance from the center of the ellipse to the second axis endpoint).

Isocircle Appears when you set the *Style* option for the **Isometric** command to Isometric. This option creates an isometric circle in the current isometric drawing plane.

Rotation   Allows you to enter an ellipse rotation value between 0 and 89.4 degrees. Imagine the ellipse to be a 2D projection of a 3D circle rotated on an axis. As the circle is rotated, its projection turns into an ellipse. The rotation value determines the rotation angle of this circle. A 0-degree value displays a full circle; an 80-degree value displays a narrow ellipse.

Set the *Pellipse* system variable to 1 for a polyline ellipse or 0 for a true ellipse. If you create an ellipse which is actually a polyline, you can edit it using **Pedit**.

See Also   Isoplane, Snap/Style, Spline; *System Variables:* Pellipse, Snapisopair

Erase

Erase deletes one or several selected objects from a drawing.

To Erase Objects

Command Line: **Erase**

Menu: Modify ➤ Erase

Modify Toolbar: Erase

Select objects: Select the objects to be erased, by picking or using any selection method.

Options

As well as the standard selection options, the following are useful with the **Erase** command:

Single   Lets you pick a single object only. From the keyboard you can also enter **Si** at the "Select objects:" prompt.

Last   Lets you erase the last entity drawn. From the keyboard you can enter **L** at the Select objects: prompt. You can also enter Previous or **P** from the keyboard to erase the previous selection set.

Oops   Lets you unerase the last erase. (See **Oops**.) (The **Undo** command will reverse the entire **Erase** sequence but not the last object erased.)

To erase an object that is overlapped or superimposed by another, hold down the Ctrl key at the "Select object:" prompt. Pick a point where two or more objects overlap, such that it is difficult to select the correct object. The prompt "<Cycle on>" appears at the command line. Continue clicking on the same point until the object you want to erase is highlighted, then press ↵.

See Also   Multiple, Oops, Select/Si, Undo

Exit

Exit ends the AutoCAD session.

To End an AutoCAD Session

Command Line: **Exit**

Menu: File ➤ Exit

NOTE If any work was done during the drawing session and the drawing was never saved or named, an AutoCAD message box displays *Save Changes to Drawing.dwg?* so you can pick the Yes, No or Cancel buttons. If no work was done to the drawing, the drawing session is terminated immediately without any warning message.

See Also Quit

Explode

Explode reduces a block, polyline, associative dimension, body, multi-line, polyface and polygon mesh, region, group, or 3D mesh or solid to its component objects.

To Explode an Object

Command Line: **Explode**

Menu: Modify ➤ Explode

Modify Toolbar: Explode

1. **<Select objects>:** Select block, 2D, 3D, or wide polyline, multiline, 3D solid, Region, Polyface mesh, circle or arc to be exploded by picking or specifying any window selection set, including *window*, *wpolygon*, *cpolygon*, and *fence*.

2. Depending on the object explodes, the results may differ:

   3D Solid Planar surfaces turn into regions and nonplanar surfaces become bodies.

   Blocks If a block is nested, **Explode** only "unblocks" the outermost block. You can also explode non-uniformly scaled blocks, but the results may be exploded into unexpected objects.

   Region A region explodes into lines, arcs and splines.

   2D/wide polyline Returns lines and arcs with width of 0 and discards tangent information.

Body Converts object into single surface body (nonplanar surfaces), regions or curves.

Polyface mesh One-vertex mesh explodes into a point object, two-meshes turn into a line and three-vertex meshes become 3D faces.

3D polyline Exploding a 3D polyline turns it into line segments.

Circle If you explode a circle in a nonuniformly scaled block, it becomes an ellipse.

Multiline Mulitines explode into lines.

Arc If you explode an arc in a nonuniform block, it turns into elliptical arcs.

Blocks inserted with **Minsert** cannot be exploded. You can't explode Xrefs and their dependent blocks unless you bind them. Mirrored blocks cannot be exploded with the **Explode** command, but may be exploded using the new Xplode command. Wide polylines lose their width properties when exploded.

See Also Select, Undo, Xplode, Xref

Extend

Extend lengthens an object to meet another object. Objects that can be extended include arcs, elliptical arcs, lines, open polylines, and rays. You can extend objects to an "implied" as well as to an actual boundary.

To Extend an Object

Command Line: **Extend**

Menu: Modify ➤ Extend

Modify Toolbar: ⟍⟋ Extend

1. **Select boundary edges: (projmode - <current value>, Edgemode - <current value> Select objects:** Select the object or use fence selection to designate the boundary objects. If you press ↵ at the "Select objects:" prompt, AutoCAD selects all objects in your drawing, then displays the prompt shown in step 2.

2. **<Select objects to extend>Project/Edge/Undo:** Select objects to be extended by picking an object, using fence selection, or entering U to undo the last extend operation. You may also enter **P** or **E** to reset the Project or Edge settings.

- If you type **P**, you will be prompted **None/Ucs/View/<current value>:.**

- If you type **E**, you will be prompted **Extend/No extend <current value>:.**

Options

Project   Specifies the projection mode for AutoCAD to use when extending objects: with *None:* only selected objects which actually intersect with the boundary are extended; UCS: specifies projection onto the XY plane of the current UCS; *View:* extends all selected objects that intersect with the boundary in the current view. This option is controlled by the system variable *Projmode*. *Projmode* settings are zero = "None"; 1 = "UCS"; 2 = "View".

Edge   Allows you to extend objects to implied as well as actual boundaries; boundary edges do not have to be exactly in the path of the objects to be extended. This option is controlled by the system variable *Edgemode*: a setting of 0 "No extend" will not extend objects to the implied boundary; a setting of 1 "Extend" will allow objects to extend to an implied boundary.

Undo   Restores the previously executed option. You cannot extend objects within blocks or use blocks as boundary edges.

See Also   Change, Lengthen, Trim; *System Variables:* Edgemode, Projmode

Extensions

AutoCAD file extensions and their meanings. When entering file names, you must include the file extension. When deleting files, take care not to delete files AutoCAD needs for its internal operation. If you or someone on your network is currently editing a file, do not delete AutoCAD temporary files with the extension .$AC, .AC$, or .$A. Table 6 lists other AutoCAD file extensions and their purposes.

TABLE 6:   AutoCAD File Extensions and Their Meanings

Standard Extension	File Description
.3DS	3D Studio file
.ADS	ADS applications file
.ADT	Audit report file

TABLE 6: AutoCAD File Extensions and Their Meanings (cont.)

Standard Extension	File Description
.AHP	AutoCAD Help files
.ARX	AutoCAD run-time extension file
.AVI	Internet file
.BAK	Drawing backup file
.BD	Display font file
.BDF	Display font file
.BKn	Emergency backup file where n=sequential number
.BMP	Bitmap files
.C	ADS Source code file
.CC	ADS Source code file
.CCP	CalComp color palette files
.CFG	AutoCAD configuration file
.CNT	(HELP DIRECTORY)
.CPM	(BONUS DIRECTORY)
.CPP	(ADSRX\SAMPLE DIRECTORY)
.CUS	Custom Dictionary file
.DCC	Dialog box color control
.DCE	Dialog box error report
.DCL	Dialog Control Language description file
.DCT	Dictionary file
.DEF	ADS source code file
.DFS	Default file setting file
.DWT	Drawing template file
.GID	(HELP DIRECTORY)
.DBF	Database file for ASE applicatons
.DIM	Dimension file
.DFS	Default file settings file
.DLL	Dynamically linked library file

TABLE 6: AutoCAD File Extensions and Their Meanings (cont.)

Standard Extension	File Description
.DOC	Document file
.DWG	Drawing file
.DXB	Binary data exchange file
.DXF	Drawing interchange file
.DXT	DXFIX translator file
.DXX	Attribute data in DXF format
.FMP	(SUPPORT DIRECTORY)
.EPS	Encapsulated PostScript file
.ERR	AutoCAD error report
.FTG	(HELP DIRECTORY)
.FTS	(HELP DIRECTORY)
.EXE	Executable file
.FLM	AutoShade filmroll file
.GID	(HELP DIRECTORY)
.GIF	(CompuServe) Graphics image format file
.GSF	(FONTS DIRECTORY)
.H	ADS include file
.HDI	Hoops Device Interface
.HLP	Windows Help file
.HDX	Help index file
.INI	(BONUS\UTILS DIRECTORY)
.INM	(DRV DIRECTORY)
.IPG	(SAMPLE DIRECTORY)
.ISU	(ACADR14 DIRECTORY)
.LIB	ADS library file
.LIN	Line type definition file
.LLI	(SUPPORT DIRECTORY)
.LST	Printer plot file

TABLE 6: AutoCAD File Extensions and Their Meanings (cont.)

Standard Extension	File Description
.MAK	(ADSRX\SAMPLE DIRECTORY)
.MAP	(SUPPORT DIRECTORY)
.MDP	(ADSRX\SAMPLE DIRECTORY)
.MID	Identification information file
.MLI	Render materials file
.MLN	Multiline library file
.MNC	Compiled menu file (Windows only)
.MND	Menu definition file
.MNL	AutoLISP functions related with a menu file
.MNR	Menu source file
.MNS	Menu source file
.MNU	Menu template file
.MNX	Compiled menu file (DOS only)
.MPR	Mass properties text output file
.OLD	Backup of a file converted from an early version of AutoCAD
.PAT	Hatch-pattern library file
.PCP	Plot-configuration settings file
.PCX	PCX raster-image file
.PFB	PostScript font file
.PFM	PostScript font metric file
.PIF	Program Interface file
.PLT	Plot file
.PM	(SUPPORT DIRECTORY)
.PS	PostScript file
.PSF	PostScript support file
.PLT	Plot file
.PWD	AutoCAD login file

TABLE 6:   AutoCAD File Extensions and Their Meanings (cont.)

Standard Extension	File Description
.REG	(ACADR14 DIRECTORY)
.RPF	Raster-pattern fill definition file (for use with Hewlett Packard printer and plotter drivers)
.SAB	ACIS Solid binary file
.SAT	Solid modeling ACIS file (ASCII format)
.SCR	Script file
.SHP	Font file
.SHX	Shape or Font file
.SLB	Slide library file
.SLD	Slide files
.STL	Stereolithography file
.SVF	(BONUS DIRECTORY)
.TGA	Truevision Format
.TIF	TIFF raster-image file
.TLB	Translation Lookaside Buffer
.TTF	TrueType font file
.TXT	Attribute extract or template file (CDF/SDF format)
.UNT	Units file
.WMF	Windows metafile
.Xn	where n = 16 or 32
.XLG	External references log file
.XMX	External message file

Extrude

See Solid Modeling

Fill

Fill turns on or off the solid fills of solids, traces, and polylines. When **Fill** is off, solid filled areas are only outlined, both on the screen and in prints. The dialog box option for solid fill is **Ddrmodes** (Tools ➤ Drawing Aids).

To Fill an Object

Command Line: **Fill** (or **'Fill** to use transparently)

ON/OFF <ON>: Enter **On** or **Off** or press ↵.

See Also Ddrmodes, Pline, Solid, Trace, System Variables, Fillmode

Fillet

Fillet uses an intermediate arc to join two nonparallel lines, a line and an arc, or segments of a polyline.

To Use Fillet

Command Line: **Fillet**

Menu: Modify ➤ Fillet

Modify Toolbar: 🗁 Fillet

1. **(TRIM mode)Current fillet radius - Polyline/Radius/Trim <Select first object>:** Pick the first line to fillet.

2. **Select second line:** Pick the second line.

   - In Step 1, if you enter **P**, the prompt "Select 2D polyline:" appears; if you enter **R**, you are prompted to "Enter fillet radius." If you enter **T**, you are prompted: "Trim/No trim:".

   - If you select multiple edges of a 3D solid, the following prompt appears: "Enter radius<current>:" Enter a distance or press Enter to display "Chain/Radius <Select edge>:" prompt. Select an edge, Enter **C** to pick adjacent edges, or enter **R** to set a new radius.

Options

Polyline   Fillets all line segments within a polyline. You are prompted to select a 2D polyline. All joining polyline segments are then filleted.

Radius   Allows you to specify the radius of the fillet arc.

Trim   Allows you to toggle the trim option *ON* or *OFF*, and set it as a temporary default (using the system variable *Trimmode*). Turning trim *OFF* allows you to add a bevel while retaining the original line segments.

Chain   Activates multiple adjacent edges selection.

Edge   Activates single edge selection.

> **NOTE**   **Fillet** joins the end points closest to the intersection. The location you use to pick objects determines which part of the object is retained. If the lines (or line and arc) already intersect, **Fillet** substitutes the specified arc for the existing corner. To connect two nonparallel lines with a corner rather than an arc, set the radius to **0**. If you select two parallel lines, fillet joins them with an arc segment. You can also fillet just a corner of a polyline by picking its adjacent segments. Both segments, however, must be part of the same polyline. Lines and polylines can be joined together with fillet. The result produces a polyline. If you are not viewing the current UCS in plan, **Fillet** may give you the wrong result. Use the **Plan** command to view the current UCS in plan before issuing **Fillet**.

See Also   Chamfer, *System Variables:* Filletrad, Trimmode

Filter

Filter opens the Object Selection Filters dialog box to generate a selection-set filter based on combinations of object properties and to save them to a file name.

To Filter Properties

Command Line: **Filter** (or **'Filter** to use transparently)

Apply coordinates, object type, color, layer, line type, block name, text style, or thickness to a filter.

Options

List Box   Displays a list box (in the upper portion of the dialog box) of the filtered objects in your current selection set.

Edit Item   Pick box used to transfer the highlighted filter shown in the list box (at the upper portion of the dialog box) to the Select Filter area below. Pick *Edit Item* to transfer additional filters from the list box to the Select Filter area for editing. You can modify and Substitute the filters and their values displayed in the edit boxes below the Select Filter area.

Delete Pick box to remove the highlighted filter from the list box.

Clear List Pick box to remove all the filters from the list box.

Named Filters Area containing options to save, restore, and delete the current filter list.

Current Popup list displaying names of saved filters.

Save As Edit box for assigning a name and saving a filter list.

Delete Current Filter List Pick box for removing the saved filtered names from the Current popup list.

Apply Exits dialog box and executes the filtering procedure.

Select Filter Area containing X, Y, and Z coordinate edit boxes, and a Select subdialog box listing object types and relational operators as well as additional pick boxes. The Select subdialog box is specific to the entity type being filtered.

Add to List Appends an object in the *Select Filter* area to the filter list in upper portion of dialog box.

Substitute Pick box to replace highlighted filter criteria with the one in the Select Filter area.

Add Selected Object Pick box temporarily exits the dialog box allowing you to select objects from the drawing and add them to the filter list.

NOTE Entering Filter transparently (**'Filter**) at the command line allows you to apply the **P** (previous) selection set to access the filtered entities. The following operands must be paired and balanced for filters to operate correctly:

Begin AND/End AND

Begin Or/End Or

Begin XOR/End XOR

Begin NOT/End NOT

Gotourl

Gotourl allows you to select an object with an attached URL and accesses the specified address assigned to the URL.

GOTOURL

To Select an Objects Attached URL

Command Line: **Gotourl**

Select objects: Select object with an attached URL and AutoCAD will automatically open your default Internet browser and go to that URL.

See Also Attatchurl, Detachurl, Listurl, Selecturl, Openurl, Inserturl, Saveurl, Inetcfg, Inethelp

Graphscr

Graphscr flips you from the text screen to the graphics screen when you are working on a single-screen system. Pressing F2 has the same effect. Although **Graphscr** can be used at the command line, its intent is for use in menu and script files when a command, such as **List**, forces display of the text screen.

To Switch to the Graphics Screen

Command Line: **Graphscr**

NOTE If the text screen is displayed, AutoCAD switches to the graphics screen.

Grid

Grid turns on the grid and sets the grid spacing.

To Turn on the Grid

Command Line: **Grid**

To Change the Grid Settings

Menu: Tools ➤ Drawing Aids...

When the Drawing Aids dialog box appears, enter the desired grid spacing or other options.

Options

Grid spacing(X) Allows you to enter the desired grid spacing in drawing units. Enter **0** to make the grid spacing match the Snap setting.

ON Turns on the grid display. (The F7 key performs the same function).

OFF Turns off the grid display. (The F7 key performs the same function.)

Snap Sets the grid spacing to match the Snap spacing. Once set, Grid spacing will dynamically follow every change in the Snap spacing.

Aspect Specifies a grid spacing in the Y axis that is different from the spacing in the X axis.

NOTE If you follow the grid spacing value with **X** at the prompt, AutoCAD interprets the value as a multiple of the **Snap** setting. For example, if you enter **2**, the grid points will be spaced two units apart, but if you enter **2X**, the grid points will be twice as far apart as the Snap settings.

NOTE At times, a grid setting may obscure the view of your drawing. If this happens, AutoCAD automatically turns off the grid mode and displays the message "Grid too dense to display." If you are using multiple viewports in Paperspace, you can set the grid differently for each viewport.

See Also Ddrmodes; *System Variables:* Gridmode, Gridunit

Grips

Grips allow you to make quick changes to objects in a drawing. With this feature turned on (using the **Ddgrips** command), you can grab endpoints, center points, and midpoints of objects, and stretch, move, copy, rotate, mirror, or scale them. To reveal the grip points, click on a single object, or select multiple objects at the command prompt. Click on a single grip to edit it, or Shift-click on more than one grip to select several points. If you select multiple grips, you must click on one of the selected grips to begin editing.

To Use Grips

Command Line: **Grips**

Menu: Tools ➤ Grips…

You may toggle grips on or off at the command line as well as via the Ddgrips dialog box.

1. At the **New value for GRIPS:** prompt, type **0** to turn off **Grips**, or **1** to turn Grips on.

- When you click on a grip, it becomes a solid color and is called a *hot grip*. The command prompt will change to tell you the current edit option. You can tell you are in a grips edit option by the asterisks that surround the option name, as in **STRETCH** or **MOVE**.

- Pressing the Tab key while right clicking the mouse button on a hot grip displays a pop-up menu for alternate selection of commands. In additon to the standard grip command option, AutoCAD includes commands such as **Properties...** (**Ai_propchk**), **Go to URL...** (**Gotourl**) and **Exit**.

> **NOTE** Once you select a grip, you see the **STRETCH** prompt along with another prompt showing the options available under **STRETCH**. To switch to the *Move*, *Rotate*, *Scale*, and *Mirror* options, press the space bar or ↵ (the options repeat after *Mirror*). The hot grip is assumed to be the base point of the edit for all of these options. To specify a new base point, enter **B** ↵ at any of the grips options. You can also copy the selected objects by entering **C** ↵, or undo the last grips option by entering **U**. To remove grips from an entity, press the Esc key.

See Also   Copy, Ddgrips, Mirror, Move, Rotate, Scale, Stretch

Group

Group opens the Object Grouping dialog box that allows you to group objects for editing purposes.

To Select Object Groups

Command Line: **Group**

Menu: Tools ➤ Object Group....

Enter information as appropriate in the dialog box.

Options

Group Name   This list box displays the names of existing groups.

Selectable   Indicates whether a group is selectable. If a group is selectable, selecting just a single group member will select all group members, except those on locked layers. If a group is unselectable, selecting a single group member will select only that object.

Group Identification   The group name, and optional description, are shown in this area when a group is selected from the Group Name list.

Create Group   Allows you to create a *New* group and specify whether it is *Selectable*. Enter a name in the *Group Identification* text box, or use the *Unnamed* check box to create an unnamed group.

Change Group   Allows you to make changes to an existing group. You may *Remove* or *Add Objects* to the group, *Rename*, or *Re-order* the group, change or add the *Description* and *Selectable* setting, or *Explode* the group.

> **NOTE**   Although a "group" has been created, you may edit individual objects within the group using **Grips**. Use **Crtl + A** to toggle grouping on or off.

See Also   Ddgrips, Grips; *System Variables:* Pickstyle

Hatch

Hatch fills an area defined by lines, arcs, circles, or polylines with either a predefined pattern, a user-defined pattern, a solid or simple hatch pattern. The equivalent dialog box command is **Bhatch**.

To Select a Hatch

Command Line: **Hatch**

1. **Enter pattern name or [?/Solid/User defined] <current pattern>:** Specify a pattern name or enter an option.

2. After you enter a pattern name, the following prompts appear:

   • **Scale for pattern <current default>:** Specify a new value or press ↵.

   • **Angle for pattern <current value>:** Specify a new value or press ↵.

   • Select hatch boundaries or press ↵ for direct hatch option.

   • **Select objects:** Pick objects that define the hatch boundary, or press ↵ for additional options. If you press ↵ the "Retain polyline? <Y/N>:" prompt appears. Entering Y retains the boundary as a polyline, otherwise N discards the boundary. Next, use the "From point:" prompt and *Arc/Close/Length/Undo/<Next point>:* options to create a boundary. Once the area is closed, the "From point or press ↵ to apply hatch:" prompt reappears for you to pick additional points or press ↵ to apply the hatch pattern.

Options

Pattern name   You may enter any valid AutoCAD pattern name as defined in the `acad.PAT` file. To list all of the patterns, use the *?* option. To fill the area with individual lines instead of a hatch block, you should precede the pattern name with an asterisk (*). In general, the pattern scale should be the same as the drawing scale. The following modifiers control how the pattern is created. To use these modifiers, enter the pattern name at the "Pattern" prompt, followed by a comma and the modifier.

N   Fills alternating areas (default option).

O   Fills only the outermost area selected.

I   Causes the entire area within the objects selected to be hatched, regardless of other enclosed areas within the selected area. Text is not hatched over.

?   Lists the names of available hatch patterns.

Solid   Specifies a solid fill.

Arc   Allows you to draw an arc as the boundary edge with the **Arc** command options *Angle/CEnter/CLose/Direction/Line/Radius/Second pt/Undo*.

Close   Closes the endpoints of a polyline.

Length   Extend a line by dragging and picking with your cursor or entering a value at the "Length of line:" prompt.

Undo   Resends the previous option.

User defined   This option allows you to define a simple user-defined hatch pattern, including **Angle for crosshatch lines <0>:** (hatch angle), **Spacing between lines <1.0000>:,** and whether or not you want a single hatch or a **Double hatch area? <N>** (cross-hatch). Cross-hatching occurs at 90 degrees to the first hatch lines. As with the predefined patterns, you may precede the **U** with an asterisk (*) to fill the area with single lines rather than hatch block, and you may append the hatch style codes (**n, o, i**) to control how the hatching is applied.

scaleXP   When entered at the scale prompt, this modifier lets you specify a hatch scale relative to Paperspace. See **Zoom/XP**.

There are 68 predefined patterns, as illustrated in Figure 12. You can create your own hatch patterns by editing the `Acad.PAT` file. This file uses numeric codes to define the patterns.

Use the **List** command to identify the pattern name, spacing, and scale.

FIGURE 12: The standard hatch patterns

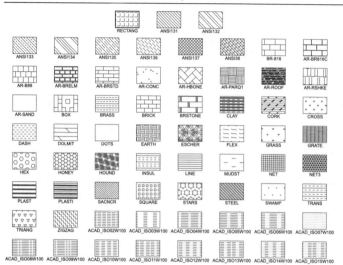

The objects that define the hatch area should be joined end-to-end and be closed. If you use lines and arcs, the end points of the objects must meet exactly end-to-end. Polylines should be closed. If you select two lines as bounding edges, AutoCAD will use the shortest line length as the limits for the hatch pattern.

To make the hatch pattern begin at a specific point, use the *Rotate* option under the **Snap** command to set the snap origin to the desired beginning point. Hatch uses the snap origin (*Snapbase* system variable) to determine where to start the hatch pattern.

The *Fillmode* system variable can be used to toggle globally the display of solid fills and hatches. AutoCAD now stores the hatch boundary information along with a pointer to the hatch definition instead of an unnamed block identifed as *X.

See Also Bhatch, Explode, Hatchedit, Snap/Rotate; *System Variables:* Fillmode, Hpang, Hpdouble, Hpname, Hpscale, Hpspace

Hatchedit

Hatchedit modifies an existing *associative* hatch block. The hatch pattern must have been associated with the hatched object, via the **Bhatch** command. If the original object is altered, you may resize the hatching to follow the object. Use **-hatchedit** to display all the prompts at the command line.

To Edit a Hatch Block

Command Line: **Hatchedit**

Menu: Modify ➤ Object ➤ Hatch

Modify II Toolbar: 🖾 Edit Hatch

1. **<Select hatch object>:** Select the hatch object you wish to modify.

2. In the *Hatchedit* dialog box, make the required modifications to the hatch pattern, and press **Apply.**

Options

Pattern Type   This section allows you to select a pattern by clicking the drop box to choose between predefined, user-defined, and custom hatch patterns, the *Pattern...* button to open the Hatch Pattern Pallette dialog box to view and choose from pattern groups or the image box to cycle through predefined patterns.

Pattern Properties   Allows you to manipulate specific properties of the chosen pattern type (see **Bhatch**).

Boundary   Allows you to edit the boundary definition (see **Bhatch**).

Preview Hatch   Displays a preview of the pattern, then returns to the dialog box (see **Bhatch**).

Inherit Properties   Allows you to select a hatch object from your current drawing and apply its properties to the hatch object that you are currently editing.

Attributes   This section contains a check box for *Associative hatching* allowing you to control whether the hatching is associated with its boundary or not and for *Exploded* which applies the old-format non-associative hatch blocks. (Only associative hatches may be edited.)

   The command line version will prompt you through the appropriate options *Disassociate/Style/<Properties>:*. The values of the hatching variables are saved as xdata in the hatch block reference.

See Also   Bhatch, Hatch, System Variable, Hpang, Hpdouble, Hpname, Hpscale, Hpspace, Snapbase

-Hatchedit

-Hatchedit displays prompts at the command line to edit an existing associated hatch.

To Edit an Associated Hatch

Command Line: **-Hatchedit**

1. **Select hatch object:** Select the hatch you wish to edit.

2. **Disassociate/Style/<Properties>:** Enter an option or press ↵ for the following prompt:

   Enter pattern name or [?/Solid/User defined] <ANSI31>: Enter a pattern name, type ? to list names of available patterns, S for a solid fill pattern or U for a user defined pattern. The U option displays additional prompts for setting *Angle for crosshatch lines, Spacing between lines* and single or *Double hatch area?*.

Options

Disassociate   Removes associativity from the hatch object.

Style   Press ↵ at the prompt Ignore/Outer/<Normal>: to fill alternating areas, enter **I** fill entire area within objects selected or **O** for outermoset area selected.

See Also   Bhatch, Hatch, Hatchedit

Help/?

Help or **?** opens up the Help dialog box to provide a brief description of how to use a particular command. You can use it on the fly by entering **'Help** or **'?** at any prompt in the command. You may press F1 to get context-sensitive Help on the current command.

To Use Help

Command Line: **Help** (or **'Help**, to use transparently)

Menu: Help ➤ AutoCAD Help Topics

Standard Toolbar: [?] Help

Options

Contents Tab   This tab displays a book icon with associated help topics. Click a topic, then pick *Open* to display branches of related help topics. Highlight a specific help topic and click *Display* to retrieve additional information, *Print...* to print the help topic and *Close* to exit the help menu.

Index Tab   This tab accesses the Help Index. Enter the first few letters of the word or use the scroll bar to locate your topic, highlight it, then click *Display*. Depending on the item selected, a Topics Found subdialog box containing additional descriptions or a Windows Help screen may appear. The Windows Help screen contains an Options menu to set controls such as *Annotate...*, *Copy to a Clipboard*, *Print Topic...*, set *Font* size or *Use System Colors*.

Find Tab   Loads a word list allowing you to search for specific words or phrases in help topics. Enter the word in an edit box or use the scroll bar to search for matching words. Click the *Clear* button to empty the edit box and the *Options...* button to open the Find Options dialog box and set radio buttons for how you search for topics. The *Find Similiar...* and *Find Now* buttons are intended to aid you in your search.

When Help is used in the middle of a command, you receive information related to the specific prompt being displayed. Pick the slide bar along the right side of the dialog box or use *Next* and *Previous* to maneuver through the description.

Hide

Hide removes hidden lines on an orthogonal or 3D view when using Vpoint, Dview, or View.

To Hide Lines

Command Line: **Hide**

Menu: View ➤ Hide

Render Toolbar: ⬚Hide

NOTE For complex 3D views, you may want to use **Mslide** to save the view with hidden lines removed. In a perspective view, use the *Hide* option under **Dview**. You can also use **Shade** to get a quick rendering of a 3D model.

See Also   Dview, Mview, Preferences, Shade, View

Id

Id displays the X, Y, and Z coordinate values of a point.

To Display a Point's Coordinates

Command Line: **Id** (or **'Id** to use transparently)

Menu: Tools ➤ Inquiry ➤ ID Point

Inquiry Toolbar: ░░░Id Point

Point: Pick a point.

A point you select with Id becomes the last point in the current editing session (stored in the *Lastpoint* variable). This can be accessed by inserting the @ sign when you are asked to pick a point.

See Also Point; *System variable:* Lastpoint

-Imageadjust

-**Imageadjust** allows you to select one or more images at the command line to adjust their contrast, fade and brightness.

To Adjust an Image

Command Line: -**Imageadjust**

1. **Select image:** Pick an image you wish to adjust.

2. **Contrast/Fade/<Brightness>:** Press ⏎ or enter an option. Contract and Brightness default values are 50; Fade defaults to 0.

See Also Imageadjust

Image

Image inserts images in different formats, such as BMP, TIF, RLE, JPG, GIF and TGA into an AutoCAD drawing file. Use -**Image** to display all commands at the command line.

To Insert an Image

Command Line: **Image**

Menu: Insert ➤ Raster Image

Insert Toolbar: ▨Image

Reference Toolbar: ▨Image

Draw Toolbar: ▨Insert Flyout ▨Image

Opens the Image dialog box for you to select a raster or bit-mapped bitonal, color image file for insertion into the drawing. Images can be 8-bit gray, 8-bit color, or 24-bit image.

Provide information as needed in the dialog box(es).

Options

List View   The image list box contains 6 drag division headings, including Image Name, Status, Size, Type, Data, and Saved path, that can be sorted alphabetically or numerically. The default sort order is alphabetical by image name. Change column widths by placing your cursor over the vertical divider line, until the heading changes to an anchor symbol, then drag it. Double click the vertical line to restore the heading default width or close the dialog box to save its size. Images can be renamed by clicking the name, then pressing the F2 key. Names are limited to 31 characters, including letters, digits, and the special characters hyphen (-) and underscore (_). Although an image in the drawing can be renamed, the actual file remains unchanged. You cannot rename an image if it is inside an external reference file.

Tree View   Pressing F3 and F4 toggles the display of images as a list of individual names or a tree structure with reference to its source. Images inserted directly into the drawing are located at the top, followed by images nested in block, then those nested in external reference files, which branch off from their xref file name are below. Their identification is similar to an xref layer, with the file and image names separated by the pipe character (|). When individual names are displayed in tree view lists, you can select multiple files using standard windows Shift and Control key methods.

Attach   Opens the Attach Image file dialog box to insert a new image object and definition to the current drawing. The **Imageattach** command opens the same dialog box. (See Imageattach).

Detach   Detaches the selected image definitions and removes all associated image objects from the drawing database and display screen.

Reload   Allows you to load a new drawing or reload an image that had been unloaded, placing its draworder on top.

Unload   Unloads an image, displaying it as a boundary and minimizing AutoCAD's memory requirement. It does not delete or permanently detach the image object from the drawing. Use *Reload* to restore the image.

Image Found At   Identifies actual drive letter, directory path, and file name for a selected image.

Browse   Opens the Attach Image file dialog box allowing you to preview as well as search and/or select an image's *File name, Directories, List of File Types* and *Drives*. Clicking *Hide preview* prevents the image from being displayed and toggles the button to *Show preview*.

Save Path Retains the new path information. If you press Escape while editing the images path, the old path is restored. If AutoCAD cannot locate the image, an alert dialog box appears with the message *Image file not found. Do you really want to use this path?* Clicking *Yes* reports Not Found in the Status column. If Save Path is not picked after the path is edited, the original image path is used the next time you load the drawing.

Details Selecting an image and clicking the button opens the Image File Details dialog box, providing you with information, such as the image name, saved path, active path, file creation date and time, file size and type, color, color depth, width and height in pixels, resolution, default size in units, and a preview image.

See Also -Image, Imageattach; *System Variables*: Sortents, Draworder.

-Image

-Image inserts .BMP, .TIF, .RLE and .JPG image files at the command line.

To Insert an Image from the Command Line

Command Line: **-Image**

? / Detach / Path / Reload / Unload / <Attach>: Enter an option or press ↵ to attach the image to your current drawing.

Options

? Alphabetically displays the image name, instances occuring and the hard-coded path.

> **Images to list <*>:** Press ↵ or an image name.

Detach Removes the named image from your drawing.

> **Image(s) to detach <*>:** Enter an image name.

Path Allows you to edit the file name and associated path of specified image.

> **Edit path for which image(s):** Enter the image name or an * for mulitple images. If you entered an asterisk (*), prompts appear *Old Path* and *New Path* to enter the current and new paths for the image.

Reload Reloads image data into memory for display and plotting. AutoCAD displays the messages:

> *Reloading...*
> *Reload image <image name>: <hard-coded path name>*
> *<image name> loaded and relinked*

Image(s) to reload: Enter an image name

Unload   Removes image data from working memory to improve performance. Unloaded images are displayed as a frame and their information remains stored with the drawing.

Image(s) to unload: Enter a loaded image name.

See Also   Image

Imageadjust

Imageadjust displays a dialog box to set control for an image's brightness, contrast, and fade values. Use **-Imageadjust** to display all commands at the command line.

To Adjust an Image

Command Line: **Imageadjust**

Menu: Modify ➤ Object ➤ Image ➤ Adjust...

Reference Toolbar: 🖼 Image Adjust

Opens the Image Adjust dialog box allowing you to use a slider button or corresponding edit boxes to adjust the *Brightness*, *Contrast* and *Fade* of an image.

Brightness   Set to higher values if you wish to brighten the image; causes pixels to become whiter.

Contrast   Use a higher value to force pixels to their primary or secondary color.

Fade   Specify a higher value to merge image with its background color.

Image Preview   Thumbnail image used to dynamically display specified adjustments.

Reset   Resets image to default values: Brightness = 50, Contrast = 50 and Fade= 0.

See Also   -Imageadjust

Imageattach

Imageattach loads an image object into memory, while attaching its definition and displaying it in the current drawing.

To Attach an Image

Command Line: **Imageattach**

Reference Toolbar: Image Attach

Opens the Attach Image dialog box directly, bypassing the Image dialog box.

Provide information as needed in the dialog box.

Image Name   Click the *Browse...* button in the Image Name section to enter a filename in the *File name* edit box, select from the list box or locate *Directories, List of File Types* and *Drives*. Use the *Hide preview* button to prevent the image from being displayed. Once the image is hidden, the button changes to *Show preview*. The drop-down box lists all the images in the current drawing. Highlighting a name displays the *Path:* below.

Image Parameters   Use an edit box to specify where the image is to be inserted *At:*, its *Scale factor*, and *Rotation*. Checking Specify On-Screen grays corresponding check boxes, allowing you to enter information at the command line when the image is inserted.

Include Path   Check this box if you wish to save the path of the image file with its definition or uncheck the box to save the image name only. AutoCAD will peruse the Project Files Search Path, stored in the *Projectname* system variable, when the box is unchecked.

Details>>   Select this button to obtain more detailed information about the image, including horizontal and vertical resolution, width and height in pixels as well as units. The units for some images, such as .TIF files, can be set to millimeters, centimeters, meters, kilometers, inches, feet, yards, miles, or unitless in the *Current AutoCAD Unit* box. The default value is unitless. The width and height of an image is automatically converted to AutoCAD units and displayed with a default size.

See Also   *System Variables:* Projectname

Imageclip

Imageclip allows you to make a clipping boundary within an image object.

To Clip an Image

Command Line: **Imageclip**

Modify: ➤ Object ➤ Imageclip

Reference Toolbar: Image Clip

1. **Select image to clip:** Pick an image object you wish to clip.

2. **ON/OFF/Delete/<New boundary>:** Specify an option or press ↵ to create a new boundary.

3. **Polygonal/<Rectangular>:** Press ↵, then pick opposite corners for a rectangular clipping boundary or type **P** to draw any closed polygon shape you define.

4. **Delete old boundary? No/<Yes>:** (This prompt appears if you select a clipped image to create a new boundary.) Press ↵ to restore the original image, then create a new boundary or **N** to exit the command.

Options

ON   Toggles clipping on and restores the images clipped area to show its previously defined boundary.

OFF   Toggles clipping off to show the entire image and frame. AutoCAD automatically turns on any image that is selected for reclipping and gives the prompt "Delete old boundary?".

Delete   Removes clipped boundary and restores original image.

Imageframe

Imageframe controls the visibility of all image frames in the current drawing at the command line.

To Turn an Image Frame Off

Command Line: **Imageframe**

Modify: ➤ Object ➤ Image ➤ Frame

Reference Toolbar: ▦ Image Frame

ON/OFF <current setting>: Enter *ON* or *OFF*.

Imagequality

Imagequality sets two controls for image quality.

To Control Image Quality

Command Line: **Imagequality**

Modify: ➤ Object ➤ Image ➤ Quality

Reference Toolbar: Image Frame

High/Draft <current setting>: Specify an option.

Option

High   Increases quality, causing images to display slower.

Draft   Decreases quality and displays the images faster.

> **NOTE** Setting image quality in the drawing does not affect their plotted output; images always plot with high quality.

Import/Export

Import and **Export** commands offer several ways to transfer data to and from other applications and file formats.

Import Functions

You can bring drawings or images from other applications into the current AutoCAD drawing by using the Import functions in the Import File dialog box. The program supports these file formats: `.DXF`, `.3DS`, `.SAT`, `.EPS`, and `.WMF`.

To Import Files Created in Other File Formats

Command Line: **Import**

Draw Toobar: Insert Flyout Import

Insert Toolbar: Import

1. Opens the Import File dialog box. Click on the required file format in the List Files of Type drop-down box, then, search Directories and/or Drives to find the file that you wish to import. A preview image displays selected images prior to importing them into your drawing. If you are unable to locate the file, click the *Find File* button to open the Browse and Search Dialog box for global further investigation.

2. Click the *Options* button to open Import Options subdialog box and set `.WMF` In toggles: **Wire Frame (No Fills)** offers the option to import objects as wire frames or filled objected and **Wide Lines** allows you to maintain line and border width or to import the file with 0 width.

Although the above steps outline the basic procedures for importing other file formats there are a number of variations and some additional prompts. Moreover, all of these file import options have equivalent command-line versions. Table 8 lists the AutoCAD import options and their command equivalents, as well as any procedural variations.

TABLE 8: AutoCAD File Import Functions

File Format	Command	Description/Comments
Drawing Exchange Format		
.DXF	DXFIN	Imports ASCII format and binary drawing exchange file. Used to transfer data from other CAD systems into AutoCAD.
3D Studio Files		
.3DS	3DSIN	Imports selected 3D Studio geometry and rendering information. Prior to import, you must provide layer- and materials-handling information in the 3D Studio File Import Options dialog box.
Solid Models		
.SAT	ACISIN	Converts geometric objects stored in ASCII (.SAT) format into AutoCAD bodies, solids, and regions.
Postscript		
.EPS	PSIN	Inserts an Encapsulated PostScript image into the current drawing as an anonymous block. You need to specify the insertion point and scale factor for the block.
Windows		
.WMF	WMFIN	Imports Windows Metafile format files. You need to specify an insertion point and scale factor when importing the file.

Export Functions

Using the AutoCAD export functions, you can convert AutoCAD drawings into several different formats. The formats can then be read by other applications: .DWF, .DWG, .DXF, .DXX, .3DS, .SAT, .STL, .EPS, .BMP, and .WMF.

To Create Other File Formats

Command Line: **Export**

Menu: File ➤ Export Data

1. Opens the Export Data dialog box. Highlight the required file format in the Save as Type drop-down box.

2. For some file formats the *Options* button ungreys allowing you to set specific controls for .DWF, .DXF and Postscript file types.

Table 9 lists the AutoCAD export options, their command equivalents, and any variations in the general procedure described above.

TABLE 9: AutoCAD File Export Functions

Format	Command	Description/Comments
Drawing Interchange Format		
.DXF	DXFOUT	Exports ASCII format drawing interchange file. Used to transfer data from AutoCAD to other CAD systems. Output types include: AutoCAD R14, R13, R12, LT95 and LT2.
3D Studio Files		
.3DS	3DSOUT	Converts selected AutoCAD geometry and rendering information into 3D Studio format. Prior to conversion, you must specify the division method and provide smoothing and welding information in the 3D Studio File Export Options dialog box.
Solid Models		
.SAT	ACISOUT	Converts AutoCAD objects, representing surfaces, solids and regions, to an ACIS file in ASCII format.
Stereolithography		
.STL	STLOUT	Outputs a single solid into an ASCII or binary format. The .STL format is compatible with Stereolithography Apparatus (SLA). The solid data is output as a triangulated mesh that represents the solid. After selecting the solid for output, you need to specify ASCII or binary format

TABLE 9: AutoCAD File Export Functions (continued)

Format	Command	Description/Comments
Windows Metafile and Bitmap Files		
.WMF	WMFOUT	Saves selected objects to Windows Metafile format, containing both vector and raster graphics.
.BMP	BMPOUT	Creates a bitmap image of selected objects in your drawing. There is no menu or dialog box option for creating bitmaps.
Drawing Web Format		
.DWF	DWFOUT	Highly compressed 2D vector file used to publish drawing on the World Wide Web.
Attribute Extract File		
.DXX	Ddattext, DXF Output File Option	Used in the Ddattext dialog box for drawing interchange file format (.DXF) to differentiate the output file from normal .DXF files.

Options

DWF   Opens the DWF Export Options dialog box, allowing you to set Low/High/Medium precision as well as Use File Compression for extraction process.

DXF   Opens an Export Options subdialog box for you to *Select objects*, then choose between ASCII or Binary formats and set Decimal places of accuracy (0–16) for your .DXF file.

EPS   Opens an Export Options subdialog box with edit boxes and radio button to set controls for PostScript output. An optional Prolog Section Name edit box is used to read from the acad.psf file when using the **Psout** command. The What to Plot section contains radio buttons for selecting different area configurations: plotting your current *Display* screen, the drawing *Extents*, and *Limits*. You can also save a *View* or create a *Window* to define the drawing area to plot. The *View* and *Window...* buttons allow you to retrieve saved images or pick points from the screen.

The Preview section allows you to specify an *EPSI, TIFF* or *None* (no preview screen image). Use the Pixels section to set your screen preview image at *128, 256* or *512*.

Use the Scale section edit boxes to specify the number of *Drawings Units* equal to *Output Units*. Check *Fit to Paper* to maximize the image for the specified paper size.

The Paper Size section has an edit box to enter a *Width* and a *Height* as well as a drop-down menu to select predefined sizes.

NOTE AutoCAD system variables and other options can be used to control the quality and precision of a number of these file conversions.

See Also Cut, Paste, Insertobj, Mslide, OLE, Olelinks; *Solid Modeling:* Ameconvert; *System Variables:* Facetres, Psquality.

Inetcfg

Inetcfg configures your Internet host for FTP login, HTTP access, Internet connection and proxy imformation.

To Configure Internet Host

Command Line: **Inetcfg**

Utilities Toolbar: Configure Internet Host

When the Internet Configuration dialog box opens, specify information as needed.

FTP Login This section contains edit boxes to enter a *User Name* and *Password* for FTP sites. You can type a personal login name or use "anonymous" and leave the password edit box empty. If you log in to a secured FTP server with files that you wish to access to open, insert, or save, toggle *Anonymous Login* off by unchecking the box, then type your user name and password for that server.

HTTP Secure Access This section contains User Name and Password edit boxes for HTTP sites. You must enter information into these edit boxes, otherwise AutoCAD displays the User Authentication dialog box and repeats the request.

Connection This section allows you to specify *Direct Connection,* if you have a direct connection to the Internet through an ISP (Internet service provider), or *Proxy Server.* A proxy server is a device that serves as a connection between a company's internal Intranet and the external Internet. Proxy servers are typically used on a secured proxy server (firewall), providing access to the outside world for individuals inside the firewall. It's main function is caching of requests and maintaining a secure means of accessing data. Direct connections do not require you to configure proxies.

Proxy Information   This section contains edit boxes to enter a *Proxy Server Name*, *FTP port* and *HTTP port* if you wish to change the default values.

NOTE The FTP password is not saved within AutoCAD sessions. If you are unfamiliar with internet requirements, contact your network system administrator or review the proxy settings in your browser. In the Netscape Navigator's Options menu, select Network Preferences, then Proxies tab; in Microsoft Internet Explorer's View menu, pick Options, then the Connection tab.

See Also   Attachurl, Detachurl, Inserturl, Listurl, Openurl, Saveurl, Selecturl, Inethelp

Inethelp

Inethelp displays online context-sensitive AutoCAD Internet Utilities Help menu.

For Internet Help

Command Line: **Inethelp**

Internet Utilities Toolbar: Internet Help

Use the Internet Utilities Help menu to display context-sensitive help information that can be viewed on the display screen or output to a printer.

Insert

Insert places a named block (or drawing) within the current file. The equivalent dialog box command is **Ddinsert**.

To Insert Blocks

Command Line: **Insert**

1. **Block name (or ?) <last block inserted>:** Enter the block or drawing name or a tilde (~) to display the Select Drawing File dialog box.

2. **Insertion point:** Enter a coordinate value, pick a point with the cursor, or enter a preset option (see "Preset Options" below).

3. **X scale factor <1> / Corner / XYZ:** Enter an X scale factor; **C** for corner; **XYZ** to specify the individual X, Y, and Z scale factors; or ↵ to accept the default X scale factor of 1.

4. **Y scale factor (default=X):** (This prompt appears if you press ↵ without entering a value or option.) Enter a Y scale factor or press ↵ to use the scale factor for the Y axis as well.

5. **Rotation angle <0>:** Enter the rotation angle for the block or pick a point on the screen to indicate the angle. (This last prompt does not appear if you use the *Rotate* preset option.)

Options

tilde (~) Entered at the "Block name..." prompt, causes the Select Drawing File dialog box to appear. The dialog box lets you select external files for insertion.

= Replaces a block with an external file.

X scale factor Scales the block in the X axis. If you enter a value, you are then prompted for the Y scale factor.

Corner Allows you to enter the X and Y scale factors simultaneously. To scale the block by a factor of 1 in the X axis and 2 in the Y axis, enter **C** at the "X scale factor..." prompt and then enter **@1,2**. Otherwise, enter a coordinate value or pick a point at the "X scale factor..." prompt to scale your block.

XYZ Gives individual X, Y, and Z scale factors. You will be prompted for the factors.

Preset Options The following options are available at the "Insertion point:" prompt. They are called Insert "presets" because they allow you to preset the scale and rotation angle of a block before you select an insertion point. Once you select a preset option, the dragged image will conform to the setting used; you will not be prompted for a scale factor after you select the insertion point.

Scale Allows you to enter a single scale factor for the block. This factor governs X, Y, and Z axis scaling.

Xscale Sets the X scale factor.

Yscale Sets the Y scale factor.

Zscale Sets the Z scale factor.

Rotate   Enters a rotation angle for the block.

Pscale   The same as *Scale,* but is used only while positioning the block for insertion to "preview" the scaled block. You are later prompted for a scale factor.

Pxscale   The same as *PScale,* but affects only the X scale factor.

Pyscale   The same as *PScale,* but affects only the Y scale factor.

Pzscale   The same as *PScale,* but affects only the Z scale factor.

Protate   The same as *Rotate,* but is used only while positioning the block for insertion. You are later prompted for a rotation factor.

If a block has previously been inserted, it becomes the default block for insertion (stored in the *Insname* system variable). Enter **?** to see a list of the blocks in the current file. Coordinate values are in relation to the current UCS.

To insert the individual entities in a block (rather than the block as a single object), type an asterisk before its name at the "Block name:" prompt. To bring the contents of an external file in as individual entities, insert the file in the normal way and use the **Explode** command to break it into its individual components. To insert a mirror image of a block, enter a negative value at either the "X scale factor..." or "Y scale factor..." prompt.

If the inserted block or file contains an attribute and the *Attreq* system variable is set to 1, you are prompted for the attribute information after you have entered the rotation angle. If the system variable *Attdia* is set to 1, a dialog box with the attribute prompts appears. (The default setting for *Attreq* is 1. *Attdia* is normally set to 0.)

You can also use **Insert** to replace or update a block with an external drawing file. For example, to replace a block named Chair1 with an external file named Chair2, enter **Chair1=Chair2** at the "Block name:" prompt. If the block and the external file names are the same (Chair1, for example), enter **Chair1=**. Note, however, that named objects in the current drawing have priority over those in an imported file.

When you attempt to replace blocks containing attributes, the old attributes will remain even though the block has been changed. To avoid them, you must delete the old block, insert the new (external) block, and reenter the attribute values. You can also use the AutoLISP utility *Attredef* (see **AutoLISP**).

Finally, an external file will be inserted with its WCS (world coordinate system) aligned with the current UCS (user coordinate system). A block will be inserted with its UCS orientation aligned with the current UCS.

See Also Attdef, Attredef, Base, Block, Ddattdef, Ddatte, Ddattext, Ddinsert, Explode, Files; *System Variables:* Attreq, Attdia, Filedia, Insname, Xplode, Xref

Insertobj

Insertobj allows you to insert a range of graphic and multimedia objects into an existing AutoCAD drawing. Objects include other AutoCAD drawings, sound clips, music clips and media clips, clip art, paint files, word-processed documents, and presentation slides. **Insertobj** works with Windows' Object Linking and Embedding (OLE). It allows you to create objects for embedding into your current AutoCAD drawing.

To Insert an Object into a Drawing

Command Line: **Insertobj**

Menu: Insert ➤ OLE Object

Draw Toolbar: 🔲Insert Flyout 🔲OLE Object

Insert Toolbar: 🔲OLE Object

1. When the Insert Object dialog box opens, double-click on the *Object Type* that you wish to embed in your drawing.

    AutoCAD starts the native Windows application associated with the type of object that you have selected. For example, if you click on Powerpoint Slide, it will open Powerpoint and allow you to create a slide file (.PPT) for insertion into your drawing. If you click on Microsoft Clip Art, it will load the Clip Art gallery and allow you to select the item you require.

2. Once you have created a new application object, choose Files ➤ Exit to simultaneously exit the application and insert the new object into your drawing.

    The new object is inserted at the upper-left corner of the drawing. To reposition it, click on the object and drag it to a new position. When you click on an object, a frame and handles appear. You may use the handles to resize the object to the desired dimensions. If you need to edit an object that you have inserted, double-click on the object. The native application will be loaded again. Make the required changes, then choose File ➤ Update... to update the changes to your drawing.

Option

Object Type This list box is on the Insert New Object dialog box. It lists all of the applications on *your* system that support Object Linking and Embedding (OLE). To delete an OLE object just right click on it and choose cut.

See Also Copyembed, Copylink, Cut and Paste, Olelinks, Pasteclip, Pastespec

---

Inserturl

Inserturl inserts an AutoCAD drawing from a URL into the current drawing:

To Insert a URL

Command Line: **Inserturl**

Internet Utilities Toolbar: Insert from URL

Provide information as needed in the dialog box(es).

Options

Insert from URL: Specify the URL in the edit box using one of the following formats, then click the *Insert* button.

- `http://servername/pathname/filename.dwg`
- `ftp://servername/pathname/filename.dwg`
- `file:///drive:/pathname/filename.dwg`
- `file:///drive|/pathname/filename.dwg`
- `file://\\localPC\pathname\filename.dwg`
- `file:////localPC/pathname/filename.dwg`
- `file://localhost/drive:/pathname/filename.dwg`
- `file://localhost/drive|/pathname/filename.dwg`

Options Opens the Internet Configuration dialog box to edit settings or use Options to execute the **Inetcfg** command and automatically set default Internet configuration settings. AutoCAD opens the Remote Transfer in Progress dialog box during insertion of the drawing from the Web site.

You are not able to insert a drawing into itself. Internet Utilities are not able to transfer files using ftp when you are connected to the Internet through a password protected proxy server.

If you use **Inserturl** to download files from the Internet, they are stored in your system's temporary C:\temp directory and should be manually deleted if not needed.

If you wish to insert a drawing into AutoCAD using drag-and-drop, hold the Control key, click on the DWF image, drag it into the AutoCAD display screen, then release the mouse button and the Control key.

See Also Attachurl, Detachurl, Inetcfg, Inethelp, Listurl, Openurl, Saveurl, Selecturl

Intersect

Intersect allows you to create a composite solid or region that contains only the common volume of two or more overlapping solid objects or regions. In effect, it joins the objects, leaving only the area or volume where the objects intersect.

To Create an Intersection Object

Command Line: **Intersect**

Modify II Toolbar: Intersect

Select objects: Click on the overlapping solids or regions for which you wish to derive the intersection.

AutoCAD removes all non-overlapping sections of the selected objects, leaving only the intersection objects created by their common areas and/or volumes.

> **NOTE Intersect** can be used only for regions or solids. You may select both regions and solids at the same time, and you may select objects from any number of planes. AutoCAD will group the selection set into subsets by region/solid and by plane before calculating the intersections and creating the intersection objects.

See Also Interfere, Subtract, Union

Isoplane

Isoplane lets you switch the cursor orientation between the left, top, and right isometric planes when the snap mode is set to the Isometric style.

To Change the Cursor Orientation

Command Line: **Isoplane** (or **'Isoplane,** to use tranparently).

Left/Top/Right/<Toggle>: Enter your choice or press ↵ to go to the next isoplane.

Current Isometric plane is: Lists the new isoplane.

> **NOTE** Ctrl+E is a toggle control key that selects the next iso-metric plane in a cycle of isometric planes.

> **NOTE** Enter the **Ddrmodes** command to open the Drawing Aids dialog box and check *On* in the Isometric Snap/Grid section to switch to an isometric view. Use the radio buttons to set the cursor orientation for *Left, Top,* and *Right* drawing planes.

See Also Ddrmodes, Snap, *System Variabxles:* Snapisopair

-Layer

-Layer must be used at the command line to create new layers, assign colors and line types to layers, set the current layer, repress editing of layers, and allow you to control which layers are displayed. The dialog box equivalents are **Ddlmodes** and **Layer**.

To Create and Modify Layers

Command Line: -**Layer** (or '-**Layer**, to use transparently)

?/Make/Set/New/ON/OFF/Color/Ltype/Freeze/Thaw/LOck/ Unlock: Enter an option.

Options

? Displays the list of existing layers. Wildcards are accepted.

Make Creates a new layer and makes it current.

Set Makes an existing layer the current layer.

New Creates a new layer.

On Turns on layers.

Off Turns off layers.

Color Sets color of a layer.

Ltype Sets line type of a layer.

Freeze   Freezes one or more layers.

Thaw   Unfreezes one or more layers.

Lock   Prevents editing of visible layers.

Unlock   Releases locked layers to allow editing.

NOTE All Layer options except *Make, Set,* and *New* allow you to enter wildcard characters (question marks and asterisks) for input. For example, if you want to turn off all layers whose names begin with G, enter **G*** at the prompt.

NOTE The option pairs *Freeze/Thaw* and *On/Off* both control whether or not a layer is displayed. However, unlike *Off, Freeze* makes AutoCAD ignore objects on frozen layers. This allows faster regenerations. *Freeze* also affects blocks differently than *Off.* Thawing layers requires a **Regen** if **Regenauto** is off.

NOTE Layer 0, the default layer when you open a new file, is white (number 7) and has the continuous line type. Layer 0 also has some unique properties. If you include objects on Layer 0 in a block, they take on the color and line type of the layer on which the block is inserted. The objects must be created with the *Byblock* option (see **Color**). The dimension layer Defpoints is also unique. When it is turned off, objects on this layer are still displayed and are not selectable, but will not appear on prints or plots. Defpoints is unique in that objects assigned to this layer will not plan or accept a color setting, everything remains white. This makes the Defpoints layer suitable for layout lines.

See Also   Color, Ddlmodes, Linetype, Regen, Regenauto, Vplayer, Wildcards; *System Variables:* Clayer

Leader

Leader creates a line-connecting annotation to an object or feature. A leader line can be either a spline or made up of straight line segments. An arrowhead can be attached if desired. In some cases, a short horizontal line, called a *hook line,* connects the text or feature control frames to the leader line. An annotation placed at the end of a leader line becomes associated with the leader line. When you move, stretch, or copy the leader line, the annotation moves with it.

To Create a Leader Line

Command Line: **Leader**

Menu: Dimension ➤ Leader

Dimension Toolbar: 🖾 Leader

1. **From point:** Specify a point (or use Object Snap) to attach the leader to an object.

2. **To point:** Specify another point.

3. **To point (Format/Annotation/ Undo) <current default>:** Specify further point(s) as required, enter an option (**F/A/U**), or press ↵.

Options

Format   Displays the prompt "Spline/STraight/Arrow/None/<Exit>:" and allows you to specify the format of the leader line Selecting *Spline* draws the leader line as a spline. *Straight* draws the leader as straight line segments. *Arrow* draws an arrowhead at the start point of the leader. *None* temporarily resets the arrow default to draw a leader with no arrowhead. *Exit* returns you to the "To point (Format/Annotation/Undo) <Annotation>:" prompt.

Annotation   Displays the prompt "Tolerance/Copy/Block/None/<Mtext>:" to insert annotation at the end of the leader line. The annotation may be text, a block, an mtext object, or a feature control frame specifying geometric tolerances. If you wish to add text, enter it at this point. The *Mtext* option allows you to define a window in the drawing, then opens the Multiline Text Editor dialog box. You may then enter the desired multiline text (Mtext) and/or format strings. When you exit the editor, the text entered is inserted into the drawing as an mtext object. The *Tolerance* option first opens the Symbol dialog box, then opens the Geometric Tolerance dialog box so you can create a feature control frame containing geometric tolerances. The feature control frame is attached to the end of the last vertex of the leader line. The *Copy* option allows you to copy any kind of annotation (text, block, feature control frame, or mtext) to the leader you are drawing. The copied annotation is associated with the leader line. The *Block* option allows you to insert a block at the end of the last vertex of the leader line. *None* ends the command without adding any annotation to the leader line.

Undo   Deletes the last line segment drawn.

NOTE The **Leader** command creates complex leader lines, unlike Dimdiameter and Dimradius, which create simple automatic leaders for circles and arcs. How Mtext is displayed is determined by the prevailing measurement units and current text style in the drawing. The Mtext is vertically centered and is aligned horizontally with the last two segments of the leader line. Text and Mtext are inserted at a location determined by the current text gap (*Dimgap* system variable).

 NOTE Leader lines are 2D objects similar to dimension objects. Like dimensions, they cannot have elevation or thickness. Although leader lines are not actually dimensions, their appearance is controlled by the same Ddim dimension variables: *Dimclrd* controls the leader color; *Dimclrt* controls the color of the annotation; *Dimblk/Dimblk1* controls the arrowheads; *Dimasz* controls the size of arrowheads; *Dimgap* controls the text gap between annotation and the hook line.

See Also   Ddim Dimensioning Commands, Insert, Mtext, Spline, Tolerance; *System Variables:* Dimasz, Dimblk, Dimclrd, Dimclrt, Dimdiameter, Dimgap, Dimradius, Dimtad

Lengthen

Lengthen changes the length of selected objects and the included angle of arcs. Closed objects cannot be lengthened.

To Lengthen an Object

Command Line: **Lengthen**

Menu: Modify ➤ Lengthen

Modify Toolbar: Lengthen

DElta/Percent/Total/DYnamic/<Select object>: Select an object to display current length or enter an option.

Options

Delta   Allows you to specify an incremental length by which to lengthen a selected object. The length is incrementally increased from the endpoint closest to the pick point. If an arc is selected, the angle of the arc is changed by the specified increment. A positive value produces an extension; a negative value trims the object.

Percent   Allows you to specify a percentage. The selected object is lengthened by that percentage. If an arc is selected, the included angle is increased by the specified percentage.

Total   Allows you to specify an absolute value for the length (or included angle) for the selected object.

Dynamic   Enters dynamic dragging mode. You may change the length or included angle by dragging one endpoint while the other remains fixed.

Undo   Allows you to undo the last specification at any point while using the command options.

See Also   Change, Extend, Grips, Trim

Limits

Limits determines the drawing boundaries. If you use a grid, it will appear only within the limits.

To Establish Drawing Boundaries

Command Line: **Limits** (or '**Limits** to use transparently).

Menu: Format ➤ Drawing Limits

AutoCAD will indicate which limits are being set with one of these prompts: "Reset Model space limits: or Reset paper space limits:".

1. **ON/OFF/<lower left corner> <0.0000,0.0000>:** Enter the coordinate for the lower-left corner, or the *On/Off* option.

2. **Upper right corner <12.0000,9.0000>:** Enter the coordinate for the upper-right corner.

Options

ON   Turns on the limit-checking function. This keeps your drawing activity within the drawing limits.

OFF   Turns off the limit-checking function. This allows you to draw objects without respect to the drawing limits.

<lower left corner>   Allows you to set the drawing limits by entering the coordinates for the lower-left corner of the desired limits.

<upper right corner>   Allows you to set the drawing limits by entering the coordinates for the upper-right corner of the desired limits.

NOTE To make the virtual screen conform to the limits of the drawing, turn on the limit-checking feature and then perform a Zoom/All operation. The **Mvsetup** command will set the limits of your drawing automatically according to the sheet size and drawing scale you select. The limits for paper space must be set independently of the Modelspace limits.

See Also Mspace, Mview, Pspace, Regen, Viewres, Zoom; *System variables:* Limcheck, Limmin, Limmax

Line

Line draws simple lines—either a single line or a series of line segments end-to-end.

To Draw a Line

Command Line: **Line**

Menu: Draw ➤ Line

Draw Toolbar: Line

1. **From point:** Select a point to begin the line.

2. **To point:** Select the line endpoint.

3. **To point:** Continue to select points to draw consecutive lines or press ↵ to exit the command.

Options

C Closes a series of lines, connecting the last start point and the last endpoint with a line.

↵ At the "From point:" prompt, lets you continue a series of lines from a previously entered line, arc, point, or polyline. If the last object drawn is an arc, the line is drawn at a tangent from the end of the arc.

U At the "To point:" prompt, deletes the last line segment.

NOTE Convert lines to polylines using the **Pedit** command.

See Also AutoLISP, Mline, Osnap, Pedit, Pline, Ray, Xline

-Linetype

-Linetype enables you to control the type of line you can draw. The
default line type is continuous Bylayer, but you can choose from several
other types, such as a dotted or dashed line or a combination of the two
(see Figure 13). Predefined line types are stored in a file called Acad.LIN.
You can list these line types by entering a question mark at the "-Linetype"
prompt, or using the **Linetype** command and clicking Load in the Layer
and Linetype Properties dialog box. **Ddltype** is the dialog box equivalent.

To Change the Line Type

Command Line: **-Linetype** (or '**-Linetype**, to use transparently)

?/Create/Load/Set: Enter the option name.

Options

? Lists available line types in a specified external line type file.

Create Creates a new line type.

Load Loads a line type from a specified line type file.

Set Sets the current default line type.

   The *Create* option first prompts you for a line type name. This name
can be any alphanumeric string of 47characters or less (although the
status line will display only the first eight characters). You are then
prompted for the name of the file in which to store your line type.
Next, you enter a description or graphic representation of the line type.
Finally, you enter the line type pattern on the next line, where you will
see an "A" (for pattern alignment) followed by a comma and the cursor.
A-type alignments force lines and arcs to start and end with a dash.
Enter a string of numeric values separated by commas. These values
should represent the lengths of lines as they will be plotted. Positive
values represent the "drawn" portion of the line; negative values represent the "pen up," or blank, portion of the line; and a zero indicates a
dot. The following code produces a line type segment with a dash .3
drawing units long and three dots spaced .05 drawing units apart:

   A,.3,-.05,0,-.05,0,-.05,0,-.05

   You can create complex line types only by editing the Acad.LIN file.

   The size of the line segments for each ISO line is defined for use with a
1 mm. pen-width. To use them with other ISO predefined pen widths,
scale the line using the appropriate value. For a pen width of 0.5 mm.,
use an ltscale of 0.5.

Several new complex line types, such as fenceline1, fenceline2, tracks, batting, hotwater, gas_line and zigzag have been added to the standard line types with Release 14. They are defined in `Ltypeshp.LIN` in Release 13, and are incorporated in `Acad.LIN` in Release 14. These linetype definitions use `Ltypeshp.SHX`.

You can assign line types to layers or to individual objects. Use the **Ltscale** command to make the scale of the line types correspond with the scale of your drawing.

A line type may appear continuous even though it is a noncontinuous type. Several things can affect the appearance of line types. For example, if the drawing scale is not 1:1, the **Ltscale** must be set to correspond with your drawing scale. If the drawing scale is "1/4" equals 1', the Ltscale must be set to 48. A low *Viewres* value can also affect appearance, making line types appear continuous onscreen even though they plot as a noncontinuous line type. Regenerating exhibits the true appearance of line types. To display a list of line types currently loaded in your drawing, use **Ddltype**.

Use the **Ltscale** command to set the global linetype scale factor, Celtscale for individual linetype scaling per object and Psltscale (with a value of 1) for viewport scaling. For global editing, it is best to define linetypes by layer and not by a property.

See Also   Change, Ddemodes, Ddlmodes, Layer, Ltscale, Viewres; *System Variables:* Plinegen, Psltscale

List

List displays most of the properties of an object, including coordinate location, color, layer, and line type. **List** informs you if the object is a block or text. If the object is text, **List** gives its height, style, and width factor. If the object is a block, **List** gives its X, Y, and Z scale and insertion point. Attribute tags, defaults, and current values are also listed, if available. If the object is a polyline, the coordinate values for all its vertices are listed. You can also use **List** to identify hatch-pattern scale and angle.

To List Properties of an Object

Command Line: **List**

Menu: Tools ➤ Inquiry ➤ List

Inquiry Toolbar: 🗐 List

Standard Toolbar: 🗐 Inquiry Flyout 🗐 List

Select objects: Pick the objects whose properties you wish to see.

> **NOTE** Listing objects causes AutoCAD to flip the screen to text mode and pause when the response is lengthy. Pressing ↵ continues you through successive screens, then returns you to the command line and the graphics mode.

See Also Dblist

Listurl

Listurl identifies which objects in your drawing have hyperlinks to Web sites.

To List URLs

Command Line: **Listurl**

Internet Utilites Toolbar: List URLs

Select objects: Select object(s) with attached URLs in the drawing you wish to list

URL for selected object is: (URL name)

> **NOTE** Entering Selecturl highlights all objects with attached URLs.

See Also Attachurl, Detachurl, Selecturl, Openurl, Inserturl, Saveurl, Inetcfg, Inethelp.

Load

Load imports a shape definition file (.SHP file) into a drawing and converts it to an .SHX file. Like text and blocks, shapes are single objects made up of lines and arcs.

To Load a Shape

Command Line: **Load**

1. Opens the Select Shape File dialog box. If *Filedia* is set to zero, you will be prompted: "Name of shape file to load (or ?):".

2. Enter the name of the shape file (.SHP) at the prompt, or, if you are using the dialog box, use the *List Files of Type* box to select and load an .SHP file.

TIP You can define shapes using Shape codes. You can include shape definitions in line type patterns in the new complex line types.

See Also Linetype, Shape, *System Variables:* Shpname

Logfileon/Logfileoff

Logfileon instructs AutoCAD to record everything that appears in the text window (both keystrokes and system prompts and responses) and writes it to an ASCII file. It continues to record until you exit AutoCAD or use the **Logfileoff** command.

To Turn On and Off the Log File

Command Line: **Logfileon**

Command Line: **Logfileoff**

NOTE A new log session begins each time you open AutoCAD. The log file grows with each session, and should be periodically edited or deleted. The default log file name is ACAD.LOG. Use the *Files* tab in the Preferences dialog box to change the name and and the *General* tab to specify a new location of the log file.

See Also Preferences

Ltscale

Ltscale controls the scale of line types. Normally, line type definitions are created for a scale of 1:1. For larger scale drawings such as 1:20, set **Ltscale** so that line types fit the drawing scale. **Ltscale** globally adjusts all line type definitions to the value you give to **Ltscale**.

To Set the Scale of Line Types

Command Line: **Ltscale** (or **'Ltscale** to use transparently)

New scale factor <current default>: Enter the desired scale factor.

NOTE **Ltscale** forces a drawing regeneration when **Regenauto** is on. If Regenauto is turned off, you won't see the effects of **Ltscale** until you issue **Regen**.

See Also   Change, Ddltype, Linetype; *System Variables:* Celtscale, Ltscale, Psltscale

Massprop

See Solid Modeling

Matchprop/Painter

Matchprop and **Painter** copy properties from a selected object to one or more objects.

To Match Properties

Command Line: **Matchprop**

Command Line: **Painter**

Menu: Modify ➤ Matchprop

Standard Toolbar: Match Properties

1. **Select Source Object:** Pick a single object.

   Current active settings = color layer ltype ltscale thickness text dim hatch

2. **Settings/<Select Destination Object(s)>:** Enter **S** to open the Property Settings dialog box to specify property settings or press ↵ to select one or more objects to change properties.

> **NOTE** The Property Settings dialog box contains a Basic Properties section allowing you to set toggles for *Color*, *Layer*, *Linetype*, *Linetype Scale* or *Thickessness* properties to be copied with the **Matchprop** or **Painter** command.

You can also click check boxes in the Special Properties Section for *Dimension*, *Text*, and *Hatch*. *Text* changes the text style of the destination object to that of the source object and is available only for line-text and paragraph-text objects. *Dimension* modifies the dimension style of the destination object to that of the source object and should be used for dimension, leader, and tolerance objects. *Hatch* only applies to hatched objects and should be used to edit the hatch pattern of the destination object to that of the source object.

Matlib

*See **Render***

Measure

Measure marks an object into divisions of a specified length. Measurement begins at the end of the object closest to the pick point. If the object does not divide evenly by the specified length, the remaining portion will be located at the end farthest from the picked point.

To Measure an Object

Command Line: **Measure**

Menu: Draw ➤ Point ➤ Measure

1. **Select object to measure:** Pick a single object.

2. **<Segment length>/Block:** Enter the length of the segments to mark or the name of the block to use for marking.

Options

Block   Establishes an existing, user-defined block as a marking device. You are prompted for a block name and asked if you want to align the block with the object.

> **NOTE**   By default, **Measure** uses a point as a marker, but a point is often difficult to see when placed over a line or arc. Use **Ddptype** to set a point style or set the *Pdmode* and *Pdsize* system variables to change the appearance of the points, or select the *Block* option and use a block in place of the point.

> **TIP**   The *Block* option is useful if you need to draw a series of objects a specified distance apart along a curved path. For example, to draw identical parking stalls for vehicles, create a block consisting of a line (or stripe) and identify the block name in step 2 above.

See Also   Block, Divide, Ddptype, Point; *System Variables:* Pdmode, Pdsize

Menu

Menu loads a custom menu file. Once you have loaded a menu into a drawing, that drawing file will include the menu file name. The next time you open the drawing file, AutoCAD will load the last menu used with the file.

To Load a Menu

Command Line: **Menu**

If the *Filedia* system variable is set to 1, the Select Menu File dialog list box appears. Use this box to select the menu file you want to use. If *Filedia* is not set to 1, respond to the following prompt at the command line:

Menu filename or for none <acad>: Enter the menu file name.

> **TIP** You can customize the `Acad.MNU` and `Acad.MNS` file using a text editor to make AutoCAD load a recompiled version of these same file names. When you load a menu file, AutoCAD looks for a corresponding `.MNL` file to load. You may place any custom AutoLISP file routines specified in this `.MNL` file.

> **NOTE** The `Acad.MNR`, `Acad.MNS`, and `Acad.MNU` menu files serve different functions. The various sections found among these menus include: pull-down menus, toolbars, cursor menu, image tile menus, screen menu, pointing device button menu, accelerator keys, and digitizer tablet menus. Use the Inet menu for the Internet Utilties commands. If you created Toolbars with custom icon buttons, the information is stored in the `.MNS` file and recompiled into the `.MNC` file. Attempting to load the `Acad.MNU` displays a message box to alert you that you are attempting to override (and consequently delete) any customization of the `Acad.MNS`.

See Also Menuload/Menuunload; *System Variables:* Menuctl, Menuecho, Menuname

Menuload/Menuunload

Menuload allows you to create custom menu groups or supplement existing menu groups with additional submenus. Both commands open the Menu Customization dialog box so you can customize, load, and unload menu groups.

To Customize and Load a New Menu Group

Command Line: **Menuload**

Command Line: **Menuunload**

1. When the Menu Customization dialog box appears, you may select a menu group.

2. To change an existing menu group or create a new group, click on the Menu Bar tab. Then add or remove submenu groups as required from the selection presented.

3. Click on the *Load* button to load the new menu into your drawing.

Type **Menuunload** to unload a previously loaded menu. When the Menu Customization dialog box appears, select the *Unload* button.

Options

Menu Group Tab   Displays list box of all existing menu files. You may enter a menu name in the *File Name* edit box or select a menu from the *Browse* pick box. Menu groups can be individually loaded and unloaded from the list box. Check *Replace all* to remove all existing menu groups.

Menu Bar Tab   Contains a pop-up list of current menu groups. When you highlight a specific menu group, the Menu area shows the sub-menus that make up the highlighted menu group. You may customize menu groups by using the *Insert* and *Remove* options to insert and remove submenus in the displayed group.

NOTE   AutoCAD Release 14 offers persistent partial menus that save and reload the partial menu the next time you start AutoCAD. If you do not want to load a menu, set the *Filedia* system variable to 0, enter **Menu** at the command line, then type a period (.) at the *Menu file name or . for none <current menu>:* prompt.

See Also   Menu

Minsert

Minsert simultaneously inserts a block and creates a rectangular array of that block. You can rotate the array by specifying an angle other than 0 at the prompt.

To Insert Multiple Objects

Command Line: **Minsert**

The prompts for **Minsert** are similar to **Insert**, except for the following:

1. **Rotation Angle <0>:** Enter the array angle.

2. **Number of rows ( ) <1>:** Enter the number of rows in the block array. If the number of rows is greater than 1, the following prompts appear:

- **Unit cell or distance between rows (—):** Enter the distance between rows. Selecting *Unit cell* requires picking two points with your cursor; after picking the First corner, you are prompted for the Other corner.

3. **Number of columns (|||) <1>:** Enter the number of columns in the block array. If the number of columns is greater than 1, the following prompt appears:

   - **Distance between columns (|||):** Enter the distance or select the distance using your cursor.

A row-and-column array of the block will then appear at the specified angle.

The entire array acts like one block. Unlike **Insert**, **Minsert** does not permit you to explode a block or use an asterisk option. Listing the **Minsert** entities will provide such information as the number of columns, number of rows, and their spacing. Inserting a block with **Minsert** groups the objects into a single object. See **Insert** for a description of the additional option prompts not described here.

See Also   Array, Insert

Mirror/Mirror3D

Mirror makes a mirror-image copy of an object or a group of objects.

To Mirror Objects

Command Line: **Mirror**

Command Line: **Mirror3D**

Menu: Modify ➤ Mirror

Menu: Modify ➤ 3D Operaton ➤ Mirror 3D

Modify toolbar: ◪ Mirror

1. Select objects: Pick the objects to be mirrored.

2. First point of mirror line: Pick one end of the mirror axis.

3. Second point: Pick the other end of the mirror axis.

4. Delete old objects? <N>: Enter **Y** to delete the originally selected objects or press ↵ to keep them.

If you selected Mirror 3D, in place of steps 2 and 3 above, you will be prompted: **Plane by Entity/Last/ZAxis/View/XY/YZ/ZX/<3 points>:** Define a plane and axis for the mirror.

Alternate: Grips

If you have enabled grips for mirroring, the sequence of steps is as follows:

1. Select the object(s) to be mirrored and the grips will appear as the objects are highlighted.

2. Pick one of the grips as your "base" point. (A base, or selected, grip appears as a solid filled rectangle.) The Stretch mode prompt then appears at the command line.

3. Cycle through the grip mode commands by pressing ⏎ or the space-bar a sufficient number of times until the following prompt appears, or by entering **mirror** or **mi**:

   MIRROR

   <Second point>/Base point/Copy/Undo/eXit:

TIP Use the Select Settings area of the Grips dialog box to enable grips.

4. To mirror the image *without* retaining the original object(s), using the selected grip as the base or first point of the mirror line, drag your cursor and pick the second point of the mirror-line axis. To mirror the image while *retaining* the original object(s), using the selected grip as the base point, enter **C** for *Copy* and pick the second point of the mirror-line axis. (You can hold the Shift key and drag your cursor to pick the second point instead of entering **C**.) Then press ⏎ to exit.

TIP To select a new base point, enter **B** before picking the second point or before entering **C**.

Options

B or Base point   Disengages the cursor from the selected grip so you can assign a new base point for the first point of the mirror-line axis.

C, Copy, or Shift   Makes a duplicate of original object(s).

U or Undo   Allows you to undo the previous operation.

X, eXit, or ⏎   Exits the command.

TIP Normally, text, attributes, and attribute definition objects are mirrored. To prevent this, set the *Mirrtext* system variable to 0. Mirroring occurs in a plane parallel to the current UCS (user coordinate system). Use the **Mirror3D** command to duplicate selected objects about an arbitrary plane.

See Also   Ddgrips, Grips; *System Variables:* Mirrtext

Mledit

Mledit allows you to edit characteristics of a multiline object. Multilines consist of multiple parallel lines. **Mledit** allows you to control the way that multilines intersect in a drawing, to add and delete vertices, and to manipulate the display of corner joints.

To Edit a Multiline

Command Line: **Mledit**

Menu: Modify ➤ Object ➤ Multiline...

Modify II Toolbar: ![icon] Edit Multiline

1. When the Multiline Edit Tools dialog box appears, double-click on the desired option in the icon menu.

2. Select mline: Select the multiline to be edited (or the vertex to be changed).

3. Select mline (or Undo): Select next multiline, enter **U** to restore mutiline or enter to exit command.

Options

The icon menu in the Multiline Edit Tools dialog box has four columns: the first column pertains to multilines which cross; the second to multilines that form a tee; the third to corner joints and vertices; and the fourth to cutting and welding multilines.

Cross   Offers three cross-intersection options: *Closed Cross, Open Cross,* and *Merged Cross.* At the "Select first mline:" prompt, select the foreground multiline. At the "Select second mline:" prompt, select the intersecting multiline.

Tee   Offers three options: *Closed Tee, Open Tee,* and *Merged Tee.* At the "Select first time:" prompt, select the multiline to trim or extend. At the "Select second mline:" prompt, select the intersecting multiline.

Corner Joint and Vertices   *Corner Join* creates a corner joint between multilines. AutoCAD trims or extends the first mline selected to its intersection with the second mline selected. Add/Delete vertex allows you to add a vertex to a multiline segment or delete an existing vertex.

Cut and Weld   The *Cut Single* and *Cut All* options allow you to cut selected (or all) elements of a multiline at specified points.

Weld All   Restores cut multiline segments. Select the break points on the multiline, and AutoCAD will weld the cut sections.

See Also   Mline, Mlstyle; *System Variables:* Cmljust, Cmlscale, Cmlsytyle

Mline

Mline draws multiple parallel lines. Multilines consist of between 1 and 16 parallel lines, or elements. Each element is offset from the origin of the multiline by an amount specified in the Multiline style invoked by Mlstyle.

To Draw a Multiline Object

Command Line: **Mline**

Menu: Modify ➤ Object ➤ Multiline...

Modify II Toolbar: Multiline

1.   Justification = Top, Scale = 1.00, Style = STANDARD

   • **Justification/Scale/Style <From point>:** Specify the first point, or select an option.

2.   Continue to pick points as required to create the multiline. When you pick a third point, you are offered the option to create a closed multiline object. Enter **C** to create a closed object, or press ↵ to exit the command.

Options

Justification   Allows you to select between *Top*, *Zero*, and *Bottom*. Top positions the top line of the multiline object at the pick point(s); Bottom positions the bottom line of the multiline object at the pick points; Zero uses the pick point(s) as the center line.

Scale   Allows you to enter a different scale value for the multilines. Scale controls the overall width (or separation) of the multiline elements.

Style   Allows you to select a different multiline style from previously created styles.

Close   Allows you to create a closed multiline by joining the last point picked to the origin point.

Undo   Allows you to undo the previous multiline segment drawn.

> **NOTE** When you are drawing a multiline, you can use the current style or you can load a style from an external file. When the style has been loaded, you can use *Mstyle* to edit it before you draw the multiline.

See Also Mledit, Mlstyle, Offset

Mstyle

Mstyle creates named styles for multilines which specify the number of lines (from two to sixteen), and the properties of each. You may use **Mstyle** to edit existing multiline styles.

To Create or Edit a Multiline Style

Command Line: **Mstyle**

Menu: Format ➣ Multiline Style

1. When the Multiline Styles dialog box appears, enter the required information. The dialog box displays a graphic representation of the current style and properties. As you define the new style or edit an existing style, the graphic displays the selected properties.

Options

Current Pop-up menu for displaying and setting current multiline styles including those stored in external reference drawings.

Name Allows you to enter a new name for the new style or rename an existing style.

Description Allows you to enter an optional description.

Element Properties Displays all of the elements in the current multiline style. The *Add* and *Delete* options allow you to add or remove a line element in the style. *Offset* specifies the offset for line elements of the multiline. *Linetype* opens the Select Linetype dialog box, and allows you to select the element's line type. *Color* opens the Select Color dialog box to select the element's color.

Multiline Properties The *Display Joints* check box allows you to select or deselect the display of a line at the joints of the multiline. *Caps* allows you to select a line or arc for each end of the multiline, and also to specify an angle for the ends. *Fill* allows you to turn on fill for the multiline and to specify a fill *Color*.

Load Loads a style from an external .MLN file.

Save   Saves the style to the external symbol table.

Add   Allows you to append a multiline style in the Name text box to the current list.

Rename   Renames an existing style after it has been edited.

NOTE   Once a multiline style has been created, all multilines drawn after that point will have the properties of that style.

See Also   Color, Linetype, Mline, Offset

Move

Move displaces a single object or a set of objects.

To Move Objects

Command Line: **Move**

Menu: Modify ➤ Move

Modify Toolbar: Move

1. **Select objects:** Select the objects to be moved.

2. **Base point or displacement:** Pick the reference or "base" point for the move.

3. **Second point of displacement:** Pick the distance and direction in relation to the base point or enter the displacement value.

Alternate: Grips

If you have enabled grips for moving, the prompts for Steps 1 and 2 and the Grips Options are the same as for **Mirror**, except for the following:

1. Cycle through the grip mode commands by pressing ↵ or the space-bar, or by entering **Move** or **M** a sufficient number of times until you see the following prompt:

   MOVE

   <Move to point>/Base point/Copy/Undo/eXit:

2. To move the object(s) with the selected grip as the base, drag your cursor and pick the second or displacement point. To move the object(s) using a new base point, enter **B** to pick your first reference point or enter coordinate values, then pick the second point of displacement.

If you chose the *displacement* option rather than picking a base point, you can enter the total amount of movement you want the object to make (in the X and Y directions) and press Enter twice.

AutoCAD assumes you want to move objects within the current UCS. However, you can move objects in 3D space by entering XYZ coordinates or using the Osnap overrides to pick objects in 3D space.

If you press ↵ at the "Second point:" prompt without entering a point value, the objects selected may be moved to a position completely off your drawing area. Use the **U** or **Undo** command to recover.

To make multiple copies of the selected object(s), follow the steps above to define your base point, then hold the Shift key while picking the first copy point (to set copy mode on), and continue by picking additional points. (Entering **C** after selecting the base point will provide the same results.) Exit the command by pressing ↵.

Pressing the Shift key in the last step to copy the first object from its source point to a destination point will set an automatic snap mode based on these two points. To apply *Multiple copy* using the snap mode, hold the Shift key down while copying additional objects.

See Also   Ddgrips, Grips

Mslide

Mslide saves the current view as a raster image in a Slide file. (Slide files have .SLD extensions.)

To Save as an *.SLD* File

Command Line: **Mslide**

When the *Filedia* system variable is set to 1, the Create Slide File dialog list box is displayed; when *Filedia* is set to zero, the "Slide File:" prompt appears. Enter a file name.

See Also   Delay, Rscript, Script, Slidelib.exe, Vslide

Mspace

Mspace lets you switch from Paperspace to a Modelspace viewport. This command works only when you are in Paperspace (**Tilemode** is set to 0). You move from Paperspace into Modelspace via previously created viewports.

To Switch from Paperspace to a Modelspace Viewport

Command Line: **Mspace**

NOTE If the **Tilemode** system variable is set to 0 but no view-ports are available in Paperspace, you will receive the message "There are no active Modelspace viewports."

Double-click MODEL in the Status Bar to toggle between **Mspace** and **Pspace**.

See Also Mview, Pspace, Tilemode

Mtext

Mtext allows you to create long, complex text entries, consisting of any number of lines or paragraphs of text. Multiline or paragraph text fits within a specified width in the drawing but may run to any length.

To Create Multiline Text

Command Line: **Mtext**

Menu: Text ➤ Multiline Text...
Draw Toolbar: **A** Multiline Text

1. **Current text style: STANDARD. Text height: 0.2000**

   • **Specify first corner:** Specify a start point for the text boundary window.

2. **Specify opposite corner or [Height/Justify/Rotation/ Style/Width]:** Enter an option or drag the window to a diagonally opposite corner and a rectangle appears to identify the location of the multiline text object. An arrow inside the rectangle indicates the direction of the paragraph's text flow

3. The Multiline Text Editor dialog box opens for you to enter and format the multiline text.

When text entry is complete, AutoCAD inserts the text into the specified text boundary.

Options

Height Allows you to enter a specific text height for the multiline text at the "Specify height <current height>:" prompt.

Justification   Controls the alignment and positioning of the multi-line text within the text window with the "Enter justification [TL/TC/TR/ML/MC/MR/BL/BC/BR] <TL>:" prompt. The two-letter options set the justification based on the combination of top, middle, or bottom, and left, center, or right. For example, TL stands for "top-left" and MC stands for "middle-center."

Rotation   Allows you to specify a rotation angle and the direction of the dragging window for the multiline text by prompting to "Specify rotation angle <0>:".

Style   Prompts to "Enter style name (or '?') <current style>:", allowing you to select a different text style from the current style.

Width   Allows you to specify the width only of the text boundary window, rather than the both corners. If you enter a zero value, the text will not wrap but will extend horizontally until you press ↵.

Additional Options

- The Multiline Text Editor dialog box contains three tabbed sections: *Character*, *Properties* and *Find/Replace*. Characters can be entered from the keyboard or imported from other files. The dialog box background color, by default, appears the same as the graphics screen but changes to white when black text is imported or pasted.

- Text imported or pasted into AutoCAD from other Windows applications with the attribute of *Auto* is changed to ByLayer.

- If you highlight text and click your return or right mouse button a cursor menu open with options to: *Undo*, *Cut*, *Copy*, *Paste*, and *Select All*.

- Click *Import Text...* to display the Open dialog box and locate the text you wish to import. If the text being imported is not in RTF (Rich Text Format) or ASCII format, the Inserting Text dialog box appears offering choices to *replace the selected text, be inserted after the selected text* or *replace all text*. Otherwise, imported text is limited to 16KB and retains its original character formatting and style properties.

Character Tab   The Character tabbed section contains drop down boxes to set controls for character formatting for text entered at the keyboard or imported into the text editor. You can edit a word or paragraph by double-clicking to select a single word, or triple-clicking to select an entire paragraph. Then click the appropriate drop down boxes to change the text's Font, Height or Color, display it as Bold, Italic, or Underlined, and/or Stacked or Unstacked (for fractions). Add a Symbol, such as *Degrees*, *Plus/Minus sign*, *Diameter*, *Non-breaking space* or pick *Other...* to open and select from Windows Unicode Characer Map dialog box. *Undo* allows you to undo the previous edit.

Properties Tab   Use the Properties tab to set text *Style*, *Width*, *Justification* or *Rotation*.

Find/Replace Tab   The Drop down boxes for *Find*, *Replace with*, *Match Case* and *Whole Word* in the Find/Replace tabbed section will help you to search for and replace specific text strings with new text. Click the *Find* or *Replace* icons to activate an action or press ↵ immediately after entering your text in these edit boxes.

TIP   You can use the Edit Mtext dialog box to quickly set properties either for the entire object or just for selected portions. Paragraph or multiline text has more options for editing than line text. You may use underlining, overlining, and apply special fonts, color, and height to single words within a paragraph.

If you have created a paragraph that is too long to fit in the text window, the text will overflow in the direction specified by the arrow's direction: top-aligned text will "spill" down, and bottom-aligned text will "flow up" from the specified boundary window; center-aligned text will spread both above and below the text window. Multiline text, no matter how many lines or paragraphs, forms a single object and can be moved, stretched, erased, copied, mirrored, or scaled.

TIP   You can use any standard text editor to create multiline text. Select the Files tab in the Preferences dilog box to specify a text editor.

See Also   Ddedit, Ddmodify, Dtext/Text, Mtprop, Preferences, Spell, Style, *System Variables:* Fontalt, Fontmap, Mtexted

Mtprop

Mtprop allows you to change Mtext properties. The command opens the Mtext Properties dialog box and allows you to modify the properties of paragraph text created using the Mtext command.

To Change Mtext Properties

Command Line: **Mtprop**

1. **Select an Mtext object:** Select a section of paragraph text.

2. In the Mtext Properties dialog box, modify the text properties as required.

NOTE The Mtext properties that may be changed are detailed more fully in the **Mtext** command option and "Notes."

See Also Ddedit, Ddmodify, Dtext/Text, Mtprop, Preferences, Spell, Style, *System Variables:* Fontalt, Fontmap, Mtexted

Multiple

Multiple causes the next command to repeat until you cancel it.

To Repeat a Command

Command Line: **Multiple**, a space, and then the command

NOTE The command repeats until you press Escape. Because **Multiple** repeats only the command itself, any options or parameters must be specified each time.

Mview

Mview creates Paperspace viewports and controls the number, layout, and visibility of viewports. This command works in Paperspace only.

To Create a Paper-Space Viewport

Command Line: **Mview**

Menu: View ➤ Floating Viewports ➤ Viewport Options

ON/OFF/Hideplot/Fit/2/3/4/Restore/<First point>: Pick a point indicating one corner of the new Paperspace viewport or enter an option. If you pick a point, you are prompted for the opposite diagonal corner. Mview then creates the viewport.

Options

ON/OFF Turns the display of Modelspace on or off within the chosen viewport.

Hideplot Controls hidden line removal for individual viewports at plot time. When you select this option, the "Select objects:" prompt appears. Pick the viewport you wish to have plotted with hidden lines removed. Selecting an entity inside the viewport will not select the viewport—you must pick the edge or border.

Fit Creates a single viewport that fills the screen.

2/3/4 Lets you create two, three, or four viewports simultaneously. Once you enter one of these options, different prompts appear, depending on the number of viewports requested. If you select **2**, you will be prompted "Horizontal/<Vertical>:"; if you select **3**, you will be prompted "Horizontal/Vertical/Above/Below/Left/<Right>:". Then you will be prompted: "Fit/<first point>:". Pick points to indicate the location of the viewports, or select the *Fit* option to force the viewports to fit in the display area.

Restore Translates viewport configurations created using the **Vport** command (Modelspace viewports) into paper-space viewport objects. You are prompted for the name of a viewport configuration. This option will not give you the same views that were in the model space vports at the time the vport configuration was saved.

> **NOTE** The *Tilemode* system variable must be set to 0 to use **Mview**. If you are in Modelspace when you issue Mview, you receive the message "Command not allowed unless TILEMODE is set to zero."

> **NOTE** Grid and snap modes, as well as layer visibility, can be set individually within each Paperspace viewport.

> **TIP** Viewports, like most other entities, can be moved, copied, stretched, or erased. You can hide viewport borders by changing their layer assignments, then turning off their layers. You can also align positions of objects in one viewport with those of another by using the **Mvsetup** utility. Viewport scale can be set using the *xp* option under the **Zoom** command.

See Also Mspace, Mvsetup, Pspace, Tilemode; *System Variables:* Psltscale, Vplayer, Vports, Zoom

Mvsetup

Mvsetup sets up the Paperspace specifications of a drawing, including viewports, drawing scale, and sheet title block.

To Set Up a Paper Space

Command Line: **Mvsetup**

MVSETUP

On a new drawing with *Tilemode* set to 1 (On), the following prompt appears: **Enable paper space?(No/<Yes>):**.

- If you enter **N**, you will be prompted to specify a Units type (Scientific, Decimal, Engineering, Architectural, Metric), Architectural Scales (480, 192, 96, 48, 24, 12, 4, 2, 1), the Scale factor, and a Paper Height and Width. AutoCAD will then draw a bounding box and exit the command.

- If you press ⏎ to accept the default **Y**, the *Tilemode* system variable is set to 0 (Off), and the following prompt appears: **Align/Create/Scale viewports/Options/Title block/Undo:**.

Options

Align   Aligns locations in one viewport with locations in another viewport. If you select Align (**A**), you will receive the "Angled/Horizontal/Vertical alignment/Rotate view/Undo?:" prompt. *Angled* aligns locations by indicating an angle and distance. You are prompted to pick a base point to which others can be aligned. Next, you are prompted to pick a point in another viewport that you want aligned with the base point. You are then prompted for a distance and angle. *Horizontal/Vertical alignment* aligns views either horizontally or vertically. You are prompted for a base point (the point to be aligned to) and the point to be aligned with the base point. *Rotate view* rotates the view in a viewport. You are prompted for a viewport and base point, and then for the angle of rotation.

Create viewports   Creates new viewports. If you select this option (C), you will receive the prompt "Delete objects/Undo/<Create viewpoints>:". *Delete object*s deletes existing viewport entities. <Create viewports> displays a list of options for creating viewports, as follows:

   0: None   Creates no viewports.

   1: Single   Creates a single viewport for which you specify the area.

   2: Std. Engineering   Creates four viewports set up in quadrants. The views that appear are for top, front, right side, and isometric. This happens automatically with this option.

   3: Array of Viewports   Creates a matrix of viewports by specifying the number of viewports in the X and Y axes. The *Add/Delete* option on the prompt adds or deletes options from the list. *Add* provides a title block for the list.

   Redisplay/<Number of entry to load>   Lets you view the list again.

Scale viewports Sets the scale between Paperspace and the viewport. For example, if your drawing in Modelspace is drawn at 1 to 1, and your title block in Paperspace is scaled to 1" = 1", and you want the drawing scaled to 1/4" = 1', you will want the scale factor of your viewport to be 48. When you select this option (**S**), the prompt "Select the viewports to scale:" appears. Once you've selected more than one viewport, the prompt "Set zoom scale factors for viewports Interactive/<Uniform>:" appears. The Interactive option sets the scale of each selected viewport individually with a request to enter the ratio of paperspace units to modelspace units. You are prompted for the "Number of paperspace units:", then the "Number of modelspace units:". In the 1/4" scale example, you would enter **1** for the paper-space units and **48** for the model-space units.

Options Allows you to set the MVSETUP preferences before you change your drawing. If you type **O**, you will receive the following prompt: *Set Layer/Limits/Units/Xref:*. Set Layer allows you to specify a layer for the title block. *Limits* allows you to reset the drawing limits by prompting *Set drawing limits?<N>*, *Units* allows you to specify the Paperspace units as feet, inches, meters, or millimeters. *Xref* allows you to specify whether the title block is to be inserted or externally referenced.

Title block Produces the prompt: *Delete objects/Origin/Undo/<Insert title block>:*. *Delete objects* deletes objects from Paperspace. *Origin* sets a new origin point for Paperspace. *<Insert title block>* displays the following:

- Available paper/output sizes:
- 0: None
- 1: ISO A4 Size (mm)
- 2: ISO A3 Size (mm)
- 3: ISO A2 Size (mm)
- 4: ISO A1 Size (mm)
- 5: ISO A0 Size (mm)
- 6: ANSI-V Size (in)
- 7: ANSI-A Size (in)
- 8: ANSI-B Size (in)
- 9: ANSI-C Size (in)
- 10: ANSI-D Size (in)

- 11: ANSI-E Size (in)

- 12: Arch/Engineering (24 X 36in)

- 13: Generic D size Sheet (24 X 36in)

- Add/Delete/Redisplay/<Number of entry to load>:

Enter the number corresponding to the title block you want to use. *Add* and *Delete* let you add or delete a title block to or from the list. Add prompts you for a title block description for inclusion in the above list, the name of the file to be used as the title block. It allows you to specify the default usable area within the title block. *Redisplay* lets you view the list again.

Undo   Undoes an option without leaving the Mvsetup utility.

When adding a title block to the list in the title block option, you must already have a title block drawing ready and in the current DOS path. The *Xp* option under the **Zoom** command can also be used to set the scale of a viewport. Mvsetup saves the current configuration to a file called Mvsetup.DFS.

See Also   Dimscale, Ltscale, Mspace, Mview, Pspace, Setup; *System Variables:* Psltscale, Tilemode, Zoom

New

New lets you start a new drawing from scratch or use an existing drawing as a template for a new drawing.

To Create a New Drawing

Command Line: **New**

Menu: File ➤ New...

Standard Toolbar: New

To Start a New Drawing

1. If changes were made to your current drawing, the Save Changes to (file name) message box appears with options for *Yes, No,* and *Cancel.* If you previously have not invoked **Save** or **Qsave**, select *Yes* to save any edited or unsaved drawings before opening a new drawing. If you wish to save your current drawing and have previously not named it, the Save Drawing As dialog box opens and you may enter a name in the File Name Edit box.

2. When the Create New Drawing dialog box opens, specify an option by clicking one of four buttons described under Options below.

If the *Filedia* system variable is set to 0, the following command line prompt appears instead of the dialog box:

> **Enter template file (or . for none) <C:\ACADR14\ template\filename.dwt>:** Specify a file name containing a .DWT or .DWG extension.

Options

Use a Wizard   Click Use a Wizard and choose between *Quick Setup* or *Advance Setup*. The Quick Setup wizard contains two tabbed sections: *Setup 1: Units* and *Step 2: Area*. The Step 1 tab is the same for both wizards and allows you to select from Decimal, Engineering, Architectural, Fractional, and Scientific units of measure. The Step 2 in Quick setup and Step 5 in Advanced Setup contains Width and Length edit boxes to help you specify your working area. The Advanced Setup dialog box offers four additional steps: *Angle Measure*, *Angle Direction*, *Title Block* and *Layout*. Each tabbed section displays a preview window showing you the results of your selection.

> *Angle Measure*   Pick a radio button or enter a value to determine the direction in which AutoCAD measures angles.

> *Angle Directon*   Set a clockwise or counter-clockwise direction for AutoCAD to measure angles.

> *Title Block*   Click drop-down boxes for *Title Block Description*, choosing among Ansi, Arch/Eng, Din, Iso, or Jis sizes or *Title Block File Name*, selecting among the various drawing files. Use *Add...* to open the Select Title Block file dialog box and append drawings to the drop down box or the *Remove* button to delete a title block file.

> *Layout*   Radio buttons *Yes* or *No* allow you to use advanced paper space layout capabilities and offer you a way to start your drawing.

Use a Template   Click this button to start a drawing based on a template. AutoCAD has created 36 template files that you can select from, serving as prototypes, some with predefined layers, dimension styles, and views for creating new drawings. AutoCAD stores template drawings as .DWT files in the C:\ACADR13\TEMPLATE directory. You can create your own templates by renaming the .DWG extension to .DWT and copying the file to the template directory. Double-click *More files...* in the list box to open the Select Template dialog box and locate a .DWG or .DWT template file from any directory or drive.

Start from Scratch   Use the *Start from Scratch* button for a drawing setup similar to the Acad.DWG prototype offered in release 13. It allows you to start a drawing quickly with either English or metric settings.

Instructions   To help you understand and decide which procedure best suites your needs, AutoCAD provides a brief description when you click the *Instructions* button.

Done   Select *Done* to exit the dialog box and start AutoCAD using the specifications you selected.

Show at startup   Toggle the Create New Drawing dialog box off if you do not want it to display when you start an AutoCAD session. To toggle it on, click *Show the Startup* dialog box in the *Capability* tab section of the Preferences dialog box.

See Also   Exit, Open, Qsave, Quit, Save; *System Variables:* Filedia, Dwgname, Dwgprefix, Dwgtitled, Savename

Offset

Offset will offset only a single object. If you have multiple, sequential lines or arcs to offset, use the **Pedit** command to join them into one polyline object before performing the offset.

To Offset a Line

Command Line: **Offset**

Menu: Modify ➤ Offset.

Modify Toolbar: 🔳Offset

   Offset distance or Through <Through>: Enter a distance value to specify a constant distance to offset, or **T** to specify an offset through-point after each object selection is made.

- Enter a distance value and press ⏎, then you are prompted to Select an object to offset. Pick the object to offset. At the next prompt, "Side to offset," pick the side on which you want the offset to appear. You can continue to offset objects at that distance or ⏎ to exit the command.

- Selecting Through by entering **T** or pressing ⏎ prompts you for the *Through point:*. Pick a point to locate the offset line.

Options

Offset Distance   If you enter a value at this prompt, all the offsets performed in the current command will be at that distance. The prompt will continue offsetting objects at the specified distance until you press ↵.

Through   Identifies a point through which the offset object will pass after you have selected the object to offset. The prompt will continue prompting for the next point until you press ↵.

> **WARNING** Very complex polylines may offset incorrectly or not at all. When this happens, it usually means that there is insufficient memory to process the offset or that the offset distance exceeds the command's ability to offset properly.

> **NOTE** You cannot perform offsets on objects unless they lie in a plane parallel to the current UCS (user coordinate system). Also, if you are not viewing the current UCS in plan, you may get an erroneous result.

> **NOTE** *Window, Crossing, Fence, WPolygon, CPolygon* and *Last* are not valid selections for Offset. The offset distance is stored in the system variable *Offsetdist* as the default. If the value is negative, it defaults to Through mode.

See Also   Copy, Grips; *System Variables:* Offsetdist

OLE

OLE (Object Linking and Embedding) lets you link AutoCAD drawings with drawings in other applications that support OLE. AutoCAD can act as an OLE client as well as a server. Objects from other OLE applications can be linked or embedded into AutoCAD drawing files.

Although the linking and the embedding processes both insert information into an AutoCAD drawing (or from an AutoCAD drawing into another application), the relationship with the source object is different. **Embed** and **Link** are comparable to the AutoCAD commands **Insert** and **Xref**, respectively. When you embed an object, you effectively insert a copy of it into the destination document, and no permanent connection with the source object remains. When you link an object, it remains connected to the original object. If the original object changes, you need only update the links and the information in the destination document will be updated. You can even set a linked object to update automatically by using **Olelinks**.

OLE

> **NOTE** Release 14 has improved support for printing OLE metafile objects, such as line drawings and spreadsheets on non-system printers. Improvements include controls for OLE visibility, printing order and proportional scaling. You can also convert OLE objects into AutoCAD raster objects using paste methods.

See Also Copy, Copyclip, Copycut, Copyhist, Paste, Insert, Insertobj, Olelinks, Xref

---

Olelinks

Olelinks allow you to update, change, and cancel existing links.

To Update Object Links

Command Line: **Olelinks**

Menu: Edit ➤ Olelinks...

Makes the required changes in the Links dialog box and allows you to modify the link information.

Options

Links Provides a list of each linked object in the current drawing. If you select a linked object and right-click on it, a cursor menu opens displays options: *Cut, Paste, Clear, Selectable, Bring to Front,* and *Send to Back.* The selected linked object is also identified so that you can edit it by accessing its source application or convert the object via the Convert dialog box.

Source Identifies objects path, file name, and source application.

Type Lists the application name.

Automatic Click this radio button to initialize an automatic update of a linked object whenever the original object is changed.

Manual If you select the Manual radio button, you will be prompted to update the link when you open the document which contains it.

Update Now Updates any selected links from the Links list box.

Open Source Opens the application containing the source file and highlights the object linked to the AutoCAD drawing.

Change Source Displays the Change Source dialog box allowing you to specify a new source location or file name.

Break Link   Breaks the connection with the source object, but retains a copy of the object in your document.

Oops

Oops restores objects that have been accidentally removed from a drawing.

To Restore an Erased Object

Command Line: **Oops**

Oops retrieves all objects erased by the last **Erase** and after executing **Bmake**, **Block**, or **Wblock**.

See Also   U, Undo

Open

Open lets you open an existing drawing.

To Open an Existing Drawing

Command Line: **Open**

Menu: File ➤ Open...

Standard Toolbar: Open

1. The Select File dialog box contains a *Files Name* edit box to enter a file name and a list box below displaying files. Use the scroll bar to select *Directories* and the drop-down box to locate *Drives*. You can open the *List Files of Type* pop-up box to show .DWG, .DXF or .DWT files in the list box.

2. A preview image is displayed in the dialog box; you may preview the drawing before loading it into the drawing area.

   If the *Filedia* system variable is set to 0, Open displays the following command-line prompt:

*   **Enter name of drawing <current default>:** Enter the name of an existing drawing.

Options

Read Only   Check this box if you wish to open a drawing in Read Only mode. Drawings that are opened in Read Only mode can be

OPEN

edited and saved to a new name. You may not save changes to the drawing's original name.

Select Initial View To open a drawing to a saved view, pick from the Select Initial View dialog box and highlight a view name or the last view.

Find File Opens the Browse/Search dialog box containing *Browse* and *Search* tabbed sections which allows you to browse or search through your drives and directories.

Search Allows you to include search criteria such as file creation date and time.

Browse Displays thumbnail images of all of the drawings in a selected directory. Once you have located the drawing you want, double-click on the image to open the drawing.

See Also Exit, New, Preview, Qsave, Quit, Save; *System Variables:* Dwgname, Dwgwrite, Filedia, Savefile, Savename, Savetime

---

Ortho

Ortho forces lines to be drawn in exactly perpendicular directions following the orientation of the crosshairs.

To Turn Ortho On or Off

Command Line: **Ortho** (or **'Ortho**, to use transparently)

Menu: Tools ➤ Drawing Aids (Modes section, Ortho)

Double-click on ORTHO in the status bar.

TIP If you enter **Ortho** through the keyboard, you are prompted to turn **Ortho ON** or **off**. Use the F8 function key or the Ctrl+O key combination to toggle between Ortho On and Ortho Off. If you pick **Ortho** from the pull-down menu, it retrieves the Ddrmodes dialog box.

TIP To force lines to angles other than 90 degrees, rotate the cursor using the *Snapang* system variable or by setting the Rotate option under the **Snap** command.

See Also Ddrmodes, Snap; *System Variables:* Orthomode, Snapang

-Osnap

-**Osnap** sets the current default Object Snap mode, allowing you to pick specific geometric points on an object. You can have several Object Snap modes active at once if you separate their names by commas. For example, to be able to select endpoints and midpoints automatically, enter **END,MID** at the "Osnap" prompt. AutoCAD knows to select the correct point (MID, END, etc.) according to which point is closer to the target box. The equivalent dialog box command is **Ddosnap** and **Osnap**.

To Pick Specific Geometric Points

Command Line: -**Osnap**

Double-click on OSNAP in the status bar.

Object snap modes: Enter the desired default Object snap mode(s).

Options

Center (CEN)   Picks the center of circles and arcs.

Endpoint (END)   Picks the endpoint of objects.

Insertion (INS)   Picks the insertion point of blocks and text.

Intersection (INT)   Picks the intersection of objects.

Apparent Intersection (APPINT)   Snaps to the apparent intersection of two objects, although they may not actually intersect in 3D space.

Midpoint (MID)   Picks the midpoint of lines and arcs.

Nearest (NEA)   Picks the point on an object nearest to the cursor.

Node (NOD)   Picks a point object. (See **Point**.)

Perpend (PER)   Picks the point on an object perpendicular to the last point.

Quadrant (QUA)   Picks a cardinal point on an arc or circle.

Quick (QUI)   Snaps to the first object snap found. It must be used along with other snap modes. *Quick* does not work in conjunction with Intersection.

Tangent (TAN)   Picks a tangent point on a circle or arc.

NONE   Disables the current default Object snap mode. Entering **Off** or pressing ↵ at the "Object snap modes:" prompt does the same.

TIP You can use the Osnap overrides whenever you are prompted to select a point or object. Unlike the Osnap mode settings, the overrides are active only at the time they are issued. Enter the first three letters of the name of the override, or pick the override from the pop-up Cursor menu.

NOTE The Cursor menu is activated in different ways depending on the pointing device that you are using: if you have a four-button device, press the *third* button (blue for some pucks); if you have a three-button device, press the *middle* button; if you have a two-button device, hold the Shift key down while pressing the Right button. The `Acad.MNU` and `Acad.MNS` files supplied with AutoCAD assigns these buttons to the Cursor menu. The Cursor menu lists snap modes, point filters, and tracking also allows you to open the Object Snap dialog box.

See Also   Aperture, Ddosnap, Point Filters, Tracking, *System Variables:* Osmode

Osnap

See Ddosnap

Pan

Pan allows you to view different parts of your drawing by moving the cursor, displayed as an open hand, in any direction. In Release 14, real-time pan is the default option for interactive panning.

To Move Around in Your Drawing

Command Line: **Pan** (or **'Pan** to use transparently)

Menu: View ➤ Pan ➤ Preset Options

Standard Toolbar: Pan Real-time

1. **Press Esc or Enter to exit, or right-click to activate pop-up menu.** Enter the command and the cursor changes to a hand cursor. Press the pick button on your pointing device to lock the cursor in its current location relative to the viewport coordinate system and the display screen moves in the same direction as the cursor. As you drag the hand your drawing moves around the graphics screen. To exit the command, press the Escape key or ↵.

To stop panning, release the pick button; to restart the process, press it again.

2. Right click the mouse button to display a pop-up menu for switching between *Exit, Pan, Zoom, Zoom Window, Zoom Previous,* and *Zoom Extents.*

See Also   -Pan, Zoom, -Zoom,

-PAN

-Pan shifts the display to reveal parts of a drawing that are off the screen. Drawings retain the same magnification.

To See Offscreen Drawing Areas

Command Line: **-Pan**

Menu: View ➤ Point/Left/Right/Up/Down

1. **Displacement**: Pick the first point of view displacement.

2. **Second point:** Pick the distance and direction of displacement.

You cannot use **-Pan** while viewing a drawing in perspective. Use the **Dview** command's *Pan* option instead.

See Also   Dview/Pan, View, Zoom

Pasteclip

Pasteclip allows you to copy and transfer information, such as AutoCAD objects, text, metafiles, bitmaps, and multimedia files stored in the Clipboard into your drawing.

To Paste Objects from the Clipboard

Command Line: **Pasteclip**

Menu: Edit ➤ Pasteclip

Standard Toolbar: Paste from Clipboard

Graphic objects are inserted at the top-left corner of the drawing area. You may click on them and drag them into position or resize them using the object "handles." Pasted Text is inserted at the top-left corner and becomes an Mtext object. Once objects have been inserted, you can edit them in their native applications by double-clicking on them in AutoCAD. The **Paste** command can also be activated by using the control key sequence Ctrl+V.

Right click your mouse button to open the cursor menu for options: *Cut, Copy, Clear, Undo, Selectable, Bring to Front, Send to Back* or *Convert* the object via the Convert dialog box.

See Also   Copyclip, Copyhist, Cutclip, OLE, Olelinks

Pastespec

Pastespec lets you insert objects from the Windows Clipboard, link objects to their source application, and/or convert the file format.

To Place a Linked or Embedded Object into a Drawing

Command Line: **Pastespec**

Menu: Edit ➤ Paste Special…

When you start the **Pastespec** command, the Paste Special dialog box opens, showing the following information and options: *Source* shows the name of the application in which the Clipboard object was created; the *Paste* and *Paste Link* radio buttons allow you to select whether to simply insert the object into the drawing or to maintain a *link* with the source file (see **OLE**); the *As* list box shows the file formats you can use to paste the Clipboard object into the current drawing. As you click each object in the list box, review the description provided in the *Result* section.

The *Display as Icon* box allows you to display the source application as an icon in your drawing so that you can double-click it to retrieve the linked or imbedded information. To modify the applications associated icon, use *the Change Icon…* button to open the Change Icon dialog box and choose from *Current, Default* and *From File* radio buttons in the Icon section. The dialog box identifies the location, file name and *Label* of the icon and allows you to *Browse…* for a replacement.

Pedit

Pedit edits 2D or 3D polylines and 3D meshes, changes the location of individual vertices in a polyline or mesh, and converts a nonpolyline object into a polyline. The editing options available depend on the type of object you select. See the following sections for information about individual **Pedit** operations.

Pedit for 2D and 3D Polylines

Pedit modifies the shape of 2D and 3D polylines. If the object you select is not a polyline, respond to the "Do you want to turn it into one? <Y>:" prompt with **Y**.

To Edit Polylines

Command Line: **Pedit**

Menu: Modify ➤ Object ➤ Polyline

Modify II Toolbar: [icon] Edit Polyline

1. Select polyline: Select the object you want to edit as a polyline.

If the object selected is a 2D polyline, the following prompt appears:
Close/Join/Width/Edit vertex/Fit/Spline/Decurve/Ltype gen Undo/eXit <X>:

If the object is a 3D polyline, the following prompt appears:
Close/Edit vertex/Spline curve/Decurve/Undo/eXit <X>:

If the polyline is closed, Open appears instead of Close in the prompts above. If the object is a standard line or arc, the following prompt appears: **Object selected is not a polyline. Do you want it to turn into one: <Y>** Enter **Y** or **N**.

Options

Close Joins the endpoints of a polyline. If the selected polyline is already closed, this option is replaced by Open in the prompt.

Open Deletes the last line segment in a closed polyline.

Join Joins polylines, lines, and arcs. The objects to be joined must meet exactly end-to-end.

Width Sets the width of the entire polyline.

Edit vertex Performs various edits on polyline vertices. See the section below on **Pedit**/Edit vertex.

Fit curve Changes a polyline made up of straight line segments into a smooth curve.

Spline curve Changes a polyline made up of straight line segments into a spline-fit curve.

Decurve Changes a smoothed polyline into one made up of straight line segments.

Ltype gen   Causes the line type to continue uniformly around the vertices of the polyline when turned on.

Undo   Cancels the last **Pedit** function issued.

eXit   Exits the **Pedit** command.

   The *Spline curve* option adjusts the "pull" of the vertex points on the curve by changing the *Splinetype* system variable. The default for *Splinetype* is 6. With *Splinetype* set to 5, the pull is greater. See **System Variables** for more details.

   You can view both the curve and the defining vertex points of a spline-fit curve by setting the *Splframe* system variable to **1.** The *Splinesegs* system variable determines the number of line segments used to draw the curve. A higher value generates more line segments for a smoother curve, but also a larger drawing file. The curve created by this process corresponds to a B-spline, but is not actually a true spline curve. You may convert a spline-fit polyline into a true B-spline (NURBS) curve by using the *Object* option on the **Spline** command.

See Also   Pedit/Edit Vertex, Pedit/3D mesh, Pline, Setvar/Splframe, Setvar/Splinesegs, Setvar/Splinetype

Pedit/Edit Vertex

Relocates, removes, moves, or inserts vertices in a polyline. Modifies a polyline's width at a particular vertex and alters the tangent direction of a curved polyline through a vertex.

To Edit a Polyline Vertex

Start the **Pedit** command, then select the polyline object you want to edit.

1. **Close/Join/Width/Edit vertex/Fit/Spline/Decurve/Ltype gen /Undo/eXit <X>:** Enter **E** for Edit vertex. An *X* appears on the first vertex of the selected polyline indicating the vertex currently editable.

2. **Next/Previous/Break/Insert/Move/Regen/Straighten/ Tangent/Width/eXit <N>:** Enter the capitalized letter of the function to be used.

Options

Next   Moves the X marker to the next vertex.

Previous   Moves the X marker to the previous vertex.

PEDIT

Break   Breaks polyline from the marked vertex. Move the X into the position where you want the break to begin and type **B** for Break. The prompt changes to "Next/Previous/Go/eXit <N>:". Move the marker to another vertex to select the other end of the break. Once the X marker is in position, enter **G** to initiate the break.

Insert   Inserts a new vertex. A rubber-banding line stretches from the vertex being edited to the cursor. Enter points either using the cursor or by keying in coordinates.

Move   Allows relocation of a vertex. A rubber-banding line stretches from the vertex being edited to the cursor. You can specify points either using the cursor or by keying in coordinates. To move a vertex, you may alternatively use the Grip editor.

Regen   Regenerates a polyline. This may be required to see effects of some edits.

Straighten   Straightens a polyline between two vertices. Move the cursor to the position where you want the straightening to begin and enter **S**. The prompt changes to "Next/Previous/Go/eXit <N>:". This allows you to move in either direction along the polyline. Once the X marker is in position, type **G** to straighten the polyline. This removes all vertices between the two markers and creates one segment instead.

Tangent   Allows you to attach a tangent direction to a vertex for later use in curve fitting. A rubber-banding line stretches from the vertex to the cursor, indicating the new tangent direction. Indicate the new tangent angle by picking the direction using the cursor or by keying in an angle value. Tangent only affects curve-fitted or spline polylines.

Width   Varies the width of a polyline segment. When you have entered this function, the prompt changes to "Enter starting width <current default width>:". This allows you to enter a new width for the currently marked vertex. When you have entered a value, the prompt changes to "Enter ending width <last value entered>:". This allows you to enter a width for the next vertex.

eXit   Exits from vertex editing.

When you invoke the *Edit vertex* option, an X appears on the polyline, indicating that the vertex is being edited. Press ↵ to issue the default **N** for *Next vertex* and move the X to the next vertex. Type **P** to reverse the direction of the X. When inserting a new vertex or using the Width function, pay special attention to the direction the X moves when you select the Next function. This is the direction along the polyline in which the new vertex or the new ending width will be inserted.

TIP You may use the Edit Vertex option to move a vertex. It is generally faster to move a vertex using the object grips. With the Grips on, click on the polyline to highlight the vertices. Click on the grip of the vertex you wish to move, and move it to the desired position.

NOTE If you select a 3D polyline, all the edit options except *Tangent* and *Width* are available. Also, point input accepts 3D points.

Pedit for 3D Meshes

Pedit smooths a 3D mesh or moves vertex points in the mesh.

To Edit a 3D Mesh

Start the **Pedit** command, then select a mesh. You will be prompted to choose one of the options described below.

> Edit vertex/Smooth surface/Desmooth/Mclose/Nclose/Undo/eXit/<X>:

Options

Edit vertex Relocates vertices of a selected 3D mesh. When you select this option, you get the prompt: **Vertex (m,n) Next/Previous/Left/Right/Up/Down/Move/REgen/eXit <N>: <option>** An X appears on the first vertex of the mesh, marking the vertex to be moved.

Next Rapidly moves the **Edit** vertex marker to the next vertex.

Previous Rapidly moves the **Edit** vertex marker to the previous vertex.

Left Moves the **Edit** vertex marker along the N direction of the mesh.

Right Moves the **Edit** vertex marker along the N direction of the mesh opposite to the Left option.

Up Moves the **Edit** vertex marker along the M direction of the mesh.

Down Moves the **Edit** vertex marker along the M direction of the mesh opposite to the Up direction.

Move Moves the location of the currently marked vertex.

Regen Redisplays the mesh after a vertex has been moved.

Smooth surface Generates a B-spline or Bezier surface based on the mesh's vertex points. The type of surface generated depends on the *Surftype* system variable.

Desmooth Returns a smoothed surface back to regular mesh.

Mclose   Closes a mesh in the M direction.

Nclose   Closes a mesh in the N direction.

Mopen   Appears when a mesh is closed to open a mesh in the M direction.

Nopen   Appears when a mesh is closed to open a mesh in the N direction.

Undo   Cancels the last **Pedit** option issued.

eXit   Exits the **Edit** vertex option or the **Pedit** command.

You can use several system variables (see **System Variables**) to modify a 3D mesh. To determine the type of smooth surface generated, use the *Surftype* variable with the *Smooth* option. A value of 5 gives you a quadratic B-spline surface; a value of 6 gives a cubic B-spline surface; and 8 gives a Bezier surface. The default value for *Surftype* is 6.

The *Surfu* and *Surfv* system variables control the accuracy of the generated surface. *Surfu* controls the surface density in the M direction of the mesh, and *Surfv* controls density in the N direction. The default value for these variables is 6.

The *Splframe* system variable determines whether the control mesh of a smoothed mesh is displayed. If it is set to 0, only the smoothed mesh is displayed. If it is set to 1, only the defining mesh is displayed.

See **Bpoly** for automatically grouping lines together into a single object by picking the internal region.

See Also   Bpoly, Grips, Pline, Spline, 3Dpoly, 3Dmesh; *System Variables:* Splframe, Surftype, Surfu, Surfv

Pface

Pface draws a polygon mesh by first defining the vertices of the mesh and then assigning 3dfaces to the vertex locations.

To Draw a Polygon Mesh

Command Line: **Pface**

1. **Vertex 1:** Pick a point for the first vertex to be used in defining the mesh. The vertex prompt repeats after each point is selected. The vertex number increases by 1 each time you pick a point. Remember the location of each vertex; you will need to know the number for the next step. When you have finished selecting points, press ↵.

2. **Face 1, Vertex 1:** Enter the number of the vertex from Step 1 that you want to correspond to the first vertex of the first face. When you enter a number, the same prompt appears with the vertex number increased by 1. You can define one face with as many of the points as you indicated in step 2. When you have defined the first face, press ↵.

3. **Face 2, Vertex 1:** Enter the number of the vertex that you want to correspond to the first vertex of the second face. When you have finished, press ↵.

Options

-(number)   Makes a face edge invisible when entered at the "Face n, Vertex n:" prompt. You must use a negative value for each overlapping edge.

Layer   Specifies the layer for the face you are currently defining. Enter Layer at the *Face n, Vertex n:* prompt.

Color   Specifies the color of the face you are currently defining. You can enter Color at the *Face n, Vertex n:* prompt.

> **NOTE** **Pface** was designed for programmers who need an object type that can easily create 3D surfaces with special properties. Pfaces cannot be edited using Pedit. However, you can use **Array**, **Chprop**, **Copy**, **Erase**, **List**, **Mirror**, **Move**, **Rotate**, **Scale**, **Stretch**, and **Explode** on Pfaces. Exploding a Pface yields 3Dfaces.

See Also   Edgesurf, Revsurf, Rulesurf; *System Variables:* Pfacemax, Tabsurf, 3DMesh

Plan

Plan displays a user coordinate system "in plan"—that is, a view perpendicular to the UCS. This allows you to create and manipulate objects in 2D more easily. **Plan** affects only the active viewport. You can set the *Ucsfollow* system variable so that whenever you change to a different UCS, you get a plan view of it.

To View in Plan

Command Line: **Plan**

Menu: ➤ 3D Viewpoint ➤ Plan View ➤ Current/World/Named

If you are using the command line, you will see the "<Current UCS>/Ucs/World:" prompt. Enter the capitalized letter of the desired option or press ↵ for the current UCS.

Options

↵   Gives you a plan view of the current UCS. This is the default option.

U   Gives you a plan view of a previously saved UCS. You are prompted for the name of the UCS you wish to see in plan. Enter a question mark to get a list of saved UCS's:

>**?/Name of UCS:** Enter **?** for a list or the name of your saved UCS.

>**UCS name(s) to list <*>:** Press ↵ to view names.

W   Gives you a plan view of the world coordinate system. This option is automatically issued when you pick PlanView (world) from the Display pull-down menu.

See Also   UCS; *System Variables:* Ucsfollow

Pline

Pline creates lines having properties such as thickness and curvature. Unlike standard lines, polylines can be grouped together to act as a single object. For example, a box you draw using a polyline will act as one object instead of four discrete lines.

To Create a Polyline

Command Line: **Pline**

Menu: Draw ➤ Polyline

Draw Toolbar: Polyline

1. **From point:** Pick the start point of the polyline.

2. **Arc/Close/Halfwidth/Length/Undo/Width/<Endpoint of line>:** Enter the desired option or pick the next point of pline.

Options

Arc   Changes Pline to **Arc** mode. The Arc options are then listed in the prompt:

>**Angle/CEnter/CLose/Direction/Halfwidth/Line/Radius/ Second pt/Undo/Width/<Endpoint of arc>:**
>You can enter either the second point, angle, center, direction, radius, or endpoint of the arc. See the **Arc** command for the use of the Arc options.

Close Draws a line from the current polyline end point back to its beginning, forming a closed polyline.

Halfwidth Specifies half the polyline width at the current point. You are first prompted for the starting half width, which is half the width of the polyline at the last fixed point. Next, you are prompted for the ending half width—half the width of the polyline at the next point you pick.

Length Draws a polyline in the same direction as the last line segment drawn. You are prompted for the line segment length. If an arc was drawn last, the direction will be tangent to the end direction of that arc.

Undo Allows you to step backward along the current string of polyline or polyarc segments.

Width Determines the whole width of the polyline. Subsequent polylines will be of this width unless you specify otherwise.

Notes To give a polyline a smooth curve shape, you must use the **Pedit** command after you create the polyline. The **Explode** command reduces a polyline to its line and arc components. Polylines with a width value lose their width once exploded. To control the uniformity of a line type that is not continuous around the vertices, set the *Plinegen* system variable to 1 or use the *Ltgen* option of **Pedit**.

See Also Bpoly, Explode, Offset, Pedit; *System Variables:* Plinegen, Plinewid

Plot/Print

Plot or **Print** opens up the Plot Configuration dialog box for sending your drawing to a plotter. You can control the plotter pen selection and speed as well as where to preview the drawing on the plotter media. **Plot** also allows AutoCAD to reduce a scale drawing to fit on the media. Once you change any of the plotter settings, they become the default settings. Several plot configurations can be saved and recalled from the dialog box.

To Plot a Drawing Using the Dialog Box

Command Line: **Plot**

Command Line: **Print**

Menu: File ➤ Print

Standard Toolbar: Print

When the *Cmddia* system variable is nonzero, the Plot Configuration dialog box opens to display various plotting default parameters and conditions.

Options

Device and Default Information   The *Device and Default Selection...* pick box opens a subdialog list box with descriptions of current plot devices assigned during configuration. Additional pick boxes are available:

- Complete (PC2) **Save...**   Saves the current default settings to a new or existing ASCII .PC2 file in the Save PC2 File dialog box.

- Complete (PC2) **Replace...**   Opens the Replace from PC2 File dialog box to replace default settings from a .PC2 file, loosing current configuration information. You can, however, add multiple configurations instead of replacing a configuration using Open on the Printer tab of the Preferences dialog box.

- Partial (PCP - R12/R13) **Save...**   Saves the current default settings to a new or existing ASCII .PCP file in the Save .PCP file dialog box.

- Partial (PCP - R12/R13) **Merge...**   Opens the Merge from .PCP file dialog box to retrieve default settings from a .PCP file and reports any errors if they exist. Pick Create Error File so that AutoCAD can create an .ERR file containing information about the error for your review in an ASCII text editor.

- Device Requirements: **Show...**   Provides configuration information about the current plotter.

- Device Requirements: **Change...**   Allows you to change configuration information for the current plotter.

Pen Parameters   The *Pen Assignment...* pick box opens a subdialog list box for specifying color, pen, line type, speed, and pen width. Highlighting one or more entries in the list box allows you to edit their values in the Modify Values edit boxes. The *Feature Legend...* pick box opens a subdialog box displaying line types available for your selected plotting device.

Optimization   This pick box opens the Optimizing Pen Motion subdialog box for fine-tuning plot performance.

Additional Parameters   This section of the dialog box contains radio buttons for selecting different area configurations: plotting your current *Display* screen, the drawing *Extents*, and *Limits*. You can also save a View or create a Window to define the drawing area to plot. The *View...* and *Window...* pick buttons allow you to retrieve saved images or pick points from the screen. Select *Text Fill* to control the filling of TrueType fonts while plotting, exporting with PSOUT and rendering, otherwise, text is output as outlines. Text Fill information is stored in the TEXTFILL system variable. A *Hide Lines* check box removes hidden lines from 3D objects and also objects drawn in Paperspace assigned with the **Mview** command. A *File Name...* pick box lets you specify a specific name or type of file if you instead opt to check *Plot to File*. Autospool sends a plot file to an assigned device for printing in the background while you continue working. Enter a value in the *Text Resolution* edit box to set the resolution, in dots-per-inch, of TrueType fonts while plotting, exporting with PSOUT, and rendering. The default value is 50: to decrease resolution and increase plotting speed, use a lower number, otherwise, a higher number will increase resolution and decrease plotting speed. Text resolution is set in the *TEXTQLTY* system variable.

Paper Size and Orientation   Button boxes let you specify plotted units by Inches or MM (Millimeters). Use the *Size...* pick box to open the Paper Size subdialog box in order to select from predefined measurements or set user-defined proportions.

Scale, Rotation, and Origin   A *Rotation and Origin...* pick box opens the Plot Rotation and Origin subdialog box to set the Plot Rotation angle and Plot Origin. Enter Plotted Inches = Drawing Units in the edit boxes when you are working with an explicit scale or pick *Scale to Fit* your drawing sheet.

Plot Preview   Select the *Preview...* button after picking the *Partial* option button to preview the placement and paper size (in red) with the effective plotting area in blue, or select the *Full* option button to see the drawing on screen as it would appear on the paper. Full preview lets you zoom and pan for closer plot inspection.

To Plot a Drawing at the Command Line

When the *Cmddia* system variable is zero, the **Plot** command prompts are as follows:

1. **What to plot—Display, Extents, Limits, View or Window <default>:** Enter the desired option. If View is chosen, you are prompted for a view name. Selecting the *Window* option prompts you to pick lower-left as *First corner:* and upper-right as the *Other corner:*. You can also simply enter the corresponding coordinates.

A description similar to the following list will appear on the text screen identifying your current plot settings:

```
Plot device is System Printer ADI 4.3 - by Autodesk, Inc
Description: Default System Printer
Plot optimization level = 0
```

Plot will NOT be written to a selected file

Sizes are in Inches and the style is landscape

Plot origin is at (0.00,0.00)

Plotting area is 7.93 wide by 10.60 high (MAX size)

Plot is NOT rotated

Area fill will NOT be adjusted for pen width

Hidden lines will NOT be removed

Plot will be scaled to fit available area

0. No changes, proceed to Plot

1. Merge partial configuration from .pcp file

2. Replace configuration from .pc2 file

3. Save partial configuration as .pcp file

4. Save configuration as .pc2 file

5. Detailed plot configuration

- Enter **0** to plot without changes.

- Enter **1** to display the Merge from PCP File dialog box to select a file to merge.

- Enter **2** to display the Replace from PC2 File dialog box to select a file to replace.

- Enter **3** to display the Save PCP File dialog box to save a partial configuration in a PCP file.

- Enter **4** to display the Save PC2 File dialog box to save configuration as PC2 file.

- Enter **5** to perform a detailed plot configuration.

Use the Control Panel to make permanent changes to a printer's configuration.

2. Prompts vary depending on the output device selected. If your plotter supports multiple pens, hardware line types, line-widths or software-controlled pen speeds, then AutoCAD displays a list of Object colors, Pen Number, Line Type, Pen Speed, and Pen Width when you enter **Y** to the following prompt:

Do you want to change any of the above parameters? <N>:

TIP Changes can be entered globally by preceding each with an asterisk, or individually as prompts appear for *Pen number <1>:*, *Line type <0>:*, *Pen speed <36>:*, and *Pen width: <0.010>:*.

Pressing ↵ advances through list; entering **C** with the specific color number moves you directly to that assignment; **S** shows the updated colors; and **X** exits the procedure.

3. **Write the plot to a file? <N>:** Enter **Y** to create a plot file or press ↵ to plot the drawing. The Create Plot File dialog list box opens when the *Filedia* system variable is nonzero or the "Enter file name for plot <default>:" prompt appears just prior to processing the plot.

4. **Size units (Inches or Millimeters) <I>:** Enter the unit equivalent of your drawing.

5. **Plot origin in Inches <0.00,0.00>:** Enter the location of the drawing origin in relation to the plotter origin in X and Y coordinates. The coordinate values should be in final plot size, not in drawing scale sizes.

6. **Rotate plot clockwise 0/90/180/270 degrees <0>:** Enter the orientation of the plot if other than 0 degrees rotation.

7. **Adjust area fill boundaries for pen width? <N>:** Enter **Y** if you want the plotter to compensate for pen width on solid filled areas. If you respond **Y** to this prompt, AutoCAD will offset the border of a filled area by half the pen width so that the area will accurately plot.

8. **Remove hidden lines? <N>:** Enter **Y** if you want a 3D view to be plotted with hidden lines removed.

9. **Specify scale by entering: Plotted Inches=Drawing Units or Fit or ? <F>:** Enter a scale factor for plot or **F** to force drawing to fit entirely on the selected sheet size.

The plot is then sent to the printer.

Because some plotters do not have built-in line types, the *Select linetype* option may not appear on your plotter. Plotter supporting pen width uses a "Pen width" prompt, which works with the "Adjust fill" prompt, allowing your plotter to compensate for the pen width during area fills. If you respond with a **Y** at the "Adjust fill" prompt, AutoCAD uses the Pen width value to offset the outline of any filled areas to half the pen width. This causes the edge of filled areas to be drawn to the center line of the fill outline. If you are using a laser printer, the Pen width value determines the thickness of a typical line.

At times, even though all of your plotter settings are correct, your plot may not appear in the proper location on your sheet, or the drawing may not be plotted at all. This often occurs when you are plotting the extents of a drawing. AutoCAD often does not recognize changes to the extents of the drawing when major portions of a drawing have been removed or edited. If you have this problem with a plot, open the file to be plotted and issue **Zoom** *Extents*. Let the drawing complete the regeneration process (it will probably regenerate twice), and try plotting again. If the problem persists, double-check your size units, plot origin, plot size, and plot scale settings.

If you have problems rotating a plot, use the **UCS** command to create a UCS that is rotated the way you want, and the **View** command to save a view of your drawing in the new UCS. Then use the *View* option under the prompt. When plotting from Paperspace, such plots include all viewports and layer settings.

See Also   Preferences, *System Variables:* Cmddia, Filedia, Plotid, Plotter

---

Point

Point creates a point object. Points can be used as unobtrusive markers that you can snap to using the Node osnap override. You may also use the **Ddptype** dialog box to select a point type.

To Draw a Point Object

Command Line: **Point**

Menu: Draw ➤ Point

Draw Toolbar: Point

Point: Enter the point location.

Options

You can set the *Pdmode* system variable to change the appearance of points. You must set *Pdmode* before drawing points. Zero is the default setting. When *Pdmode* is changed, all existing points are updated to reflect the new setting. The setting values are as follows:

Pdmode Value	Object
0	A dot
1	Nothing
2	A cross
3	An x
4	A vertical line upward from the point selected

Adding 32, 64, or 96 to the values above selects a shape to draw *around* the point in addition to the figure drawn through it:

Pdmode Value	Object
32	A circle
64	A square
96	A circle inside a square

NOTE You can combine the different *Pdmode* variables to create 20 different types of points. For example, to combine a cross (2) within a circle (32), set Pdmode to 34 (2 + 32).

See Also   Ddptype, Divide, Measure, *System Variables:* Pdmode, Pdsize

Point Selection

You can enter a point by direct distance entry, tracking, picking it with your cursor, keying in an absolute or relative coordinate value, or keying in a relative polar coordinate. You can also use modifiers called filters to align points in an X, Y, or Z axis. On the command line, whenever a point selection is required, type **.x**, **.y**, or **.z**, or a combination of these modifiers (e.g., **.xy**).

Options

Direct distance entry   Specify a point then move your pointing device to indicate a direction, and then you enter a distance at they keyboard. Setting orthomode to On, makes locating vertical and horizontal points easy.

Tracking   Use tracking to locate a point relative to previous or base point.

Absolute coordinate   Specifies points by giving the X, Y, and Z coordinate values separated by commas, as follows:

Select point: 6,3,1

The X value is 6, the Y is 3, and the Z is 1. If you omit the Z value, AutoCAD assumes the current default Z value (see the **Elev** command to set the current Z default value). Absolute coordinates use the current UCS's origin as the point of reference.

Relative coordinates   Entered like absolute coordinates, except that an at sign (@) precedes the coordinate values, as follows:

Select point: @6,3,1

If you omit the Z value, AutoCAD assumes the current default Z value (see the **Elev** command for setting the current Z default value). Relative coordinates use the last point entered as the point of reference. To tell AutoCAD to use the last point selected, simply enter the at sign by itself at a point selection prompt.

Relative polar coordinates   Specify points by giving the distance from the last point entered, preceded by an at sign (@), the distance, and followed by a less-than sign (<) and the angle of direction, as follows:

Select point: @6<45

This entry calls for a relative distance of 6 units at a 45-degree angle from the last point entered.

Filters   Align a point along an X, Y, or Z axis by first specifying the axis on which to align, then selecting an existing point on which to align, and then entering the new point's remaining coordinate values. The following example aligns a point vertically on a specific X location:

To Use Point Filters

Pop-up Cursor Menu: Point Filters ➤ .X, .Y, .Z, .XY, .XZ, and .YZ filters

1. **Point:** Enter **.x** or select a known point to which you want to align vertically. For precision, use the Osnap overrides.

2. **(need yz):** Select a Y-Z coordinate. Again, you can use Osnap overrides to align to other geometries.

The cursor menu is activated in different ways depending on the pointing device that you are using: If you have a four-button device, press the *third* button (blue for some pucks); if you have a three-button device, press the *middle* button; if you have a two-button device, hold the Shift key down while pressing the right button. The Acad.MNU and Acad.MNS files supplied with AutoCAD assigns these buttons to the cursor menu. The cursor menu lists snap modes as well as point filters.

You can also enter **.xy**, **.yz**, or **.xz** at the prompt. For example, you can first pick an X-Y location and then enter a Z value for height.

NOTE   To override the current angle units, base, and direction settings (set using the **Units** command), use double or triple lesser-than signs (<):

<<   Enters angles in degrees, default angle base (east), and direction (counterclockwise), regardless of the current settings.

<<< Enters angles based on the current angle format (degrees, radians, grads, etc.), default angle base (east), and direction (counterclockwise), regardless of the base and direction settings.

You can enter fractional units regardless of the unit style setting. This means you can enter **5.5"** as well as **5'6"** when using the architectural format.

See Also Ddosnap, Ddunits, Filter, Osnap, Tracking, Units

Polygon

Polygon allows you to draw a regular polygon of up to 1,024 sides. To define the polygon, you can specify the outside or inside radius, or the length of one side. The polygon is actually a polyline that can be exploded into its individual component lines. Use the **Pedit** command to edit a polygon's width.

To Draw a Polygon

Command Line: **Polygon**

Menu: Draw ➢ Polygon

Draw Toolbar: 🔲 Polygon

1. **Number of sides:** Enter the number of sides.

2. **Edge/<Center of polygon>:** Enter **E** to select Edge option or pick a point to select the polygon center. If you select the default center of a polygon, the following prompts appear:

    Inscribed in circle/Circumscribed about circle (I/C): Enter the desired option.

    Radius of circle: Enter the radius of circle defining polygon size.

Options

Edge Determines the length of one face of the polygon. You are prompted to select the first and second endpoint of the edge. AutoCAD then draws a polygon by creating a circular array of the edge you specify.

Inscribed Forces the polygon to fit inside a circle of the specified radius; the endpoints of each line lie along the circumference.

Circumscribed Forces the polygon to fit outside a circle of the specified radius; the midpoint of each line lies tangent to the circumference.

Radius of circle   Sets the length of the defining radius of the polygon. The radius will be the distance from the center to either an endpoint or a midpoint, depending on the *Inscribed/Circumscribed* choice.

See Also   Pedit, Pline, *System Variables:* Polysides

Preferences/Config

Preferences allows you to set a range of variables that control AutoCAD's appearance and functioning. This command opens a series of tabbed dialog boxes to allow modification of an extensive set of controls: *Files, Performance, Compatibility, General, Display, Pointer, Printer* and *Profiles*.

To Set AutoCAD Preferences

Command Line: **Preferences**

Command Line: **Config**

Menu: Tools ➤ Preferences…

Right click your mouse button over the command line for the cursor menu, then select *Preferences…*

Once you customize the settings in the Preferences dialog box, click *Apply* to immediately see your new configurations. Pick OK to exit the dialog box.

Options

Files Tab   Use this tabbed subdialog box to specify AutoCAD search paths for Support files, Drivers, Menus, Project Files (xref's), Help files, Log files, a Text Editor, Dictionary, Font File Names, Print File, Spooler, Prolong Section Names, Printer Spooler File Locations, Prototypes (templates), Temporary Drawing File Locations, and Texture Map Search Paths.

   Browse   Depending upon your selection in the list, opens the Browse for Folder or Select a File dialog box.

   Add   Adds a new search path under the selected directory.

   Remove   Removes selected search path or file from directory.

   Move Up   Allows you to move your directory up the search path.

   Move Down   Allows you to move your directory down the search path.

   Set Current   Lets you set the selected Project or Dictionary current.

Performance Tab   Use this tabbed subdialog box to set controls for appearance of Solid Objects, Text Objects, Raster Images, Dragged Objects, Arcs and Circles. Values can also be set for full or incremental saves, maximum number of viewports as well as how xref's are loaded.

> *Solid Model Object Display*   Specify a value *for Rendered Object Smoothness* and *Contour Lines per Surface.* Use the check box *to Show Silhouettes in Wireframe.*

> *Display Object Being Dragged*   Pick a radio button for *Do not display, Display when requested* or *Display automatically.* When you move an object and dragging is on, you can see object being dragged. This setting is saved in the *Dragmode* system variable.

> *Show Text Boundary Frame Only*   Displays text objects as frames instead of the actual text.This setting is stored in the *Qtextmode* system variable and requires a **Regen** to restore as text object.

> *Show Raster Image Content*   Controls how raster images are displayed while being moved. The corresponding system variable is *Rtdisplay.*

> *Arc and circle smoothness*   Specify a value; high values generate smoother objects but require more time to regenerate. Smoothness is controlled by the *Viewres* command.

> *Segments per polyline curve*   Enter a value to set the number of lines segments you wish to generate for each polyline curve or use the *Splinesegs* system variable.

> *Incremental save %*   Enter a number for the percentage of wasted space allowed in a drawing file and AutoCAD will determine when to perform a full save instead of incremental saves. You can also use the *Isavepercent* sysem variable and set it to 0, making all saves perform a full save.

> *Maximum active viewports*   Specify the maximum number of active viewports you desire; the maximum number is 48. This settings is stored in the *Maxactvp* system variable. Viewports that are not active appear empty and do not regenerate.

> *External Reference File Demand Load*   Controls methods for loading external reference files and whether indexes are used.

> *Reset*   Restores all values to system defaults.

Compatibility Tab   Use this tabbed subdialog box to control loading and display of third party applications and the startup dialog box. It also allows you to set a priority for coordinate data entry.

Load ARX Applications on Demand   Determines appropriateness for AutoCAD to demand load third party applications if a drawing has custom objects created in that application. Demand load values are stored in the *Demandload* system variable.

Show Proxy Information dialog box   Toggles display of the dialog box on and off.

Proxy images for custom objects   Select from among *Do not show proxy graphics*, *Show proxy graphics* or *Show proxy bounding box* radio buttons.

Priority for accelerator keys   Pick a radio button to set *Windows standards* or *AutoCAD classic* mode for AutoCAD to interpret keystrokes.

Priority for coorindate data entry   Specify your priority among *Running object snap*, *Keyboard entry* or *Keyboard entry except scripts*. You can use the *Osnapcoord* system variable to store this value.

Show the Start Up dialog box   Allows you to turn the display of the Start Up dialog box on and off.

Reload AutoLISP between drawings   Reminds AutoCAD to load AutoLISP-defined functions and variables for the duration of each drawing session. It applies to those custom commands that are auto loaded at start up, not to custom routines that are loaded into drawing sessions.

General Tab   Use this tabbed subdialog box to set and specify automatic save methods, extension for network node names and maximum number of items to sort. You can set toggles to create backups, CRC validation, audits, log files, thumbnail preview images and alarm beeps.

Drawing session safety precautions   Toggles allow you to set an *Automatic save* and control the number of *Minutes between saves*. You can also specify the following: *Create backup copy with each save; Full-time CRC validation, Audit after each DXFIN or DXBIN* and *Maintain a log file*.

Save thumbnail preview image   Checking this saves the image that is displayed in the Preview area of the Select File dialog box and stores the value in the *Rasterpreview* system variable.

Beep on error in user input   If this box is checked, AutoCAD beeps when it detects an invalid entry.

File extension for temporary files   To specify a unique network node name, enter an extension in the edit box. The default is .AC$.

Maximum number sorted symbols   Specifies alphabetical
order for maximum number of items to sort and save it to the
Maxsort system variable. If you set this number to 0, items appear in
the order they are created.

Reset   Restores all values to system defaults.

Display Tab   Use this tabbed subdialog box to toggle the display of
scroll bars or to maximize the AutoCAD window. You can set the number of lines that appear at the command line and text window. Pick
boxes open subdialog boxes to set screen colors and fonts.

Drawing Window Parameters   Toggles allow you *to Display
screen menu in drawing session, Display scroll bars in drawing window*
and *Maximize the AutoCAD window upon startup.*

Text window parameters   Specify the *Number of lines to show in
docked command line window* and the *Number of lines of text window
to keep in memeory.*

AutoCAD window format   Click the **Colors...** button to *set
Colors for drawing area, screen menu, text window and command line*
and the **Fonts...** button to specify *Fonts for screen menu, text window
and command line.*

Pointer Tab   Use this tabbed subdialog box to display and select the
current AutoCAD pointing device. Toggles allow you to set mouse or
digitizer input methods and cursor size.

Current pointing device driver   The list box displays the names
of the pointing device drivers.

Set Current   Click the button to set a pointing device shown in
the list box current.

Accept Input From   Toggle a radio button for *Digitizer only* or
Digitizer and mouse. (Only available if you select a digitizer)

Cursor size   Specify a value to set the cursor size based on
Percentage of screen size. A value of 100 extends the vertical and horizontal crosshairs to the ends of the graphics screen; the default is 5.

Printer Tab   Use this tabbed subdialog box to display, set, create, add,
remove, edit, describe and save plot configuration settings.

Current printer   This list box displays the name of your current
printers and plotters.

Set Current   Click this box to set a printer or plotter current.

Modify...   Opens the Reconfigure a Printer dialog box to *Reconfigure* the selected printer and include a *Description*.

New...   Displays the *Add a Printer* dialog box to view and select available printer drivers. Use the edit box to *Add a description*.

Open...   Opens the Replace from PC2 File dialog box to select a configuration file for the device you wish to use.

Save As...   Displays the Save PC2 File dialog box, allowing you to specify a directory and file name to save configuration information.

Remove   Deletes selected printer from the list box.

Profiles Tab   Use this tabbed subdialog box to list, set, copy, rename, describe, export or import profiles. A profile is a user-defined windows setup configuration.

Set Current   Sets and displays name of current profile.

Copy...   Opens the Copy Profile dialog box to enter a profile name and description.

Rename...   Displays the Change Profile dialog box to edit an existing profile's name and description.

Delete   Allows you to remove a profile from the list box.

Export...   Opens the Export Profile dialog box to export a profile on the same or a different computer.

Import...   Displays the Import Profile dialog box to import the profile created with *Export*.

Reset   Restores all values to system defaults.

See Also   System Variables referred to within this command

Preview

Preview shows you a full-page view of the current drawing similar to other Windows applications. The view displayed is set in the **Plot** command, based on your current plot configuration.

To Preview Your Plot

Command Line: **Preview**

Press Esc or Enter to exit, or right click to activate pop-up menu.

A symbol displayed as a magnifying glass with a plus and minus sign helps you zoom in and out of your preview. Right click to display the pop-up menu allowing you to switch between *Exit*, *Plot*, *Pan*, *Zoom*, *Zoom Window* and *Zoom Previous*. Press the Escape key or press ↵ to cancel the preview and not plotting your drawing.

See Also   Plot, Preferences

Psdrag

Psdrag controls the appearance of the PostScript image as you drag it into position using the **Import/Export** command **Psin**.

To Display the PostScript Image

Command Line: **Psdrag**

PSIN drag mode <0>: Enter 0 or 1, or press ↵.

Options

0   Displays only the image's bounding box and file name while the image is being dragged.

1   Displays the rendered PostScript image while the image is being dragged into place. If the *Psquality* system variable is set to 0, this drag mode option has no effect. Only the bounding box is shown.

See Also   Import/Export: Psfill, Psin, *System Variables:* Psquality

Psfill

Psfill fills 2D polyline outlines with any PostScript pattern defined in the Acad.PSF PostScript support file. The pattern is not visible on the screen but is output with the **Psout** command.

To Use a PostScript Fill Pattern

Command Line: **Psfill**

1. **Select polyline:** Pick the two dimensional polyline outline.

2. **PostScript fill pattern (.=none)<.>/?:** Enter a pattern name.

Entering **?** displays the following list of available patterns: *Grayscale RGBcolor AIlogo Lineargray Radialgray Square Waffle Zigzag Stars Brick Specks*. The prompt is then repeated with the pattern name displayed in the brackets.

The appearance of fill patterns is controlled by a range of parameters. Depending upon the pattern you select, you will be prompted to specify the relevant parameters. AutoCAD does not display the patterns on screen, but **Psout** recognizes and exports them.

See Also   Import/Export: Psin/Psout, Psdrag

Pspace

Pspace lets you move from Modelspace back to Paperspace when you are working from Paperspace through viewport into Modelspace. Paperspace must be enabled before you use **Pspace**.

To Switch from a Modelspace Viewport to Paperspace

Command Line: **Pspace**.

Menu: View ➤ Paperspace

Double-click MODEL/PAPER on the status bar.

NOTE   You use Modelspace in AutoCAD to do drafting and design work. Paperspace is an alternative work space that lets you arrange views of your Modelspace drawing and scale or size them for plotting. You can create viewports in Paperspace that are like windows into Modelspace. Layers, Snap, and Grid modes can be set independently for each viewport. You can also accurately control the scale of a viewport for plotting purposes.

TIP   To get into Paperspace in a new drawing, set Tilemode to 0. You can toggle Tilemode On and Off by double-clicking TILE on the status bar. Your screen will go blank and the UCS icon will change to a triangle. Use the **Mview** command to set up viewports so you can display your Modelspace drawing in Paperspace. Use the Xp option under the **Zoom** command to set the scale of a viewport display. Use **Mvsetup** for easier interface and setup procedures.

TIP   Viewports in Paperspace can be resized, moved, copied, and even overlapped using standard AutoCAD editing commands.

NOTE   In Release 14, regenerations following zoom or pan have been almost eliminated. You can perform transparent and realtime Zoom's and Pan's in paperpace (tilemode = 0).

See Also   Mspace, Mview, Mvsetup, Tilemode, Vplayer, Vports, Zoom/xp

Purge

Purge allows you to remove unreferenced blocks, layers, line types, dimension styles, shape files, or text styles. These objects and settings can increase the size of the drawing file, making the drawing slow to load and difficult to transport.

To Purge Elements from the Drawing File

Command Line: **Purge**

Menu: Files ➤ Drawing Utilities ➤ Purge ➤ Preset Options

Purge unused Blocks/Dimstyles/LAyers/LTypes/SHapes/ STyles/Mlinestyles/All: Select the type of element you wish to purge.

When you select the element type, AutoCAD displays each element name of the type specified. Enter a **Y** to purge the element or **N** to keep it. The All option purges all elements regardless of type.

Release 14 allows you to purge all objects at once:

Names to purge <*>: Enter name of variable to purge.

Verify each name to be purged? <Y> Enter **N** if you wish to purge all objects, or **Y** for a list to selectively choose objects to purge.

The layer 0, the continuous line type, the standard text style, UCS, views, and viewport configurations cannot be purged. Nested blocks are removed only by repetitious purging and exiting of the drawing. The **Wblock** command describes an alternative and more effective method for purging.

See Also Wblock

Qsave

Qsave saves a named drawing quickly without asking for a file name. If saving an unnamed drawing, **Qsave** works like **Saveas**, enabling you to name the drawing before saving it.

To Save a Drawing

Command Line: **Qsave**

Menu: File ➤ Save

Standard Toolbar: 💾Save

See Also   Save, Saveas; *System Variables:* Dwgtitled, Savename, Savetime

Qtext

Qtext helps reduce drawing regeneration and redraw times by making text appear as a rectangular box instead of readable text. The rectangle approximates the height and length of the text.

To Display Text as a Rectangular Box

Command Line: **Qtext**

Menu: Tools ➤ Drawing Aids... ➤ Qtext Text check box

ON/OFF <Off>: Enter the desired option.

   You do not see the effects of **Qtext** until you issue the **Regen** command.

See Also   Dtext, Regentext; *System Variables:* Qtextmode

Quit

Quit exits a drawing and allows you to save or discard changes from the last save or an unsaved drawing.

To Exit a Drawing

Command Line: **Quit**

Menu: File ➤ Exit

   If no changes were made to the current drawing, AutoCAD exits the program. If changes were made and not saved, a dialog box opens to pick *Yes, No,* or *Cancel.* If the drawing is unnamed and you pick Yes, the Save Drawing As dialog box will open, giving you an opportunity to name the drawing.

See Also   Exit, Qsave, Save, Saveas; *System Variables:* Dbmod

Ray

Ray creates the "semi-infinite" lines that are generally used as construction lines in a drawing. The ray extends from a selected point to infinity.

To Create a Ray

Command Line: **Ray**

Menu: Draw ➤ Ray

1. **From Point:** Specify a start point for the ray.

2. **Through Point:** Specify the point through which you want the ray to pass.

3. Continue to specify points to create multiple rays, if required, and then press ⏎.

See Also Xline

Recover

Recover salvages as much of a file as possible and allows AutoCAD to read the file. A drawing may become corrupted because of problems with your hard disk drive or floppy disk. If the header information is damaged, AutoCAD will attempt to recover the file with the Open command.

To Recover Corrupted Files

Command Line: **Recover**

Menu: File ➤ Drawing Utilities ➤ Recover...

If the *Filedia* system variable is set to 1, the Select File dialog box is displayed so you can enter the drawing name that you wish to recover. Otherwise, the following command-line prompt appears:

Recover<*current filename*>: Enter file name to recover.

A series of messages appears indicating the action AutoCAD is taking to recover the file. An AutoCAD Alert dialog box opens after recovery to report whether the audit detected any errors in the recovered database. If so, the recovery is processed and reported to the screen.

See Also Audit, *System Variables:* Auditctl

Rectang

Rectang allows you to draw a rectangular polyline with chamfered or filleted corners, thickness, elevation and/or width.

To Draw a Rectangle

Command Line: **Rectang**

Menu: Draw ➤ Rectangle

Draw Toolbar: 🔲 Rectangle

1. **Chamfer/Elevation/Fillet/Thickness/Width/<First corner>:**
   Specify a point, or type one of the uppercase letters as indicated in
   steps 3 - 7.

2. **Other corner:** Specify the opposing corner.

3. If you entered a **C**, your are prompted for a chamfer distance or
   press ⏎ at the prompts "First chamfer distance for rectangles
   <0.0000>:" and "Second chamfer distance for rectangles <0.0000>:".

4. If you specified **E**, you can enter the **Elevation for rectangles
   <0.0000>:**.

5. To set the **Fillet radius for rectangles <0.0000>:**, type **F** and
   enter a value.

6. If you wish to set a **Thickness for rectangles <0.0000>:**, type **T**
   and specify a thickness.

7. You can set the **Width for rectangles <0.0000>:** by typing the
   letter **W, pressing** ⏎, then specifying a value.

NOTE The *Elevation* and *Thickness* options need to be used
with caution. If you're doing only 2D drafting hen you should not
use them—they will cause problems.

See Also Pline, Thickness, Chamfer, Fillet; *System Variables:* Filetrad,
Thickness, Chamfera, Chamferb, Plinewid

Redefine/Undefine

Undefine suppresses any standard AutoCAD command. For example,
if you load an AutoLISP **Copy** command you have written and then
enter **Copy** at the command prompt, you will still get the standard
Copy command. However, if you use **Undefine** to suppress the standard **Copy** command, you can use the AutoLISP **Copy** program.
Redefine reinstates a standard command that has been suppressed.

To Suppress or Reinstate a Standard Command

Command Line: **Undefine** or **Redefine** (as appropriate)

> **NOTE Command name:** Enter the command name.To enter
> the standard AutoCAD **Copy** command when an AutoLISP version
> might already be defined, precede the command with a period at
> the command prompt, as follows:

Command Line: **Copy⏎**

Select objects:

This is the only way to use an undefined command with the AutoLISP
Command function.

Redo

Redo restores a command you have undone using **U** or **Undo**. Redo
must immediately follow the U or Undo. You are allowed only one
Redo per command. If you enter a series of three *U*s (that is, three Undo
1's), only the last U can be restored.

To Undo Your Undo

Command Line: **Redo**

Menu: Edit ➤ Redo

Standard Toolbar: Redo

Here is the most effective approach for restoring undo's:

undo 6

If this undoes too much, then try **redo**. If this undoes too much, then
try **undo 4**. Otherwise, enter **u**.

See Also   U, Undo; *System Variables:* Undoctl

Redraw and Redrawall

During the drawing and editing process, an operation may cause an
object to partially disappear. Often, the object was previously behind
other objects that have since been removed. **Redraw** and **Redrawall**
refresh the screen and restore such obscured objects. These commands
also clear the screen of blips that may clutter your view.

To Redraw the Display

Command Line: **Redraw/Redrawall** or (**'Redraw/'Redrawall** to use transparently).

Menu: Redraw

Standard Toolbar: Redrawall

> **NOTE** **Redraw** will act only on the currently active viewport. **Redrawall**, on the other hand, refreshes all viewports on the screen at once. These commands affect only the virtual screen, not the actual drawing database.

See Also Regen, Viewres

Regen and Regenall

These two commands update the drawing editor screen to reflect the most recent changes in the drawing database.

To Regenerate the Drawing and Refresh Your View

Command Line: **Regen** or **Regenall**

Menu: View ➤ Regen/Regen All

> **NOTE** If you make a global change in the drawing database and **Regenauto** is turned on, a regeneration occurs automatically. If you have **Regenauto** turned off, regeneration will not occur automatically, so changes to the drawing database are not immediately reflected in the drawing you see. If you need to see those changes, use **Regen** to update the display.

See Also Regenauto, Viewres

Regenauto

Regenauto automatically regenerates the screen display to reflect the most recent drawing changes. For complex drawings, regeneration can be very time-consuming. Regenauto enables you to turn off automatic regeneration. Regenauto is on by default.

To Control Regeneration

Command Line: **Regenauto** (or **'Regenauto** to use transparently)

REGENAUTO

ON/OFF/ <current status>: Enter **ON** or **OFF** as required.

Options

On   Causes the display to be automatically regenerated when required to reflect global changes in the drawing database. Your display will reflect all the most recent drawing changes.

Off   Suppresses the automatic regeneration of the display. This can save time when you are editing complex drawings. When a command needs to regenerate the drawing, a prompt allows you to decide whether or not to regenerate the display.

See Also   Regen; *System Variables:* Regenmode, Viewres

Region

The **Region** command allows you to create 2D enclosed areas from existing overlapping closed shapes (called *loops*). The loops can be combinations of lines, polylines, circles, arcs, ellipses, elliptical arcs, and splines. They must be closed or form closed areas.

To Create Regions

Command Line: **Region**

Menu: Draw ➤ Region

Draw Toolbar: 🔲 Region

1.   **Select objects:** Select the objects you wish to combine into a region.

2.   Press ⏎ to end the command. The command line shows how many loops were detected and how many regions were created.

You can create composite regions by subtracting, combining, or finding the intersection of regions.

To Create Composite Regions

Command Line: **Union**

Command Line: **Subtract**

Command Line: **Intersect**

1.   **Select objects:** Select the regions you wish to combine into a composite region.

2.   Press ⏎ to end the command.

You may select objects in any order to unite them with the **Union** command or to find the intersection with the **Intersect** command.

When you wish to subtract one region from the other, you must first select the region from which you want to subtract.

NOTE Regions may not be created from open objects that intersect to form a closed area, such as intersecting arcs or self-intersecting curves. (The related **Boundary** command allows you to create polyline boundaries from any intersecting objects.) Objects in a region must be in the same plane.

NOTE Regions are useful for calculating area properties for facilities management purposes (see the **Area** command). You can also hatch and shade regions, using the **Bhatch** or **Shade** commands, and analyze other properties.

See Also Bhatch, -Boundary, Boundary, Intersect, Shapes, Subtract, Union

Reinit

Reinit opens the Re-initialization dialog box to re-initialize the Input/Output ports, digitizer, display, and Acad.PGP file.

To Reinitialize Ports, Digitizer, Display, and *.PGP* File

Command Line: **Reinit**

Options

I/O Port Initialization This section contains check boxes for resetting the I/O port for your digitizer and plotter.

Device & File Initialization This section contains check boxes to reinitalize your digitizer, display, and .PGP file.

NOTE If you edit your Acad.PGP file with an ACII text editor, check the .PGP File box to activate those changes in your current drawing. If your cursor does not appear on the screen to permit you to select the check boxes, you can use the *Re-init* system variable and specify the sum of several reinitialization values. For example, enter **Re-init** and enter a value of **5** (1 = Digitizer + 4 = Digitizer reinitialization) for a digitizer analog failure. See system variables for additive values.

See Also *System Variables:* Re-init

Rename

Rename renames any namable drawing element, such as a block, dim-style, layer, line type, text style, etc. The dialog box equivalent command is **Ddrename**.

To Assign a New Object Name

Command Line: **Rename**

1. **Block/Dimstyle/LAyer/LType/Style/Ucs/VIew/VPort:** Enter the type of drawing element to be renamed.

2. **Old (object) name:** Enter old name of object.

3. **New (object) name:** Enter new name of object.

See also   Ddrename, Layer, Linetype

Render

Render uses light sources and surface settings to render a 3D model. Surfaces can be adjusted for reflectance, shininess, and smoothness. Multiple light sources can be added to the drawing to enhance the rendering, and the intensity of these light sources is adjustable. Render produces an image using information from a named scene, the current selection set, or the current view.

To Render a Scene, Objects, or View

Command Line: **Render**

Menu: View ➢ Render ➢ Render... (on the drop-down Render menu)

Render Toolbar: Render

1. In the Render dialog box, you may set the Rendering Type as required; select a Scene to Render; set Screen Palette options (shading, materials, and smoothing variables); and choose the Destination for the rendered output (Viewport, Render Window, or File).

2. Click on either the Render Scene or Render Objects button.

If you choose the *Render Objects* button, you will be prompted to Select objects: before the rendering can begin. If no scene or selection set is specified, **Render** will use the current view. If there are no lights in the drawing, **Render** will use a standard "over-the-shoulder" light source with an intensity of 1.

Preset Options

The following options are available on the Render toolbar. Their command-line equivalents are shown at the command line.

Hide   Initiates a hide for a 3D model with hidden lines suppressed

Command Line: **Hide**

Menu: View ➤ Hide

Render Toolbar: Render

Shade   Displays a flat-shaded image of the drawing in the current viewport.

Command Line: **Shade**

Menu: View ➤ Shade➤ Shade Color Options

Render Toolbar: Shade

Scenes   Brings up a Scenes dialog box that lets you set up a scene you can later recall.

Command Line: **Scene**

Menu: View ➤ Render ➤ Scene...

Render Toolbar: Scenes

Lights   Brings up the Lights dialog box that lets you adjust, delete, or create a light source. You can set the intensity of the Ambient light and set the lighting drop-off to be inverse linear or inverse square

Command Line: **Light**

Menu: View ➤ Render ➤ Light...

Render Toolbar: Scenes

Materials   Brings up a dialog box that lets you create a new finish, or import, delete, export, or modify an existing finish. A preview sphere gives you a sample view of what your finish looks like.

Command Line: **Rmat**

Menu: View ➤ Render ➤ Materials...

Render Toolbar: Materials

Materials Library   Brings up a dialog box that shows a list of all the materials finishes available. You may select materials subsets and store them as named materials library (.MLI) files.

Command Line: **Matlib**

Menu: View ➤ Render ➤ Materials Library...

Render Toolbar: Materials Library

Mapping Prompts to **Select objects:**, then Opens the Mapping dialog box to assign mapping coordinates and projection Mapping dialog box.

Command Line: **Setuv**

Menu: View ➤ Render ➤ Mapping…

Render Toolbar: Mapping

Fog Displays the Fog/Depth dialog box to emulate distances for objects with white (for fog), black (for traditional depth cueing) or blends of color combinations.

Command Line: **Fog**

Menu: View ➤ Render ➤ Fog…

Render Toolbar: Fog

Landscape New Opens the Landscape New dialog box to select a landscape object.

Command Line: **Lsnew**

Menu: View ➤ Render ➤ Landscape New…

Render Toolbar: Landscape New

Landscape Edit Opens the Landscape Edit dialog box to edit a landscape object.

Command Line: **Lsedit**

Menu: View ➤ Render ➤ Landscape Edit…

Render Toolbar: Landscape Edit

Landscape Library Opens the Landscape Library dialog box. Lets you maintain libraries of landscape objects.

Command Line: **Lslib**

Menu: View ➤ Render ➤ Landscape Library…

Render Toolbar: Landscape Edit

Render Preferences Brings up the Rendering Preferences dialog box that lets you set the rendering preferences for the following: Rendering Procedures defaults; Screen Palette or color mapping techniques; Icon scale for Lights; Rendering (display) options; Render Quality and Face controls.

Command Line: **Rpref**

Menu: View ➤ Render ➤ Preferences…

Render Toolbar: Render Preferences

Statistics   Provides information about the last scene rendered (**Stats** command).

Command Line: **Stats**

Menu: View ➤ Render ➤ Statistics...

Render Toolbar: 🖼️Statistics

Resume

See Script

Revsurf

Revsurf draws an extruded curved surface that is rotated about an axis, like a bell, globe, or drinking glass, as shown in Figure 14. Before you can use **Revsurf**, you must define both the shape of the extrusion and an axis of rotation. Use arcs, lines, circles, or 2- or 3D polylines to define this shape. The axis of rotation can be a line.

FIGURE 14:   Extruded curved surface drawn by Revsurf

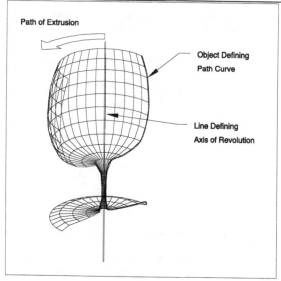

To Draw an Extruded Surface

Command Line: **Revsurf**

Menu: Draw ➤ Surfaces ➤ Revolved Surface

Surfaces Toolbar: Revolved Surface

1. **Select path curve:** Pick an arc line, circle, 2D polyline, or 3D polyline defining the shape to be swept.

2. **Select Axis of revolution:** Pick a line representing the axis of rotation.

3. **Starting Angle <0>:** Enter the angle from the object selected as the start point of the sweep.

4. **Included angle (+=ccw, ~=cw) <Full circle>:** Enter the angle of the sweep.

> **NOTE** The point you pick on the object in step 3 determines the positive and negative directions of the rotation. You can use the "right-hand rule" illustrated in Figure 15 to determine the positive direction of the rotation. Imagine placing your thumb on the axis line, pointing away from the end closest to the pick point. The rest of your fingers will point in the positive rotation direction. The rotation direction determines the N direction of the surface while the axis of rotation defines the M direction.

FIGURE 15: Determining the positive direction of rotation

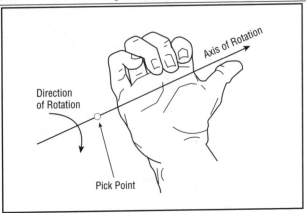

You can control the number of facets used to create the Revsurf by setting the *Surftab1* and *Surftab2* system variables. *Surftab1* controls the number of facets in the M direction, while *Surftab2* controls the facets

in the N direction. You can set these variables or by entering them at the command prompt. Resetting a higher value in *Surftab1* or *Surftab2* will not affect already drawn surfaces.

See Also   3Dmesh, Pedit; *System Variables:* Splframe, Surftab1, Surftab2

Rotate

Rotate rotates an object or group of objects to a specified angle.

To Rotate Objects

Command Line: **Rotate**

Menu: Modify ➤ Rotate

Modify Toolbar: Rotate

1. **Select objects:** Select as many objects as you like.

2. **Base point:** Pick the point about which objects are to be rotated.

3. **<Rotation angle>/Reference:** Enter the angle of rotation or **R** to specify a reference angle.

Options

Reference   Allows you to specify the rotation angle in reference to the object's current angle. If you enter this option, you get the prompts:

Reference angle <0>: Enter the current angle of the object or pick two points representing a base angle.

New angle: Enter a new angle or pick an angle with the cursor.

NOTE   Rotate is also a grips option.

See Also   Ddgrips, Grips

Rotate3D

Rotate 3D rotates an object or group of objects about an arbitrary 3D axis.

To Rotate Objects

Command Line: **Rotate3D**

Menu: Modify ➤ 3D Operation ➤ Rotate3D

1. **Select objects:** Select as many objects as you like.

2. **Axis by object/Last/View/Xaxis/Yaxis/Zaxis/<2points>:** Specify a point or select an option.

3. **<Rotation angle>/Reference:** Enter the angle of rotation or **R** to specify a reference angle.

Options

Axis by Object   Allows you to align the axis of rotation with an existing object (line, circle, arc, or 2D polyline).

Last   Uses the last axis of rotation.

View   Aligns the axis of rotation with the viewing direction of the current viewport that passes through a selected point. At the "Point on view direction axis <0,0,0>:" prompt, select a point.

X\Y\Zaxis   Aligns the axis of rotation with one of the axes (X, Y, or Z) that pass through the selected point. At the "Point on (X, Y, or Z) axis <0,0,0>:", select a point.

2Points   Allows you to specify two points to define the axis of rotation. You will be prompted *1st point on axis:* and *2nd point on axis :.* Select two points.

Rscript

*See **Script***

Rulesurf

Rulesurf generates a surface between two curves. Before you can use Rulesurf, you must draw two curves defining opposite ends of the desired surface (see Figure 16). The defining curves can be points, lines, arcs, circles, 2D polylines, or 3D polylines.

To Use Curves to Define a Surface

Command Line: **Rulesurf**

Menu: Draw ➤ Surfaces ➤ Ruled Surface

Surfaces Toolbar: Ruled Surface

1. **Select first defining curve:** Pick the first curve.

2. **Select second defining curve:** Pick the second curve.

SAVE

FIGURE 16: Defining the opposite ends of a surface for Rulesurf

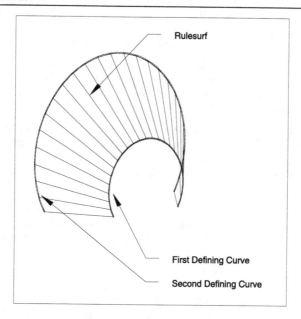

Rulesurf

First Defining Curve

Second Defining Curve

NOTE The location of your pick points on the defining curves affects the way the surface is generated. If you want the surface to be drawn straight between the two defining curves, pick points near the same position on each curve. If you want the surface to cross between the two defining curves in a corkscrew fashion, pick points at opposite positions on the curves.

The *Surftab1* system variable controls the number of faces used to generate the surface.

See Also Pedit; *System Variables:* Surftab1

Save

Save stores your currently open file to disk. Use **Save** to save changes to your drawing under the same name.

To Save Your Drawing

Command Line: **Save**

If the *Filedia* system variable is set to 1 and your drawing has not yet been named, the Save Drawing As dialog list box opens. Enter a drawing name in the File edit box. The next time you enter Save, the Save Drawing As dialog box reappears. Click the OK button to save the drawing to the same file name or specify a new file name, directory, and/or path.

If the *Filedia* system variable is set to 0, the following command line prompt appears: **Save Drawing As <C:\ACADR14\<drawing.dwg>:**. Enter a new <drive><path><file name> or press ↵ to accept the default current file name.

If you save the drawing into the same location with the same name you will get another dialog box telling you that a file with that name already exists and do you want to overwrite it. *Yes* overwrites the existing file. *No* stops the save and puts you back at the Save Drawing As dialog box.

NOTE Use the **Savetime** command to set a time interval for automatically saving your drawing. The current drawing is saved to the default file name Auto.sv$.

Options

Options   Displays Export Options tab with check box to *Save Proxy Images of Custom Objects*. Click the drop down box for *None, Layer, Spacial* and *Layer and Spacial*.

See Also   Preferences, Qsave, Saveas; *System Variables:* Savefile, Savename, Savetime

Saveas

Saveas saves an unnamed drawing with a file name or allows you to rename your drawing, making it the current drawing.

To Save An Existing Drawing as the Current Drawing

Command Line: **Saveas**

Menu: File ➤ Saveas

If the *Filedia* system variable is set to 1 and your drawing has not yet been named, the Save Drawing As dialog list box opens. Press ↵ to save the drawing as the same name in the File edit box or enter a new file name, directory and/or path.

If the *Filedia* system variable is set to 0, the following command line prompt appears:

1. **R12(LT2)/R13(LT95)/Template/ <R14>:** Press ↵ to save the drawing in AutoCAD Release 14 format or enter an option.

2. **Save Drawing As <C:\ACADR14\test4.dwg>:** Press ↵ to save the drawing as the same name or enter a new <drive><path><filename>.

Options

R14   AutoCAD Release 14 Drawing (.DWG)

R13(LT95)   AutoCAD Release 13/LT 95 Drawing (.DWG)

R12(LT2)   AutoCAD Release 12/LT 2 Drawing (.DWG)

Template   Drawing Template File (.DWT)

> **NOTE** See **Save** for Options

See Also   Preferences, Qsave, Saveas; *System Variables:* Savefile, Savename, Savetime

Saveasr12

Saveasr12 allows you to save a current AutoCAD Release 13 drawing in Release 12 format.

To Save a Drawing in Release 12 Format

Command Line: **Saveasr12**

Save As Release 12 Drawing: Enter name of drawing.

> **NOTE**   Exporting a drawing to Release 12 format may lose some AutoCAD Release 14-specific information. AutoCAD creates a drawing log, displayed in the text window, which lists any information that is lost or changed.

See Also   Save, Saveas

Saveimg

Saveimg saves a rendered image to a .BMP, .TIFF or .TGA file format after rendering a model to a viewport.

To Save an Image

Command Line: **Saveimg**

Tools menu: Display Image ➤ Save

Provide information as needed in the Dialog Boxes

In Format section, click a radio button to save the image in .BMP, .TGA or .TIFF file format. Clicking the *Options...* button for .TGA or .TIFF displays a subdialog box for with compression options for None, .RLE or PACK. .RLE provides run-length-encoded image compression for .TGA and PACK uses Macintosh packbits, run-length-encoded image compression) for .TIFF files.

The Portion section includes an Active viewport image box. You can click two diagonal points to define the lower-left and upper-right coordinates for the image area or enter values in the *Offset* and *Size* edit boxes. Picking points away from the extreme lower left corner (0,0) or upper right (default XY) of image selection area sets the Image's Offset and Size. Click the *Reset* button to restore the default 1002x569 value.

Scale

Scale changes the size of objects in a drawing. You can also scale an object by reference.

To Resize Objects

Command Line: **Scale**

Menu: Modify ➤ Scale

Modify Toolbar: ⬚ Scale

1. **Select objects:** Pick the objects to be scaled.

2. **Base point:** Pick a point of reference for scaling.

3. **<Scale factor>/Reference:** Enter the scale factor, move the cursor to visually select new scale, or enter **R** to select the *Reference* option.

Options

Reference Allows you to scale the selected objects based on a reference length and a specified new length. When using the Reference option, at the "Reference length <1>:" prompt specify a distance, or scale factor. At the "Newlength:" prompt, specify a new distance, or scale factor. If the new length is longer than the reference length, the object(s) will be enlarged, and vice versa.

As with **Mirror** and **Stretch**, you can work with grips by selecting objects and selecting the **Scale** command. AutoCAD will display the object with grips and, after you issue the command, will show the following prompt:

SCALE

<Scale factor>/Base point/Copy/Undo/Reference/eXit:

Except for *Reference* (discussed above), the options here are similar to those available when working with the **Mirror** command. You can cycle through the options shown by pressing the spacebar.

See Also   Block, Change, Insert, Lengthen, Select

Script

Script "plays back" a set of AutoCAD commands and responses recorded in a script file. Script files, like DOS batch files, are lists of commands and responses entered exactly as you would enter them while in AutoCAD.

To Invoke a Script File

Command Line: **Script** (or **'Script** to use transparently)

Menu: Tools ➤ Run Script

If the *Filedia* system variable is set to 1, the Select Script File dialog list box opens. Enter a script file name in the File edit box.

If the *Filedia* system variable is set to 0, the following command-line prompt "Script file <current file name>:" appears:. Enter the script file name.

Options

Delay <milliseconds>   When included in a script file, makes AutoCAD pause for the number of milliseconds indicated.

Rscript   When included at the end of a script file, repeats the script continuously.

Resume   Restarts a script file that has been interrupted using the Backspace or Escape key.

Backspace   Interrupts the processing of a script file (you can also press Escape to do this).

SCRIPT

NOTE You can use Script files to set up frequently used macros to save lengthy keyboard entries or to automate a presentation. Another common use for scripts is to manage layering setups.

Section

See **Solid Modeling**

Select

Select provides a variety of options for selecting objects and returns you to the command prompt once you have made your selection. The objects selected become the most recent selection in AutoCAD's memory.

To Select Objects

Command Line: **Select**

Select objects: Choose an object selection method.

Options

Window/W   Selects objects completely enclosed by a rectangular window by prompting for *First corner:* and *Other corner:*. Enter **W** at the "Select objects:" prompt, or pick two points from left to right to automatically create a window selection set.

Crossing/C   Selects objects that cross through a rectangular window. Enter **C** at the "Select objects:" prompt, or pick two points from right to left and automatically create a crossing window selection set.

Group/G   Prompts to *Enter group name:*. Select all objects within a named group.

Previous/P   Selects last set of objects selected for editing. You can use *Previous* to pick the objects you have picked with Select when a later command prompts you to select objects. The *Previous* option is useful when you want several commands to process the same set of objects, as in a menu macro.

Last/L   Selects last object drawn or inserted.

All   Selects all objects on thawed layers.

Remove/R   Removes objects from the current selection of objects and displays the "Remove object:" prompt. Entering **A** returns to Add mode and restores the "Select object:" prompt. You can also hold down the Shift key and pick objects to remove them from a selection set.

Add/A   Adds objects to the current selection of objects. You will usually use this option after you have issued the **R** option. The Remove and Add modes will remain in effect only during the specific command's execution and can be interchanged as often as necessary.

Multiple/M   Allows you to pick several objects at one time before highlighting them and adding them to the current selection of objects.

Undo/U   Removes the most recently added object from the current selection of objects.

BOX   Allows you to use either a crossing or a standard window, depending on the orientation of your window pick points. If you pick points from right to left, you will get a crossing window. If you pick points from left to right, you will get a standard window.

Auto/AU   Allows you to select objects by picking them or by using a window, as you would with the *BOX* option. After you issue the *AUto* option, you can pick objects individually, as usual. If no object is picked, AutoCAD assumes you want to use the *BOX* option, and a window appears that allows you to use either a crossing or standard window to select objects.

Single/SI   Selects only the first picked object or the first group of windowed objects.

Wpolygon/WP   Selects objects that are contained within any shape you define. The shape assumes a closed polyline. There are certain restrictions. For example, you cannot include intersecting rubber-band lines, and you cannot place a vertex on an existing polygon segment.

Cpolygon/CP   Similar to *WPolygon*, except it selects objects that cross or enclose any shape you define. The shape assumes a closed polyline. There are certain restrictions. For example, you cannot include intersecting rubber-band lines, and you cannot place a vertex on an existing polygon segment.

Fence/F   Similar to *CPolygon*, except it selects intersecting or crossing objects with one or more rubber-band lines you define, including lines that intersect themselves.

> **NOTE** The **Select** command maintains a selection set only until
> you pick a different group of objects at another "Select object:"
> prompt. Entering the AutoLISP command **(setq set1 (ssget))** at
> the command prompt allows you to create a selection set that you
> can return to again and again during the course of the current edit-
> ing session. Whenever you want to select this group of objects
> again, enter **!set1** at the "Select objects:" prompt.

See Also Aperture, Ddselect; *System Variables:* Pickadd, Pickauto

Selecturl

Selecturl locates all objects that have URLs attached to them in a
drawing.

To Select a URL

Command Line: **Selecturl**

Internet Toolbar: Selecturl

> **TIP** Invoking **Selecturl** highlights all URL's in your current drawing.

Setvar

See System Variables

Shade

Shade produces a quick "Z buffer" shaded view of a 3D model by
removing hidden lines. This command should not be confused with
AutoShade, which is a separate program from AutoCAD.

To Shade a 3D Object

Command Line: **Shade**

Menu: View ➤ Shade, preset options

Render Toolbar: Shade

The *Shadedge* and *Shadedif* system variables give you some control over
the way a model is shaded.

TIP You can't directly plot images that were created using **Shade**. However, you can output a shaded image to a slide using the **Mslide** command. On systems that support fewer than 256 colors, **Shade** produces an image with hidden lines removed and 3dfaces in their original color. However, **Shade** can produce an image faster than the **Hide** command, and might be used where speed is a consideration. On systems with 256 colors or more, **Shade** produces a shaded image for which the light source and viewer location are the same.

See Also *System Variables:* Shadedge, Shadedif

Shape

Shape allows you to insert custom shapes, such as text font characters, into your drawing. Before you use **Shape**, you must load the file containing the shape(s). Use the **Load** command to load the Select Shape file dialog box, and select and load the desired file. Shapes act like blocks, but you can't explode them or attach attributes to them.

To Insert Custom Shapes

Command Line: **Shape**

1. **Shape name (or ?) <default>:** Enter the name of the shape or a question mark and the prompt "Shape(s) to list <*>:" appears to list available shapes.

2. **Start point:** Pick the insertion point.

3. **Height <1.0>:** Enter the height value or select a height using the cursor.

4. **Rotation angle <0.0>:** Enter or visually select the angle.

NOTE Because shapes take up less file space than blocks, you may want to use shapes in drawings that do not require the features offered by blocks.

See Also Compile, Load, Wildcards; *System Variables:* Shpname

Shell/Sh

Shell and **Sh** allow you to use any DOS command and run other programs with low memory requirements without exiting AutoCAD.

To Open a DOS Shell

Command Line: **Shell**

OS Command: Enter a standard DOS command or press ↵ to shell out to DOS.

> **NOTE** If you want to use external DOS commands or programs, you must, *before* starting AutoCAD, either specify or set a path to the drive and directory where the commands or programs are located. If you press ↵ at the "OS Command:" prompt, the DOS prompt appears and you can enter any number of external commands. Type **Exit** and press ↵ whenever you are ready to return to the AutoCAD command prompt.

Showmat

Showmat identifies an objects material type and attachment method.

To list an objects material type

Command Line: **Showmat**

Select object: Select the object, then depending on the method used to attach a material to an object, one of the following descriptions appear:

- Material <material name> is explicitly attached to the object.

- Material <material name> is attached by ACI to ACI <color number>.

- Material <material name> is attached by layer to layer <layer name>.

- Material *GLOBAL* is attached by default or by block.

See Also Render

Sketch

Sketch allows you to draw freehand. (It actually draws short line segments end-to-end to achieve this effect.) The lines Sketch draws are only temporary lines that show the path of the cursor. To save the line, you must use the *Record* and *eXit* options.

To Draw Freehand

Command Line: **Sketch**

1. **Record increment:** Enter a value representing the distance the cursor must travel before a line segment is generated along the sketch path.

2. **Pen eXit Quit Record Erase Connect:** Start your sketch line or enter an option.

Options

Pen   As an alternative to the pick button on your pointing device, you can press **P** from the keyboard to toggle between the pen-up and pen-down modes. With the pen down, the short temporary line segments are drawn as you move the cursor. With the pen up, no lines are drawn.

eXit   Saves any temporary sketch lines and then exits the **Sketch** command.

Quit   Exits the **Sketch** command without saving temporary lines.

Record   Saves temporary sketched lines during the time you are using the Sketch command.

Erase   Erases temporary sketched lines.

Connect   Allows you to continue from the end of a sketch line.

Period(.)   Allows you to draw a long line segment while using the **Sketch** command. With the pen up, place the cursor at the location of the long line segment, then type a period.

> **TIP**   To draw using polylines with Sketch instead of standard lines, use the **Setvar** command to set the *Skpoly* system variable to 1.

The easiest way to use **Sketch** is with a digitizer equipped with a stylus. You can trace over other drawings or photographs and refine them later. The stylus gives a natural feel to your tracing.

The "Record increment:" prompt allows you to set the distance the cursor travels before AutoCAD places a line. The Record increment value can greatly affect the size of your drawing. If this value is too high, the sketch line segments are too apparent and your sketched lines will appear "boxy." If the increment is set too low, your drawing file becomes quite large, and regeneration and redrawing times increase dramatically.

When AutoCAD runs out of RAM in which to store the lines being sketched, it must pause for a moment to set up a temporary file on your disk drive before it continues to store additional sketch lines in RAM.

Your computer will then beep and display the message "Please raise the pen." If this occurs, press **P** to raise the pen. (You may have to press **P** twice.) When you get the message "Thank you. Lower the pen and continue," press **P** again to proceed with your sketch. Setting Record increment to a low value increases your likelihood of running out of RAM.

Turn the **Snap** and **Ortho** modes off before starting a sketch. Otherwise, the sketch lines will be forced to the snap points, or drawn vertically or horizontally. The results of having the Ortho mode on may not be apparent until you zoom in on a sketch line. If you prefer, you can sketch an object and then use the **Pedit** command with the **Fit** option to smooth the sketch lines.

See Also   Pedit, Pline; *System Variables:* Sketchinc, Skpoly

Slice

See **Solid Modeling**

Slidelib.EXE

Slidelib.EXE is an external AutoCAD program that runs independently from AutoCAD. Use it to combine several slide files into a slide library file. You use slide libraries to create icon menus and to help organize slide files.

To Build a Slide Library

At the DOS prompt, enter the following:

Slidelib slide-library-name < ascii-list ↵

> **NOTE** Before you can create a slide library, you must create an ASCII file containing a list of slide-file names to include in the library. Do not include the .SLD extension in the list of names. You can give the list any name and extension. You can then issue the Slidelib program from the DOS prompt.

See Also   Delay, Mslide, Script, Vslide

Snap

Snap controls the settings for the Snap mode. The Snap mode allows you to accurately place the cursor by forcing it to move in specified increments.

To Set Snap Mode

Command Line: **Snap**

Snap spacing or ON/OFF/Aspect/Rotate/Style <default spacing>: Enter the desired snap spacing, or select an option.

Options

Snap spacing   Allows you to enter the desired snap spacing. The Snap mode is turned on and the new snap settings take effect.

ON   Turns on the Snap mode. Has the same effect as pressing the F9 key, Ctrl+B or double-clicking Snap on the status bar.

OFF   Turns off the Snap mode. Has the same effect as pressing F9, Ctrl+B or double-clicking Snap on the status bar.

Aspect   Enters a Y-axis snap spacing different from the X-axis snap spacing.

Rotate   Rotates the snap points and the AutoCAD cursor to an angle other than 0 and 90 degrees.

Style   Allows you to choose between the standard orthogonal snap style and an isometric snap style.

> **NOTE**   You can use the *Rotate* option to rotate the cursor; the Ortho mode will conform to the new cursor angle. This option also allows you to specify a snap origin, allowing you to accurately place hatch patterns. The *Snapang* system variable also lets you rotate the cursor.

> **NOTE**   If you use the **Isometric** *Style* option, you can use the **Isoplane** command to control the cursor orientation. Also, the **Ellipse** command allows you to draw isometric circles. You can set many of the settings available in the **Snap** command using the **Ddrmodes** dialog box.

See Also   Ddrmodes, Ellipse, Hatch, Isoplane; *System Variables:* Snapang, Snapbase, Snapisopair, Snapmode, Snapunit

Solid

Solid creates solid-filled polygons. You determine the area by picking points in a crosswise, or "bow tie" fashion. Solid is best suited to filling rectangular areas. Polylines are better for filling curved areas. Solids are filled only when the *Fillmode* system variable is set to On, and the view is set to Plan.

To Fill an Area

Command Line: **Solid**

Menu: Draw ➤ Surfaces ➤ 2D Solid.

Surfaces Toolbar: 2D Solid

1. **First point:** Pick one corner of the area to be filled.

2. **Second point:** Pick the next, adjacent corner of the area.

3. **Third point:** Pick the corner diagonal to the last point selected.

4. **Fourth point:** Pick the next, adjacent corner of the area or press ↵ to create a filled triangle.

NOTE AutoCAD repeats "Third point:" and "Fourth point:" prompts to create further connected triangles and four-sided polygons as a single solid object. Continue to pick points until you have defined the area to be filled.

TIP In large drawings that contain many solids, you can reduce regeneration and redrawing times by setting the **Fill** command to *Off* until you are ready to plot the final drawing.

See Also   Fill, Pline, 3dface, Trace

Solid Modeling

A full range of solid modeling commands provide an easy method to building 3D models. As well as creating basic solids (solid primitives), you can additionally create solids from 2D objects by extruding and revolving them (swept solids), and create more complex solids out of either of these by adding and subtracting volumes and calculating interferences. Solids are native AutoCAD objects, which means that they compute faster than AME objects and generally respond to standard AutoCAD commands—for example, **Chamfer**, **Fillet**, and **Scale**.

Solid objects resemble surface objects and are created in approximately the same way. The critical difference is that the solid objects have mass, which allows measurement based upon volume. It also allows edits that change the mass by addition, subtraction, and by combination with other solid objects.

> **TIP** The Solids commands that create composite objects (**Union**, **Subtract**, **Intersect**) can also be used to manipulate 2D regions.

Solid Primitives

The six solid primitives—box, cone, cylinder, sphere, torus, and wedge—are basic 3D objects, which can be used to build more complex solids.

To Draw a Box

The **Box** command creates a 3D solid box. The command line is **Box.**

Command Line: **Box**

Menu: Draw ➤ Solids ➤ Box ➤

Solids Toolbar: Box

1. **Center/<Corner of box><0,0,0,>:** Pick the first corner point (or Enter **C** for the center point) for your box, or enter a value.

2. **Cube/Length/<other corner>:** Pick a second corner point, or enter a value or enter **C** or **L**. See Options below.

3. **<Height>:** Provide the box height by dynamically picking two points or entering a value.

Options

Center Allows you to create a 3D box using a specified center point.

Cube Allows you to create a 3D box with all sides equal.

Length Allows you to enter values for *Length, Width,* and *Height.*

To Draw a Cone

Cone offers several methods for drawing a 3D solid cone. The default is to choose a center point, then pick or enter the diameter/radius and apex.

Command Line: **Cone**

Menu: Draw ➤ Solids ➤ Cone

Solids Toolbar: Cone

1. **Elliptical/<center point> <0,0,0>:** Pick a center point, or enter **E**.

2. **Diameter/<Radius>:** Provide a Diameter or Radius (or Axis end-point for an elliptical cone by dynamically picking or entering a value).

3. **Apex/<Height>:** Provide an apex or height by dynamically picking the point(s) or entering a value.

Options

Center   Allows you to create a cone with a circular base.

Elliptical   Allows you to create a cone with an elliptical base.

Apex   Allows you to specify the apex of the cone solid.

Height   Allows you to specify the height of the cone solid.

To Draw a Cylinder

Cylinder offers several methods for drawing a 3D solid cylinder. The default is to choose a center point, then pick or enter the diameter/radius and apex.

Command Line: **Cylinder**

Draw ➤ Solids ➤ Cylinder

Solids Toolbar: [icon] Cylinder

1. **Elliptical/<center point> <0,0,0>:** Pick a center point, or enter **E**.

2. **Diameter/<Radius>:** Provide a Diameter or <Radius> (or an Axis endpoint for an elliptical cylinder) by dynamically picking or entering a value.

3. **Center of other end/<Height>:** Provide a cylinder top or height by dynamically picking the point(s) or entering a value, or enter **C**.

Options

Center   Allows you to create a cylinder with a circular base.

Elliptical   Allows you to create a cylinder with an elliptical base.

Center of other end   Allows you to specify the top end of the cylinder.

Height   Allows you to specify the height of the cylinder.

To Draw a Sphere

Sphere creates a 3D solid sphere with its central axis parallel to the Z axis of the current UCS. The overall dimensions of the sphere can be specified using either the radius or the diameter.

Command Line: **Sphere**

Menu: Solids ➤ Sphere

Solids Toolbar: [icon] Sphere

1. **Center of sphere <0,0,0>:** Pick a center point.

2. **Diameter/<Radius> of sphere:** Provide a diameter or radius by dynamically picking or entering a value.

Options

Radius   Allows you to specify the overall dimension of the sphere using its radius.

Diameter   Allows you to specify the overall dimension of the sphere using its diameter. Type **D** at step 2 to use this option.

To Draw a Torus

Torus creates a 3D donut-shaped solid. The torus is defined by specifying two radius (or diameter) values, one from the center of the torus to the center of the tube, and one for the actual tube. You can create a torus with no center hole (a self-intersecting torus) by specifying the radius of the tube greater than the radius of the torus.

Command Line: **Torus**

Menu: Draw ➣ Solids ➣ Torus

Solids Toolbar: [icon] Torus

1. **Center of torus <0,0,0>:** Pick a center point

2. **Diameter/<Radius> of torus:** Provide a diameter or radius for the torus by dynamically picking or entering a value.

3. **Diameter/<Radius> of tube:** Provide a diameter or radius for the tube by dynamically picking or entering a value.

Options

Radius   Allows you to specify the overall dimension of the torus or the tube using its radius.

Diameter   Allows you to specify the overall dimension of the torus or the tube using its diameter. Type **D** at step 2 or step 3 to use this option.

To Draw a Wedge

Wedge creates a 3D wedge-shaped solid. The base is parallel to the Z axis and the sloped face is tapered along the X axis. You may create a wedge based on the first corner point, or on a specified center point.

Command Line: **Wedge**

Menu: Draw ➣ Solids ➣ Wedge

SOLID MODELING

Solids Toolbar: Wedge

1. **Center/ <corner of wedge> point> <0,0,0>:** Specify a corner point, or type **C** and pick a center point.

2. **Cube/ Length <other corner>:** Pick a point for the other corner.

3. **Height:** Provide height by dynamically picking the point(s) or entering a value.

Options

First Corner   Allows you to create a cylinder starting from the first corner point.

Center   Allows you to create a wedge centered on a specified point.

Cube   Allows you to create a cubic (equal-sided) wedge. Only one length value is required to create this type of wedge.

Length   Allows you to create a wedge by specifying separately the length, width, and height.

To Create Swept Solids

Solid objects can also be created from 2D objects. You can draw new solids by extruding (adding height) to a 2D object along a specified path or by revolving a 2D object about an axis. For example, extruding a circle produces a cylinder, and revolving a circle about an axis produces a torus. These commands create a solid object from a common profile and are particularly useful for profiling objects that have fillets or chamfers which would otherwise be very difficult to profile.

To Create a Solid by Extruding a 2D Object

You can extrude closed objects such as circles, ellipses, closed splines and polylines, polygons, rectangles, donuts, and regions, but not 3D objects, objects wit1hin a block, and polylines that self-cross or intersect or are not closed.

Command Line: **Extrude**

Menu: Draw ➤ Solids ➤ Extrude

Solids Toolbar: Extrude

1. **Select Objects:** Select the object(s) to extrude.

2. **Path <Height of Extrusion:>** Specify the height or enter **P** and pick an object that describes the path.

3. **Extrusion taper angle <0>:** Enter a value for tapering the extruded object, if required, or press ↵.

NOTE If you wish to extrude an object that contains lines or arcs, you should first join them using the **Pedit** command to form a single polyline object, or make them into a region before you extrude them. If you are extruding a polyline, it must contain at least 3 but not more than 500 vertices. If an object you have selected to extrude has width or thickness (in the case of a polyline), AutoCAD will ignore it. A thick polyline is extruded from the center of its path.

To Create a Solid by Revolving a 2D Object

Revolve works with the same kinds of objects as **Extrude**. You can revolve closed objects such as circles, ellipses, splines and polylines, polygons, rectangles, donuts, and regions, but not 3D objects, objects within a block, and polylines that self-cross or intersect or are not closed.

Command Line: **Revolve**

Menu: Draw ➤ Solids ➤ Revolve

Solids Toolbar: Revolve

1. **Select Objects:** Select the object(s) to revolve.

2. **Axis of revolution-Object/X/Y/<Start point of axis>:** Specify the start point and endpoint of the axis; type **X** or **Y** to specify the X axis or Y axis; or type **O** and select an object as the axis of revolution

3. **Angle of revolution <full circle>:** Specify the required angle of revolution, or press ↵ to accept the default (360 degrees).

To Create Composite Solids

Complex solids can be created from both Solid Primitives and Swept solids. Boolean operations can be used to create composite solids from two or more solids.

Options

Union   Allows you to combine the volume of two or more solids (or regions) into one. Select the objects to join, and AutoCAD creates a single composite object. (See **Union**)

Subtract   Allows you to remove the common area shared by two sets of solids (or regions). You must first select the solid(s) from which to subtract and then the solid(s) which are to be subtracted. (See **Subtract**)

Intersect Allows you to create a composite solid that contains only the common volume of two or more overlapping solids (or regions). It effectively joins the solids, leaving only the area where the solids intersect. (See **Intersect**)

Interference Performs essentially the same operation as the **Intersect** command. Interfere, however, allows you to keep the original objects after it has created a further object based on their overlapping volumes. The original objects are kept, minus the overlapping areas. (See **Interference**)

To Slice a Solid

Slice allows you to create a new solid or set of solids by slicing an existing solid with a plane and removing a selected side. You may choose to keep only one or both sides of the solids.

Command: **Slice**

Menu: Draw ➤ Solids ➤ Slice

Solids Toobar: Slice

1. **Select objects:** Pick the required objects.

2. **Slicing plane by Object/Zaxis/View/XY/YZ/ZX/<3points>:** Specify a point or enter an option.

3. Specify additional points at the **2nd point on plane:** and **3rd point on plane: promts**.

4. **Both sides/<Point on desired side of the plane>:** Press ⏎ to select side to keep, or enter **B** to retain both.

> **NOTE** By default, you specify 3 points to define the cutting plane: the first point defines the origin of the slicing plane; the second point defines the X axis; and the third point defines the Y axis. You may also define the cutting plane using another Object, or by the current View, the Z axis, or the XY, YZ, or ZX plane.

To Create a Cross-Section of a Solid

Section allows you to create a cross-section through any solid.

Command Line: **Section**

Menu: Draw ➤ Solids ➤ Section

Solids Toobar: Section

1. **Select objects:** Pick the required objects.

2. **Section plane by Object/Zaxis/View/XY/YZ/ZX/<3points>:**
Specify a point or enter an option.

3. Specify additional points at the **2nd point on plane:** and **3rd point on plane:** prompts.

To Convert an AME Solid Model

Ameconvert allows you to convert solid models created using the AutoDESK Advanced Modeling Extension into AutoCAD solid objects.

Command Line: **Ameconvert**

Select objects: Pick the solid models you wish to convert.

NOTE If the objects are not regions or solids created using AME Release 2 or 2.1, AutoCAD ignores them. Improved accuracy in the solid modeler may cause AME models to display differently, particularly filleted and chamfered objects.

To Calculate a Solid's Mass Properties

Massprop calculates and displays the mass properties of 2D and 3D objects. For Solids, it provides volumetric information such as center of gravity principal axes and moments of inertia.

Command Line: **Massprop**

Menu: Tools ➤ Inquiry ➤ Mass Properties

Inquiry Toolbar: ▨ Mass Properties

1. **Select objects:** Pick the solid model(s) you wish to analyze. Massprop will display all of the properties of the object(s) on the text screen.

2. **Write to a file <N>:** If you want the information written to a file, type **Y** and provide a file name, or press ↵ to return to the command prompt.

NOTE The **Massprop** command can be used to list the properties of 2D regions as well as solid objects.

See Also Import/Export, Stlout, Pedit, Pline, Solid; *System Variables:* Isolines

Soldraw

Soldraw creates profiles and sections in viewports constructed exclusively from Solview.

To Create Profiles and Sections

Command Line: **Soldraw**

Menu: Draw ➤ Solids ➤ Setup ➤ Drawing

Solids Toobar: ![Setup Drawing icon] Setup Drawing

Select viewports to draw:

Select objects: Pick one or more viewports to draw or redraw profiles and sections.

NOTE AutoCAD uses visible and hidden lines that represent the silhouette and edges of solids in the viewport to create a plane perpendicular to the viewing direction. For crosshatching in sectional views, current values of the *Hpname*, *Hpscale*, and *Hpang* system variables are used.

Solview

Solview uses orthographic projection with floating paperspace viewports to lay out multi- and sectional-view drawings of 3D solid and body objects, saving view-specific information during creation. The data collected is then used by **Soldraw** for final generation of the drawing view

To Set up Multi- and Sectional-Views

Command: **Solview**

Menu: Draw ➤ Solids ➤ Setup ➤ View

Solids Toobar: ![Setup View icon] Setup View

   Ucs/Ortho/Auxiliary/Section/<eXit>: Press ↵ or enter an option.

Option

UCS   Press ↵ or enter a suboption at the "Named/World/?/<Current>:" prompt.

   Name   Enter the "Name of UCS to restore:", then "Enter view scale <1.0>:" to emulate paper space scaled viewports. Prompts then appear to specify a point for the "View center:", to "Clip first corner:" and "Clip other corner:", then provide a "View name:".

   World   Prompts are similar to *Name*; the profile view created uses the XY plane of the WCS.

   ?   Press ↵ or use wild-card combinations at the "UCS names to list <*>:" prompt for names of existing user coordinate systems.

Current   Prompts are similar to *Name*; the profile view created uses the XY plane of the current UCS.

Ortho   Select a viewport edge at the "Pick side of viewport to project:" prompt, then specify information as described for *Name* above to generate a folded orthographic view from an existing view.

Auxiliary   Specify points in the same viewport to obtain the auxiliary view's Inclined plane's 1st point and Inclined plane's 2nd point:. Then select a point for the Side to view from and a rubber-band line perpendicular to the inclined plane appears to pick a View center. The next prompt sequences are the same as *Name* above.

Section   Use the original viewport and specify two points at the "Cutting plane 1st point:" and "Cutting plane 2nd point:" prompts to define the sectioning plane. Then Define the viewing side by specifying a point on one side of the cutting plane by picking a point at the "Side of cutting plane to view from:" prompt. The remaining prompt sequences are the same as *Name* above.

NOTE AutoCAD appends layer names Vis, Hid and Hat to your defined view names as shown in table 9.

TABLE 9:   Layer and Object name conventions

Layer Name	Object Type
View name-Vis	Visible lines
View name-Hid	Hidden lines
View name-Dim	Dimensions
View name-Hat	Hatch patterns (for sections)

WARNING These layer names are reserved for **Soldview**; AutoCAD automatically purges the information stored on these layers when you use **Soldraw**.

Solprof

Solprof generates profile images of 3D solids in floating viewports and shows the edges and silhouettes of curved surfaces of a solid for the current view.

To Create 3DProfiles

Command Line: **Solprof**

Menu: Draw ➤ Solids ➤ Setup ➤ Profile

Solids Toobar: Setup Profile

1. **Select objects:** Select object(s) in active modelspace viewport.

2. **Display hidden profile lines on separate layer? <Y>:**
   Pressing ↵ instructs AutoCAD to create two separate unnamed profile blocks, one for visible lines and another for invisible lines. If the
   Hidden linetype is loaded, the visible profile block is created using
   the Bylayer linetype and the hidden block uses the Hidden linetype;
   otherwise, linetypes are all continuous. If you entered **N**, all profile
   lines are stored in a block for each solid and created as visible lines.
   Visible profile blocks assume the same linetype as the original solid.

3. **Project profile lines onto a plane? <Y>:** Press ↵ to generate
   the profile lines with 2D objects. The 3D profile is projected onto a
   plane normal to the viewing direction, passing through the origin
   of the UCS. AutoCAD evaluates the 2D profile, removes lines parallel to the viewing direction then changes arcs and circles viewed on
   edge to lines. Entering **N** creates the profile lines with 3D objects.

4. **Delete tangential edges? <Y>:** Press ↵ to retain tangential edges
   or enter N to have them removed.

TABLE 10:   Layer names and object types

Layer Name	Object type
Pv-viewport handle	Visible profile layer
Ph-viewport handle	Hidden profile layer

Spell

Spell checks the spelling of text in your drawing, including dimension
text. You may select between several different dictionaries, which are
available in different languages. You can customize any of the main dictionaries to include words that you commonly use.

To Check Spelling

Command Line: **Spell**

Menu: Tools ➤ Spelling

Standard Toolbar: Spelling

1. Select the objects you want to check or type **all** to select all text objects.

2. If a misspelled word is found, the Check Spelling dialog box identifies the misspelled word.

3. Choose one of the options offered.

Options

Current dictionary   Identifies name of current dictionary.

Current word   Displays misspelled word being checked.

Suggestions   List box shows replacement word.

Ignore   Leaves a flagged word unchanged.

Ignore All   Does not flag further instances of the word.

Change   Allows you to select a word from the Suggestions list box or type in the correct spelling.

Change All   Changes all instances of the flagged word without further prompting.

Add   Leaves the flagged word unchanged and adds it to a custom dictionary. This button is not selectable if you are using a standard dictionary.

Lookup   Checks the spelling of a word in the Suggestions list box.

Change Dictionaries   Opens the Change Dictionaries subdialog box and allows you to change dictionaries during a spell check. Click the *Main dictionary* drop down box for alternates. Enter a drive, directory and dictionary name in an edit box, or use the *Browse...* button to replace the current custom dictionary. Use the *Add* or *Delete* buttons to append or remove custom dictionary words to the dictionary.

Context   Displays selected sentence or phrase of word being checked.

Cancel   Allows you to exit the Check Spelling dialog box.

TIP   To create a new dictionary, select the Change Dictionaries button and enter the new dictionary name, using .CUS as a file extension.

See Also   *System Variables:* Dctcust, Dctmain

SPLINE

Spline

Spline fits a smooth curve to a set of points within a defined tolerance. The particular kind of spline created by AutoCAD is a NURBS (nonuniform rational B-spline) curve. Splines can be used to produce irregularly shaped curves for mapping.

To Draw a Spline

Command Line: **Spline**

Menu: Draw ➤ Spline

Draw Toolbar: Spline

1. **Object/<Enter first point>:** Specify a point.

2. Continue to enter points until you have defined the spline curve. After the second point, you will be prompted: **Close/Fit Tolerance/<Enter point>:**. Enter **C** to close the spline; **F** to change the tolerance, or continue to enter points.

3. When you have added all of the required spline segments, press ↵.

4. **Enter start tangent:** If desired, specify the tangency of the spline or press ↵.

5. **Enter end tangent:** Pick a point or press ↵ to terminate the spline.

Options

Object   This option allows you to convert 2D or 3D spline-fit polylines to corresponding splines. In step 2 above, type **O**, then select the polyline objects you wish to convert. If the *Delobj* system variable is set to zero, the original polylines will be deleted.

Close   Closes the spline curve so that the last point coincides with the first point and is tangent to the joint.

Fit Tolerance   Allows you to change the tolerance for fitting the spline curve. Tolerance defines how closely the spline fits the set of points you specify. A lower tolerance produces a closer fit to the specified points. When you adjust the tolerance, the current spline curve is redrawn so that it still fits the specified points, but is adjusted per the new tolerance.

Tangent   Allows you to redefine the spline start- and endpoint tangents. You may do this dynamically by picking a point, or enter **Tan** or **Perp**. Using these object snaps, you may make the spline tangent or perpendicular to existing objects. The spline is redrawn through the defined points.

> **NOTE** Once you have created a spline object, you can manipulate it easily using **Grips**. The spline retains the smoothness of the curves no matter where you position the grips.

See Also Grips, Polyline, Splinedit; *System Variables:* Delobj

Splinedit

Splinedit allows you to edit spline objects. You can add or delete fit points and control points, remove fit points or control vertices, open or close a spline, change the fit tolerance, and edit the start and end fit point tangents.

To Edit a Spline

Command Line: **Splinedit**

Menu: Modify ➤ Object➤ Spline

Modify II Toolbar: Edit Spline

1. **Select Spline:** Select a spline. Grips appear on the control points and also on fit data points, if they have not been purged.

2. **Fit Data/Close/Move Vertex/Refine/rEverse/Undo/eXit<X>:** Enter an option, then press ↵.

Options

Fit Data Displays prompt "Add/Close/Delete/Move/Purge/Tangents/ toLerance/eXit <X>:" to edit the spline fit data. Fit data includes all fit points' fit tolerance, and all tangents associated with the spline. If a spline has no fit data, the fit Data option does not appear in the prompt. Type **F** to edit fit data. To add a fit point, type **A** at the next prompt, then select an existing fit point (grip). The grips for this point and the next point are highlighted with a rubber-banding line. Enter a new point. AutoCAD interpolates the new point between the two highlighted points and refits the spline curve. To delete a fit point, type **D**, then select the point(s) you wish to delete. The spline is redrawn to fit the remaining fit points. To move fit points to a new position, type **M**, to display the "Next/Previous/Select Point/eXit/<Enter new location> <N>:" prompt then type **N** (Next) or **P** (Previous) to move sequentially along the fit points until you reach the desired point, or type **S** (Select Point) and pick a specific point; pick a new point or enter a coordinate to relocate the fit point. To Purge the fit data from the drawing, type **P**.

SPLINEDIT

To change the start or end tangent of the spline, type **T**, and then specify a new point or type **S** to accept the System Defaults. Type **X** to return to the main prompt.

Close   Closes an open spline and creates a smooth curve through the start/endpoint. Type **C** and select the spline to close it. A spline may have the same start- and endpoint and still be an open spline. It will, however, lack the smoothness (tangent continuity) of a closed spline.

Open   Opens a closed spline.

Move Vertex   Moves the control points on the spline. When you select this option, the start point of the spline is highlighted. Type **N** (Next) or **P** (Previous) to move sequentially along the control vertices until you reach the desired point, or type **S** (Select Point) and pick a specific vertex. Pick a new point or enter a coordinate to relocate the control point. Type **X** to return to the main prompt.

Refine   Allows you to increase the accuracy of a spline's definition. You may increase the number of points on a given portion or across the whole spline, or manipulate the distance between the spline and the control points. The *Add control point* option allows you to increase the number of control points by picking them directly. The *Elevate Order* option allows you to increase the number of control points on the spline by a specified order of magnitude (up to 26). The *Weight* option allows you to assign a greater "weight" to any selected control point. Selecting a point will pull the spline more to that point.

Reverse   Reverses the direction of the spline.

Undo   Cancels the last edit performed using **Splinedit**.

Exit   Exits the current Splinedit mode.

> **NOTE**   A spline can lose its fit data, if it is purged or refined. It may also lose its fit data if you fit the spline to a tolerance and then move its control vertices, or open or close the spline.

See Also   Pedit, Pline, Spline

Status

Status displays the current settings of a drawing, including the drawing limits and the status of all drawing modes. It also displays the current memory usage.

STATUS

To Display Current Drawing Settings

Command Line: **Status**

Menu: Tools ➤ Inquiry ➤ Status

Returns the following information:

- Model or Paper space limits
- Model or Paper space uses
- Display shows
- Insertion base is
- Snap resolution is
- Grid spacing is
- Current space
- Current layer
- Current color
- Current linetype
- Current elevation
- Thickness
- Fill, Grid, Ortho, Qtext, Snap, Tablet
- Object Snap modes
- Free dwg disk space
- Free physical memory
- Free swap file space

> **NOTE** AutoCAD uses many defaults and modes. They are all displayed using the **Status** command. All measurements are shown in the standard units specified for the drawing.

> **NOTE** Modelspace limits and Modelspace uses change to Paper-space limits and Paperspace uses when you are in the Paperspace mode.

See Also Layers, Settings, Time

StIout

See Import/Export

Stretch

Stretch moves vertices of objects while maintaining the continuity of connected lines.

To Stretch an Object

Command Line: **Stretch**

Menu: Modify ➤ Stretch

Modify Toolbar: Stretch

1. **Select objects to stretch by crossing window or -polygon:**

    *   Enter **W** (Window) to select objects that lie entirely within a specified window. This option will move the entire object.

    *   Enter **C** (Crossing window) to select objects that lie wholly or partially within a specified window.

    *   Enter **CP** (Crossing polygon) to select only objects that lie wholly or partly with a user-specified polygon.

2. **Select objects:** Enter **R** to remove objects from the set of selected objects or press ↵ to confirm your selection.

3. **Base point:** Pick the base reference point for the stretch.

4. **New point:** Pick the second point in relation to the base point, indicating the distance and direction you wish to move.

    You cannot stretch blocks or text. If the insertion point of a block or text is included in a crossing window, the entire block will be moved.

See Also   Copy, Move

-Style

-Style allows you to create a text style by specifying the AutoCAD font on which it is based, its height, its width factor, and the obliquing angle. You can change a font to be backwards, upside down, or vertical. You can also use Style to modify an existing text style.

To Create a Text Style

Command Line: **-Style**

1. **Text style name (or ?) <current style>:** Enter a style name or a question mark to display a list of styles that have been defined in the drawing. Wildcards are accepted.

2. **Font file <default font file>:** Enter a font file name, select one from the Select Font File dialog box, or press ↵ to accept the default.

3. **Height <default height>:** Enter the desired height or press ↵ to accept the default.

4. **Width factor <default width factor>:** Enter the desired width factor or press ↵.

5. **Obliquing angle <default angle>:** Enter the desired width obliquing angle or press ↵.

6. **Backwards? <N>:** Enter **Y** if you want the text to read backward, or press ↵ to accept N, the default.

7. **Upside-down? <N>:** Enter **Y** if you want the text to read upside-down or press ↵ to accept N, the default.

8. **Vertical? <N>:** Enter **Y** if you want the text to read vertically, or press ↵ to accept N, the default.

Options

Text style name   Allows you to enter either a new name to define a new style or the name of an existing style to redefine the style.

Font file   Allows you to choose from several fonts. In Windows you can select from a set of predefined fonts by picking Find File from the Select Font File dialog box to open Browse/Search dialog boxes.

Height   Allows you to determine a fixed height for the style being defined. A value of 0 allows you to determine text height as it is entered.

Width factor   Allows you to make the style appear expanded or compressed.

Obliquing angle   Allows you to "italicize" the style.

Backwards   Allows you to make the style appear backwards.

Upside down   Allows you to make the style appear upside-down.

Vertical   Allows you to make the style appear vertical.

-STYLE

NOTE If you modify a style's font, text previously entered in that style is updated to reflect the modification. If any other style option is modified, previously entered text is not affected. Once you use the **Style** command, the style created or modified becomes the new current style.

NOTE A 0 value at the "Height:" prompt causes AutoCAD to prompt you for a text height whenever you use this style with the **Dtext** or **Text** commands. At the "Width factor:" prompt, a value of 1 generates normal text. A greater value expands the style; a smaller value compresses it. At the "Obliquing angle:" prompt, a value of 0 generates normal text. A greater value slants the style to the right, creating italics. A negative value slants the style to the left.

See Also   Change, Ddedit, Ddstyle, Dtext, Qtext, Text, Wildcards

Subtract

Subtract allows you to remove the common area shared by two sets of solids (or regions) and create a new composite region or solid. You must first select the object(s) from which to subtract and then the object(s) that are to be subtracted.

To Subtract Solids or Regions

Command Line: **Subtract**

Menu: Modify ➤ Boolean➤ Subtract

Modify II Toobar: Subtract

1. **Select solids and regions to subtract from:** Click on the overlapping solid(s) or region(s) that will form the basis of the new object.

2. **Select solids and regions to subtract:** Click on the objects you wish to subtract.

   AutoCAD removes all of the objects selected in step 2 above.

NOTE Subtract can be used only for regions or solids. In steps 1 and 2 above, you may select both regions and solids at the same time, and you may select objects from any number of planes. AutoCAD will group the selection set into subsets by region/solid and by plane before subtracting the common areas and creating the new object.

See Also Intersect, Union

System Variables/Setvar

The system variables control AutoCAD's many settings. Many of the settings controlled by the system variables can be adjusted by the user. At the command prompt, type the name of the system variable you wish to manipulate.

To Adjust System Variables

Command Line: **Setvar** (or **'Setvar** to use transparently)

Menu: Tools ➤ Inquiry ➤ Set Variables

You may use the **Setvar** command to list and/or set system variables:

Variable name or ?: Enter the desired system variable name, a question mark for a list of variables or the appropriate integer value or decimal value. (Values are usually numeric, but in some cases you may also use Off and On in place of 0 and 1 values.)

Options

Table 11 lists all of the system variables. They fall into two categories: adjustable variables and read-only variables. Read-only system variables such as *DWGNAME* cannot be directly modified by the user, but are modified by AutoCAD program. Each adjustable variable has a specific set of values. The meaning of that value depends on the nature of the variable.

TABLE 11: System Variables

Variable	Description
Acadmaxobjmem	Controls the object pager. See **Maxobjmem**.
Acadprefix	Read-only. Displays the name(s) of the directory path or paths saved in the DOS environment variable *Acad*, using the DOS command **SET**.
Acadver	Read-only. Displays the AutoCAD version number.
Acisoutver	Controls the ACIS version of **SAT** files created using the ACISOUT command. Only supports a value of 16 for ACIS version 1.6.
Aflags	Controls the attribute mode settings: 0 = no mode, 1 = invisible, 2 = constant, 4 = verify, 8 = preset. For more than one setting, use the sum of the desired settings. See **Attdef**.

TABLE 11: System Variables (continued)

Variable	Description
Angbase	Controls the direction of the 0 angle. Can also be set with the **Units** command.
Angdir	Controls the positive direction of angles: 0 = counter-clockwise, 1 = clockwise. Can also be set with the **Units** command.
Apbox	Controls the AutoSnap aperture box: 0 = not displayed, 1 = displayed, default = 1.
Aperture	Controls the Osnap cursor target height in pixels. Can also be set with the **Aperture** command.
Area	Read-only. Displays the last area computed. See **Area, List** commands.
Attdia	Controls the attribute dialog box for the **Insert** command: 0 = no dialog box, 1 = dialog box.
Attmode	Controls the attribute display mode: 0 = off, 1 = normal, 2 = on. Can also be set with the **Attdisp** command.
Attreq	Controls the prompt for attributes. 0 = no prompt or dialog box for attributes. Attributes use default values. 1 = normal prompt or dialog box upon attribute insertion. Can also be set with the **Units** command.
Auditctl	Controls the creation of Audit log (.ADT) files. 0 = create, 1 = do not create. See **Audit**.
Autosnap	Controls the display of the AutoSnap marker and SnapTip and turns the AutoSnap magnet on or off: 0 = Turns off the marker, SnapTip, and magnet; 1 = Turns on the marker; 2 = Turns on the SnapTip; 4 = Turns on the magnet ; Bit values are additive:, default = 7.
Aunits	Controls angular units: 0 = decimal degrees, 1 = degrees- minutes-seconds, 2 = grads, 3 = radians, 4 = surveyors' units.
Auprec	Controls the precision of angular units determined by decimal place. Can also be set with the **Units** command.
Backz	Displays the distance from the Dview target to the back clipping plane. See **Dview**.
Blipmode	Controls the appearance of blips: 0 = off, 1 = on. See **Blipmode**.

TABLE 11: System Variables (continued)

Variable	Description
Cdate	Read-only. Displays calendar date/time read from DOS. See **Time**.
Cecolor	Displays/sets current object color. See **Color**.
Celtscale	Displays/sets current global line type scale for objects. See **Linetype, Ltscale**.
Celtype	Displays/sets current object line type. See **Linetype**.
Chamfera	Displays/sets first chamfer distance. See **Chamfer**.
Chamferb	Displays/sets second chamfer distance. See **Chamfer**.
Chamferc	Displays/sets thirdchamfer distance. See **Chamfer**.
Chamferd	Displays/sets fourth chamfer distance. See **Chamfer**.
Chammode	Chamfer method. 0 = two distances, 1 = one distance plus angle. See **Chamfer**.
Circlerad	Sets a default value for circle radius. Enter 0 for no default.
Clayer	Displays/sets current layer. See **Layer** and **Ddlmodes**.
Cmdactive	Read-only. Shows status of commands, scripts, and dialog boxes: 1 = ordinary command is active, 2 = ordinary and transparent commands are active, 4 = script is active, 8 = dialog box is active. If more than one setting is active, the variable shows the active sum.
Cmddia	Controls dialog box for **Plot** command: 1 = use dialog box, 0 = use command-line prompts.
Cmdecho	Used with AutoLISP to control what is displayed on the prompt line. 0 = not echoed to screen, 1 = echoed. See the AutoLISP manual for details.
Cmdnames	Displays in English current active command name, including transparent command.
Cmljust	Multiline object justification. 0 = Top, 1 = Middle, 2 = Bottom.
Cmlscale	Scales the width of a multiline object. 0 = single line. < 0 reverses line sequence.
Cmlstyle	Displays/sets the multiline object style name.

TABLE 11: System Variables (continued)

Variable	Description
Coords	Controls coordinate readout: 0 = coordinates are displayed only when points are picked. 1 = absolute coordinates are dynamically displayed as cursor moves. 2 = distance and angle are displayed during commands that accept relative distance input. Also controlled by the F6 function key.
Cvport	Shows/sets ID number for current viewport
Date	Read-only. Displays Julian date/time. See **Time**.
Dbmod	Read-only. Identifies drawing database modification status: 0 = drawing database not modified, 1 = entity database modified, 2 = symbol table modified, 4 = database variable modified, 8 = window modified, 16 = view modified.
Dctcust	Display/sets custom spelling dictionary (.DCT).
Dctmain	Display/set main spelling dictionary (.DCT).
Delobj	Controls retention of polyline when coverting splinefit polylines to the new spline objects. 0 = delete, 1 = retain.
Diastat	Read-only. Dialog box exit method: 0 = via Cancel, 1 = via OK.
Dispilh	Controls display of silhouette curves in 3D objects. 0 = on, 1 = off.
Distance	Read-only. Displays last distance read using **Dist.** See **Dist**.
Donutid	Sets inside diameter default value for **Donut** command.
Donutod	Sets outside diameter default value for **Donut** command.
Dragmode	Controls dragging: 0 = no dragging, 1 = on if requested, 2 = automatic drag. See **Dragmode**.
Dragp1	Controls regen-drag input sampling rate.
Dragp2	Controls fast-drag input sampling rate. Higher values force the display of more of the dragged image during cursor movement, and lower values display less.
Dwgcodepage	Current drawing code page.
Dwgname	Read-only. Displays drawing name. See **Status**.

TABLE 11: System Variables (continued)

Variable	Description
Dwgprefix	Read-only. Displays drive and directory prefix or path for the current drawing file.
Dwgtitled	Read-only. Drawing name status: 0 = drawing is unnamed, 1 = drawing is named.
Edgemode	Controls definition of boundary edge for **Trim** and **Extend**. 0 = as selected, 1 = extend selected edge to apparent intersection.
Elevation	Controls current three-dimensional elevation. See **Elev**.
Errno	Displays/sets code for errors from AutoLISP and ADS applications.
Expert	Controls prompts, depending on level of user's expertise. 0 issues normal prompts. 1 = suppresses the About to Regen: and Really want to turn the current layer off? prompts and the Verify Regenauto OFF setting. 2 = suppresses previous prompts plus Block already defined...Redefine it? and A drawing with this name already exists. 3 = suppresses previous prompts plus line type warnings. 4 = suppresses previous prompts plus **UCS** and **Vports** *Save* warnings. 5 = suppresses previous prompts plus DIM Save and DIM Override warnings.
Explmode	Controls exploding of non-uniformly scaled blocks. 0 = explode, 1 = do not explode
Extmax	Read-only. Displays upper-right corner coordinate of drawing extent.
Extmin	Read-only. Displays lower-left corner coordinate of drawing extent.
Facetres	Control resolution of 3D objects. Values are 0.01 to 10.0.
Filedia	Controls use of dialog boxes. 0 = off unless requested by ~ (tilde), 1 = on.
Fillmode	Controls fill status: 0 = off, 1 = on. See **Fill**.
Filletrad	Stores the current fillet radius, default value = 0.5000
Fontalt	Defines alternate font to be used when font specified in drawing is not found.

TABLE 11: System Variables (continued)

Variable	Description
Fontmap	Defines location of substitute fonts to be used in place of fonts defined in drawing.
Frontz	Displays the distance from the Dview target to the front clipping plane. See **Dview**.
Gridmode	Controls grid: 0 = off, 1 = on. See **Grid**.
Gridunit	Controls grid spacing. See **Grid**.
Gripblock	Sets the appearance of grips in blocks: 0 = grip appears at block insertion only (default value), 1 = grips assigned to all entities within blocks.
Gripcolor	Sets color for nonselected grips.
Griphot	Sets color for selected grip.
Grips	Displays grips for **Stretch**, **Move**, **Rotate**, **Scale**, and **Mirror**: 0 = grips off, 1 = grips on.
Gripsize	Sets grip box size. Default value is 3.
Handles	Read-only. Handles status. On is the only valid option with R13.
Highlight	Controls object-selection ghosting: 0 = no ghosting, 1 = ghosting.
Hpang	Sets default hatch pattern angle.
Hpbound	Sets object type created by **Hatch** and **Boundary**. 0 = region, 1 = polyline
Hpdouble	Sets default double hatch for user-defined pattern: 0 = single hatch, 1 = double hatch.
Hpname	Sets default hatch pattern name and style.
Hpscale	Sets default hatch pattern scale.
Hpspace	Sets default line spacing for user-defined hatch pattern.
Indexctl	Controls layer and spatial indexes in drawing files: 0 = no indexes created; 1 = layer index created; 2 = spatial index created; 4 = layer and spatial indexes created, default is 0.
Intelocation	Stores the Internet location used by the **Browser** command. Default value: "www.autodesk.com/acaduser".

TABLE 11: System Variables (continued)

Variable	Description
Isavebak	Improves speed of incremental saves, 0 = no .BAK is created (even for a full save); 1 = Created .BAK
Isavepercent	Controls tolerance for wasted space in a drawing file.default = 50;values = 0 to 100.
Insertctl	Controls whether layer and spatial indexes are created and saved in drawing files. 0 = No indexes; 1= Layer index is created; 2 = Spatial index is created; 3 = Layer and spatial indexes are created.
Insbase	Controls insertion base point of current drawing. See **Base**.
Insname	Default block name for **Ddinsert** or **Insert** command.
Isolines	Sets number of lines displayed per surface on solids: default = 4, values = 0 to 2047.
Lastangle	Read-only. Displays the end angle of last arc or poly arc.
Lastpoint	Displays coordinates of last point entered. Same point referenced by at sign (@).
Lastprompt	Read-only. Stores the last command line entry.
Lenslength	Displays the current lens focal length used during the **Dview** command *Zoom* option.
Limcheck	Controls limit checking: 0 = no checking, 1 = checking. See **Limits**.
Limmax	Stores the coordinate of drawing's upper-right limit. See **Limits**.
Limmin	Stores the coordinate of drawing's lower-left limit. See **Limits**.
Lispinit	Controls loading of AutoLISP-defined functions and variables: 0 = saved in AutoCAD session, from drawing to drawing; 0 = saved in current drawing only
Locale	Displays ISO language code of the version of AutoCAD.
Logfilename	Saves path for the log file. Default: "c:\acadr14\acad.log"
Logfilemode	Sets log file on and off; 0 = file not created; 1 = file is created
Loginname	Read-only. Displays user's login name set during configuration.

TABLE 11:   System Variables (continued)

Variable	Description
Ltscale	Global line type scale factor. See **Psltscale, Celtscale**.
Lunits	Controls unit styles: 1 = scientific, 2 = decimal, 3 = engineering, 4 = architectural, 5 = fractional. See **Units, DDunits**.
Luprec	Stores unit accuracy by decimal place or size of denominator. See **Units**.
Maxactvp	Number of viewports to regenerate at one time. Maximum = 48.
Maxobjmem	Controls object pager, specifying allotment of virtual memory and begins paging to disk into the object pager's swap files; default 0 = off.
Maxsort	Sets the maximum number of symbol or file names to be sorted by any listing command.
Measurement	Sets drawing units as English or metric for hatch patterns and linetypes for existing drawings. 0 = English;1 = Metric.
Menuctl	Controls swapping of the screen menus whenever a command is entered: 0 = doesn't switch, 1 = switches.
Menuecho	Controls the display of commands and prompts issued from the menu. A value of 1 suppresses display of commands entered from menu (can be toggled on or off with Ctrl-P); 2 suppresses display of commands and command prompts when command is issued from AutoLISP macro; 3 is a combination of options 1 and 2; 4 disables Ctrl-P menu echo toggle; 8 enables the printing of all input and output strings to the screen for debugging DIESEL macros.
Menuname	Stores the current menu file name. See **Menu**.
Mirrtext	Controls text mirroring: 0 = no text mirroring, 1 = text mirroring.
Modemacro	Allows display of text or special strings like current drawing name, time, date, or specials modes at the status line. See DIESEL macro language in AutoCAD Customization manual.
Mtexted	Name of program for text editing.
Offsetdist	Offset default distance. Negative value = offset through point.

TABLE 11: System Variables (continued)

Variable	Description
Olehide	Controls display of OLE objects: 0 = All objects visible; 1 = visible in paper space only; 2= visible in model space only; 3 = objects not visible
Orthomode	Controls the Ortho mode: 0 = off, 1 = on. See **Ortho**.
Osmode	Sets the current default Osnap mode: 0 = none, 1 = endpoint, 2 = midpoint, 4 = center, 8 = node, 16 = quadrant, 32 = intersection, 64 = insert, 128 = perpendicular, 256 = tangent, 512 = nearest, 1024 = quick, 1028 = appint. If more than one mode is required, enter the sum of those modes. See **Osnap**.
Osnapcoord	Controls entry of coordinates at command line: 0 = running object snap settings override keyboard coordinate entry; 1 = keyboard entry overrides object snap settings; 2 = keyboard entry overrides object snap settings except in scripts
Pdmode	Sets the display style for point object. See **Point, Ddptype**.
Pdsize	Controls the display size of the point object. See **Point**, **Pdmode**.
Pellipse	Controls the type of ellipse created with the ellipse command. 0 = true ellipse, 1 = polyline ellipse.
Perimeter	Read-only. Displays the perimeter value currently being read by Area, List, or Dblist. See **Area**, **List**, and **Dblist**.
Pfacevmax	Read-only. Defines maximum number of vertices for mesh entity faces.
Pickadd	Controls ability to add or remove entities from a selection set using the Shift key. 0 = disabled, 1 = enabled.
Pickauto	Controls automatic windowing for "Select objects:" prompt: 0 = disabled, 1 = enabled
Pickbox	Sets object selection target height in screen pixels.
Pickdrag	Controls how a selection window is drawn: 0 = click mouse at each corner, 1 = Click mouse at one corner, hold mouse down while dragging, then release at other corner.
Pickfirst	Lets you select first, then use an edit/inquiry command: 0 = disabled, 1 = enabled.

TABLE 11: System Variables (continued)

Variable	Description
Pickstyle	Sets group and associative hatch selection. 0 = None, 1 = Group, 2 = Associative hatch, 3 = Group and Associative hatch.
Platform	Read-only. Message indicating AutoCAD version, such as Microsoft Windows, 386 DOS Extended, Apple Macintosh.
Plinegen	Controls line type pattern to adjust its appearance between vertices. 0 = line type displays dash at vertices, 1 = line type continuous around vertices.
Plinetype	Sets 2D polylines optimization for pre-R14 drawing versions: 0 = not converted, old-format used; 1 = not converted, pline is optimized; 2 = Older drawings converted and optimizes polylines.
Plinewid	Default polyline width.
Plotid	Changes default plotter based on text description.
Plotter	Changes default plotter based on its assigned configuration number.
Plotrotmode	Sets plot orientation, 0 = landscape, 1 = portrait.
Plotter	Changes default plotter using its assigned configuration number.
Polysides	**Polygon** command's default for number of sides, can be 3 to 1024.
Popups	Read-only. Displays the availability of the Advanced User Interface based on the display driver. 0 = not available, 1 = available.
Projmode	Sets projection mode for **Trim/Extend**. 0 = True 3D (no projection), 1 = XY plane of the current UCS, 2 = Current view plane.
Projectname	Assigns project name to drawing for search path of xref and images.
Proxygraphic	Controls images of proxy objects in drawing: 0 = displays bounding box, image not saved; 1 = image saved. default = 1
Proxynotice	Sets proxy notification: 0 = No proxy warning; 1= Proxy warning displayed. default = 1. default = 1

TABLE 11: System Variables (continued)

Variable	Description
Proxyshow	Controls proxy objects: 0 =not displayed; 1 = graphic images displayed; 2 = bounding box displayed.
Psltscale	Sets line type scale for Paperspace. 0 = regular line type scaling, 1 = adjust all line types to use the current ltscale, including XREF's, viewed from Paperspace.
Psprolog	Assigns a name for the prologue section in file acad.PSF for **Psout** command.
Psquality	Sets rendering quality PostScript image when imported into a drawing. 0 = disabled.
Qtextmode	Controls the Quicktext mode: 0 = off, 1 = on. See **Qtext** command.
Rasterpreview	Controls BMP preview images: 0 = off, 1 = on. default = 1.
Regenmode	Controls the Regenauto mode: 0 = off, 1 = on. See **Regenauto**.
Re-init	Resets I/O ports, digitizer, display, plotter, and Acad.PGP file.
Rtdisplay	Controls display of raster images while performing a realtime part zoom: 0=Display image, 1=Display outline.
Savefile	Read-only. Displays current auto-save file name.
Savename	Read-only. File name assigned to the currently saved file.
Savetime	Automatic-save time interval: 0 = disabled.
Screenboxes	Read-only. Number of boxes displayed on screen menu of graphics area.
Screenmode	Read-only. Controls grpahics/text screens: 0 = text screen, 1 = graphics mode, 2 = dual screen. Values are additive.
Screensize	Read-only. Reads the size of the graphics screen in pixels.
Shadedge	Sets shading parameters: 0 = faces shaded, edges not highlighted, 1 = faces shaded with edges drawn using background color, 2 = faces unfilled with edges in entity color, 3 = faces in entity color, edges with background color.

TABLE 11: System Variables (continued)

Variable	Description
Shadedif	Sets the ratio (in percent) of diffuse reflective light to ambient light.
Shpname	Stores default shape name.
Sketchinc	Sets the sketch record increment. See **Sketch**.
Skpoly	Controls whether the **Sketch** command uses regular lines or a connected lines in a polyline. 0 = lines, 1 = polyline.
Snapang	Controls snap and grid angle. See **Snap**.
Snapbase	Controls snap, grid, and hatch pattern origin. See **Snap**.
Snapisopair	Controls isometric plane: 0 = left, 1 = top, 2 = right. See **Snap** command.
Snapmode	Controls snap toggle: 0 = off, 1 = on. See **Snap** command.
Snapstyl	Controls snap style: 0 = standard, 1 = isometric. See **Snap**.
Snapunit	Sets snap spacing given in *X* and *Y* values. See **Snap**.
Sortents	Controls entity sorting order: 0 = disabled, 1 = object selection, 2 = object snap, 4 = redraws, 8 = Mslide slide creation, 16 = regens, 32 = plotting, 64 = PostScript output. Values are additive.
Splframe	Controls the display of spline vertices, surface-fit three-dimensional meshes, and invisible edges of 3dfaces. 0 = no display of Spline vertices of invisible 3dface edges. Displays only defining mesh or surface-fit mesh. 1 = display of Spline vertices or invisible 3dface edges. Displays only surface-fit mesh.
Splinesegs	Controls the number of line segments used for each spline patch.
Splinetype	Controls the type of curved line generated by the **Pedit Spline** command. 5 = quadratic B-spline, 6 = cubic B-spline.
Surftab1	Controls the number of mesh control points for the **Rulesurf** and **Tabsurf** commands and the number of mesh points in the M direction for the **Revsurf** and **Edgesurf** commands.

TABLE 11: System Variables (continued)

Variable	Description
Surftab2	Controls the number of mesh control points in the N direction for the **Revsurf** and **Edgesurf** commands.
Surftype	Controls the type of surface fitting generated by the **Pedit Smooth** command. 5 = quadratic B-spline, 6 = cubic B-spline, and 8 = Bezier surface.
Surfu	Controls the accuracy of the smoothed surface models in the M direction.
Surfv	Controls the accuracy of the smoothed surface models in the N direction.
Syscodepage	Read-only. Indicates system code page of *Acad.XMF*.
Tabmode	Sets tablet mode: 0 = disabled, 1 = enabled.
Target	Read-only. Displays the coordinate of the target point used in the **Dview** command.
Tdcreate	Read-only. Displays time and date of drawing creation. See **Time**.
Tdindwg	Read-only. Displays total editing time. See **Time**.
Tdupdate	Read-only. Displays time and date of last save. See **Time**.
Tdusrtimer	Read-only. Displays user-elapsed time. See **Time**.
Tempprefix	Read-only. Displays the name of the directory where temporary AutoCAD files are saved.
Texteval	Controls whether prompts for text and attribute input to commands are taken literally or as AutoLISP expressions. 0 = literal, 1 = text you input with left parens and exclamation points will be interpreted as AutoLISP expression. **Dtext** takes all input literally, regardless of this setting.
Textfill	Controls the display of TrueType fonts. 0 = outline, 1 = filled.
Textqlty	Controls the resolution of TrueType fonts. values are 0 to 100.
Textsize	Controls default text height except for styles with an assigned fixed height. See **Dtext**, **Text**, and **Style**.
Textstyle	Sets the current text style. See **Style**.
Thickness	Controls 3D thickness of objects being drawn. See **Elev**.

TABLE 11:   System Variables (continued)

Variable	Description
Thickness	Sets current 3D thickness.
Tilemode	Toggle between Paperspace and Modelspace: 0 = enable paper space, 1 = exit paper space.
Tooltips	Controls the display of tooltips (windows only). 0 = off, 1 = on.
Tracewid	Sets default trace width. See **Trace**.
Treedepth	Lets you set a four-digit integer coding that ultimately affects AutoCAD's quickness for searching a database to execute commands. Changing the value of this variable forces a drawing regeneration regardless of **Regenauto** setting.
Treemax	Limits memory (RAM) usage during regen operations.
Trimmode	Controls whether corner lines are trimmed during **Chamfer** and **Fillet** commands. 0 = no trim, 1 = trim.
Ucsfollow	Controls whether changing the current UCS automatically displays the plan view of the new current UCS. 0 = displayed view does not change, 1 = automatic display of new current UCS in plan.
Ucsicon	Controls UCS icon display: 0 = off, 1 = on, 2 = at origin and off, 3 = at origin and displayed when origin is visible.
Ucsname	Read-only. Displays the name of the current UCS. See **UCS**.
Ucsorg	Read-only. Displays the current UCS origin point. See **UCS**.
Ucsxdir	Read-only. Displays the X direction of the current UCS. See **UCS**.
Ucsydir	Read-only. Displays the Y direction of the current UCS. See **UCS**.
Undoctl	Read-only. Displays state of **Undo**: 1 = set if Undo enabled, 2 = set for one undo, 4 = set if Auto-group mode enabled, 8 = set if group currently active.
Undomarks	Read-only. Displays the number of Undo's by *Mark* and *Back* options placed in the current drawing.

TABLE 11: System Variables (continued)

Variable	Description
Unitmode	Sets how fractional, feet-and-inches, and surveyors' angles are displayed on the status line. 0 = normal (for example, 1~'– 6~FS1/2~"). 1 = same as input format (for example, 1~'6– 1/2~").
Useri1-5	Five variables for storing integers for custom applications.
Userr1-5	Five variables for storing real numbers for custom applications.
Users1-5	Five variables for storing text strings for custom applications.
Viewctr	Read-only. Displays the current UCS coordinates of the center of the current viewport.
Viewdir	Read-only. Displays the view direction of the current view port. This also describes the camera point as a 3D offset from the TARGET point.
Viewmode	**Controls** view mode for current viewport: 1 = perspective on, 2 = front clipping plane on, 4 = back clipping plane on, 8 = UCS follow mode on, 16 = front clipping plane not at eye level.
Viewsize	Read-only. Displays the height of the current view in drawing units.
Viewtwist	Read-only. Displays the view twist angle for the current viewport. See **Dview**.
Visretain	Stores Xref freeze/thaw, on/off, color and line-type layer settings. 0 = Xref layer settings are as defined in the Xref drawing itself. 1 = Xref layer settings are controlled and stored by the current drawing. One xref may be called into multiple drawings with different layer settings, if Visretain is set in the calling drawing, the Xref's will conform to each of the called layer definitions.
Vsmax	Read-only. Displays the 3D coordinate of the upper-right corner of the current viewport's virtual screen relative to the current UCS.
Vsmin	Read-only. Displays the 3D coordinate of the lower-left corner of the current viewport's virtual screen relative to the current UCS.
Worlducs	Read-only. Displays the status of the world coordinate system. 0 = WCS is not current, 1 = WCS is current. See **UCS**.

TABLE 11: System Variables (continued)

Variable	Description
Worldview	Controls whether point input to the **Dview** and **Vpoint** commands is relative to the WCS or the current UCS. 0 = commands use the current UCS to interpret point value input, 1 = commands use WCS to interpret point value input.
Xclipframe	Sets controls for visibility of xref clipping boundaries: 0= not visible; 1 = visible
Xloadctl	Toggles xref demand loading and controls whether it opens the original drawing or a copy: 0 = Off, entire drawing is loaded; 1 = On, reference file is kept open; 2 =On; a copy of the reference file is opened
Xloadpath	Creates path for storing temporary copies of demand-loaded xref files.
Xrefctl	Controls creation of external .XLG files: 0 = not written, 1 = written.

Syswindows

Syswindows allows you to arrange (tile or cascade) the AutoCAD windows or arrange the window icons. It works in AutoCAD in the same way as the Window menu in the Windows Program Manager works.

To Arrange AutoCAD Windows

Command Line: **Syswindows**

Cascade/tileHorz/tileVert/Arrangeicons: Select an option.

Options

Cascade Overlaps the windows with visible title bars.

TileHorz Arranges the windows horizontally, in non-overlapping tiles.

TileVert Arranges the windows vertically, in non-overlapping tiles.

Arrangeicons Arranges the window icons.

Tablet

Tablet is useful only if you have a digitizing tablet. Use it to set up your tablet for accurate tracing.

To Set Up a Tablet

Command Line: **Tablet**

Menu: Tools ➤ Tablet ➤ On/Off/Calibrate/Configure

1. **Option (ON/OFF/CAL/CFG):** Enter an option. If you do not have a digitizing tablet, you will get the message "Your pointing device cannot be used as a tablet."

Options

ON/OFF Toggles the Calibrated mode on or off. When on, you cannot access the screen menus. Use the F4 key to toggle On/Off. Alternatively, you may set the *Tabmode* system variable: 0=Off, 1=On. Pressing **Ctrl+T** on some systems turns Tablet mode on and off.

CAL Allows you to calibrate a tablet so distances on the tablet correspond to actual distances in your drawing. The calibration is effective only for the space (Paper/Modelspace) in which it is performed. After calibrating the tablet, set the transformation to Orthogonal, Affine, or Projective, depending on the drawing dimensions and the digitizing requirements.

CFG Allows you to configure your digitizing tablet for a tablet menu like the one provided by AutoCAD.

> **Orthogonal** Requires two calibration points to set translation, uniform scaling, and rotation. Appropriate for dimensionally accurate paper drawings and paper drawings in which the portion to be digitized is long and narrow, and points are confined to single lines.

> **Affine** Useful when specifying arbitrary linear transformation in two dimensions consisting of translation, independent X and Y scaling, rotation, and skewing with three calibration points. Applicable when horizontal dimensions in a paper drawing are exaggerated with respect to vertical dimensions, and lines that are supposed to be parallel actually are parallel.

> **Projective** Sets a transformation representing a perspective projection of one plane in space onto another plane with four calibration points. Adjusts parallel lines that appear to converge.

The *CAL*, or Calibrate, option allows you to set specific distances on the tablet to correspond to actual distances in your AutoCAD drawing. You are prompted to pick a first known point on the tablet and enter its corresponding coordinate in your AutoCAD drawing. This point should be at the lowest-left corner of a known origin—for example, one corner of a property line. Then you are prompted to pick a second known point on your tablet and enter its corresponding coordinate in your drawing. This second point should be the upper-right end of the line of known length. For best results, this line should be as long as possible and should be horizontal or vertical, not diagonal. You may want to include a graphic scale in your drawing to be digitized just for the purpose of calibrating your tablet.

You may not be able to calibrate your tablet if you have configured it to have menus and a small screen pointing area. If this is the case, you may have to reconfigure it so that its entire surface is designated for the screen pointing area.

The *CFG*, or Configure, option allows you to control the location and format of tablet menus as well as the pointing area on your tablet. You are first prompted for the number of tablet menus you want. The AutoCAD tablet menu contains four menus. Then you are prompted to pick the upper-left, lower-left, and lower-right corners of the tablet menus. The AutoCAD template shows a black dot at these corners. Next, you are prompted for the number of columns and rows that each menu contains. Finally, you are asked if you want to specify the screen pointing area. This is the area on the tablet used for actual drawing. If you answer Yes to this prompt, you are prompted to pick the lower-left and upper-right corners of the pointing area.

To Use the Tablet Menu

The Tablet menu allows you to use a pointing device to activate commands from a digitizing tablet. To use it, load the Tablet menu. You can activate a command from the tablet by moving your pointing device to a box that represents the desired command and pressing the pick button. Commands you pick from the tablet menu often display a corresponding screen menu to allow you to pick the command options. The blank area at the top of the tablet menu is reserved for additional custom menu options.

See Also Preferences (Pointer Tab), Sketch; *System Variables:* Tabmode, Tablet Mole Mode

Tabsurf

Tabsurf draws a surface by extruding a curve in a straight line, as shown in Figure 17. Before using **Tabsurf**, you must draw a curve defining the extruded shape and a line defining the direction of the extrusion (the direction vector).

FIGURE 17: A curve extruded in a straight line

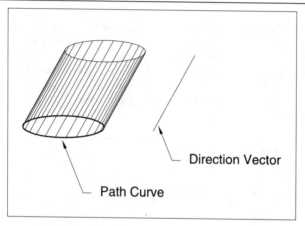

Direction Vector

Path Curve

To Straighten a Curved Surface

Command Line: **Tabsurf**

Menu: Draw ➤ Surfaces ➤ Tabulated Surface

Surfaces Toolbar: Tabulated Surface

1. **Select path curve:** Pick a curve defining the surface shape.

2. **Select direction vector:** Pick a line defining the direction of the extrusion.

The point at which you pick the direction vector at the "Select direction vector:" prompt determines the direction of the extrusion. The endpoint nearest the pick point is the base of the direction vector, and the other end indicates the direction of the extrusion.

You can draw the curve with a line, arc, circle, 2D polyline, or 3D polyline. The direction vector can be a 3D line. Tabsurf has an effect similar to changing the thickness of an object, but extrusions using Tabsurf are not limited to the Z axis. The *Surftab1* system variable will affect the number of facets used to form the surface.

See Also Pedit, *System Variables:* Surftab1

Text

See Dtext

3D

3D creates basic 3D surface objects. You may select from a predefined set of 3D shapes: box, cone, dish, dome, mesh, pyramid, sphere, torus, or wedge. The objects initially display as wire-frame objects, although they are actually faceted surfaces. You may use **Hide**, **Shade**, or **Render** on them to simulate solid objects. At the command line you can enter **3D** and choose an option, **Box, Cone, Dish, Dome, Mesh, Pyramid, Sphere, Torus or Wedge**.

NOTE If you enter **box** at the command prompt you get a 3D Solid.

To Create a Simple 3D Surface Object

Command Line: **3D**

Menu: Draw ➤ Surfaces ➤ 3D Surfaces

Surfaces Toolbar: ⊞Box △Cone ◎Dish ◎Dome ◈3Dmesh ◆Pyramid ◉Sphere ◈Torus ◇Wedge

1. **Box/Cone/Dish/DOme/Mesh/Pyramid/Sphere/Torus/ Wedge:** Select a 3D surface. When you select 3D Surfaces... from the menu, the 3D Objects icon menu displays the predefined surface objects for selection.

TIP The simple mesh option is available from the icon menu.

2. Depending on the 3D surface chosen, you will be prompted for **Diameter, Radius, Height**, etc.

3. **Number of Segments <current value>:** Enter the number of facets desired on the surface. This prompt appears only for curved surface objects, not for flat-sided objects such as a box or pyramid. For dish, dome, and sphere, you will be prompted for both latitudinal and longitudinal segments; for torus you will be prompted for segments around tube circumference and segments around torus circumference.

NOTE Surface objects fall somewhere between wire-frame models and solid objects. They initially display as wire-frames, but can be shaded or rendered to appear as solid objects. Unlike solids, they provide no information about physical properties (such as mass, weight, or center of gravity), cannot be combined into more complex shapes, or used to calculate interferences.

See Also Hide, Render, Shade, Solid Modeling, 3D mesh

3Dface

3Dface draws a 3D face in 3D space. 3D faces are surfaces defined by four points in space picked in circular fashion. Although they appear transparent, 3D faces are treated as opaque when you remove hidden lines from a drawing. After the first face is defined, you are prompted for additional third and fourth points, which allow the addition of adjoining 3D faces.

To Draw a 3D Face

Command Line: **3Dface**

Menu: Draw ➤ Surfaces ➤ 3D Surfaces

Surfaces Toolbar: 3D Face

1. **First point:** Select the first corner.

2. **Second point:** Select the second corner.

3. **Third point:** Select the third corner.

4. **Fourth point:** Select the fourth corner.

5. **Third point:** Continue to pick pairs of points defining more faces or press ↵ to end the command.

Entering **Invisible** or **I** at the first point of an edge makes that edge of the 3D face invisible.

NOTE Use the *Invisible* option if you want to hide the joint line between joined 3D faces. Do this by entering **I** just before you pick the first defining point of the side to be made invisible. Make invisible edges visible by setting the *Splframe* system variable to a nonzero value. See **System Variables** for more on *Splframe*.

NOTE The **Edge** command can also be used to change the visibility of 3D faces. All meshes are composed of 3D faces. If you explode a 3D mesh, each facet of the mesh will be a 3D face.

See Also Edge, Solid Modeling; *System Variables:* Pfacevmax, Splframe

3Dmesh

3Dmesh draws a 3D surface mesh using coordinate values you specify. **3Dmesh** can be used when drawing 3D models of a topography or performing finite element analysis. **3Dmesh** is designed for programmers who want control over each node of a mesh. You may also use **3Dmesh** along with scripts and LISP routines to automate the process.

To Draw a Rectangular Mesh

Command Line: **3Dmesh**

Menu: Draw ➤ Surfaces ➤ 3Dmesh

Surfaces Toolbar: 3Dmesh

1. **Mesh M size:** Enter the number of vertices in the M direction (2 to 256).

2. **Mesh N size:** Enter the number of vertices in the N direction (2 to 256).

3. **Vertex (0,0):** Enter the XYZ coordinate value for the first vertex in the mesh.

4. **Vertex (0,1):** Enter the XYZ coordinate value for the next vertex in the N direction of the mesh.

5. **Vertex (0,2):** Continue to enter XYZ coordinate values for the vertices.

TIP To use 3Dmesh to generate a topographical model, arrange your XYZ coordinate values in a rectangular array, roughly as they would appear in the plan. Fill any blanks in the array with dummy or neutral coordinate values. Start the 3Dmesh command and use the number of columns for the mesh M size and the number of rows for the N size. At the prompts, enter the coordinate values row by row, starting at the lower-left corner of your array and reading from left to right. Include any dummy values. 3Dmesh creates a polygon mesh which is open in both directions (M and N).

See Also   Mface, Pedit, Pface, Solid Modeling; *System Variables:* Surftype, Surfu

3Dpoly

3Dpoly draws a polyline in 3D space using XYZ coordinates or object snap points. 3D polylines are like standard polylines, except that you can't give them a width or use arc segments. Also, you cannot use the **Pedit** command's *Fit curve* option with 3dpoly. To create a smooth curve using 3D polylines, use the **Pedit** *Spline* option. This creates a Spline fit curve. To convert this into a true spline, use the **Spline** command *Object* option.

To Draw a 3Dpolyline

Command Line: **3Dpoly**

Menu: Draw ➤ 3D Polyline

1. **From point:** Enter the beginning point.

2. **Close/Undo/<Endpoint of line>:** Enter the next point of the line.

3. **Close/Undo/<Endpoint of line>:** Continue to pick points for additional line segments or press ↵ to end the command.

Options

Close   Connects the first point with the last point in a series of line segments.

Undo   Moves back one line segment in a series of line segments.

See Also   Pedit, Pline, Spline

Tilemode

Tilemode allows you to toggle between Modelspace and Paperspace in AutoCAD. Modelspace is where you do basic design and drafting. In Paperspace you can create and manipulate different views of your model for plotting. When Tilemode is On (=1), you are working in Modelspace and the Modelspace UCS icon is visible in the lower-left corner. When Tilemode is Off (=0), you are in Paperspace and the triangular Paperspace icon is visible in the lower-left corner.

While you are in Paperspace (Tilemode = 0), you may create *floating viewports* of your Modelspace drawing using **Mview**, and then switch to *floating Modelspace* (Tilemode still = 0) to edit the views.

To Turn On Paper Space

Command Line: **Tilemode**

Menu: View ➤ Paper Space

The above menu option performs two functions. It moves you from regular Modelspace to Paperspace, and it can also be used to switch from floating Modelspace back into Paperspace. So it activates both the **Tilemode** toggle and starts the **Pspace** command.

You can use the status bar to turn on Paperspace. Double-click on the MODEL button. The button changes to PAPER.

To Switch to Floating Modelspace

Command Line: **Mspace / MS**

Menu: View ➤ Modelspace (Floating)

This menu option activates the **Mspace** command, and allows you to work in Modelspace via a floating Paperspace viewport. You may edit the Modelspace objects while keeping the Paperspace layout visible.

You can use the status bar PAPER/MODEL button to toggle back and forth between Paperspace view and the floating Modelspace. Note that as long as you are in Paperspace, MODEL on the status bar indicates floating Modelspace, not regular Modelspace.

TIP When you wish to return to regular Modelspace, you may either reset Tilemode to 1 (On), or choose View ➤ Model Space [Tiled] to perform the same function.

NOTE Floating viewports and tiled viewports should not be regarded as the same. In floating viewports you have more control over the contents of each view. You can turn off layers within different floating viewports, and scale and align views with more flexibility.

See Also Mspace, Mvsetup, Pspace

Time

Time keeps track of the time you spend on a drawing. The time is displayed in military format, using the 24-hour count.

To Display Drawing-Time Data

Command Line: **Time** (or '**Time** to use transparently)

Menu: Tools Inquiry ➤ Time

1. Current time: Enter date and time.

2. Times for this drawing:

- **Created** Displays date and time.

- **Last updated** Displays date and time.

- **Total editing time** Displays days and time.

- **Elapsed time** Displays days and time.

- **Display/On/Off/Reset** Enter an option.

Options

Display Redisplays time information.

On Turns elapsed timer on.

Off Turns elapsed timer off.

Reset Resets elapsed timer to 0.

See Also *System Variables:* Tdcreate, Tdindwg, Tdupdate, Tdusrtimer

Tolerance

Tolerance allows you to specify maximum allowable variations of
form, profile, orientation, location, or runout from those that are
defined by the geometry shown in the drawing. These geometric tolerances define the maximum variations on the specified dimensions that
will still allow the drawn object to function and to fit as required.
AutoCAD positions the specified tolerances on the drawing in a *feature
control frame*.

To Add Geometric Tolerances to Object Dimensions

Command Line: **Tolerance**

Menu: Dimension ➤ Tolerance...

Dimension Toolbar: Tolerance

1. When the Symbols dialog box appears, select the desired feature
control symbol, then choose OK.

2. When the Geometric Tolerance subdialog box appears, enter the relevant tolerance information for the feature selected. In addition to the tolerance value, you may add a diameter symbol and supplementary datums and symbols pertaining to material conditions and projected tolerances. Choose OK when you have entered all of the required information.

3. **Enter tolerance location:** Pick the point at which the tolerance information is to be located. The symbol(s) selected, surrounded by a standard frame, will appear at the selected location.

Options

Feature Control Symbols   The Symbols dialog box provides an icon menu of the geometric feature symbols: the first three symbols pertain to *Location* (position, concentricity, and symmetry); the next three symbols to *Orientation* (parallelism, perpendicularity, and angularity); the next three symbols to *Form* (flatness, roundness, and straightness); then come two symbols for *Profile* (surface profile and line profile); and the final two symbols pertain to *Runout* (circular runout and total runout). When you select a feature symbol, AutoCAD closes the Symbols dialog box and inserts the symbol into the Sym text box in the Geometric Tolerance subdialog box.

Tolerance 1/Tolerance 2   You may enter up to two tolerance values for the object dimension. The tolerance *Value* specifies the amount by which the dimensions of the built object may deviate from the dimensions indicated on the drawing. Two additional modifiers may be added to value. You may optionally insert a diameter symbol (if appropriate) before the value by clicking on the Dia box. You may also add material condition information; clicking on the MC box opens the Material Condition subdialog box and allows you to specify *maximum material condition* (symbol M), *least material condition* (symbol L) or *regardless of feature size* (symbol S). Material conditions apply to features that can vary in size.

Datum 1/2/3   You may add up to three optional *datum reference letters* (A, B, C) after the tolerance values. Each datum represents a point, axis, or plane from which you can measure and verify dimensions. Usually these are three mutually perpendicular planes called the *datum reference frame*. Each datum may be followed by a material condition modifier symbol (M, L, or S) as described immediately above.

Height/Projected Tolerance Zone   You may define projected tolerances in additional to positional tolerances to increase accuracy. Specify a Height value. This value specifies the minimum projected tolerance zone. Selecting the Projected Tolerance Zone box will add the projected tolerance symbol (P) after the height value.

Datum Identifier   Allows you to specify a datum-identifying symbol. This identifier consists of a reference letter preceded and followed by a dash (-A-).

> **NOTE**   AutoCAD inserts all of the tolerance information and symbols into a feature control frame. A feature control frame will at minimum contain two elements: the symbol of the geometric characteristic being defined and the tolerance value. The tolerance value field will additionally contain all modifiers and datum references selected. The projected tolerance height and P symbol (if any) are inserted in a frame below the feature control frame, and the datum identifier is placed in a frame below these frames.

> **TIP**   Feature control frames are a single AutoCAD object, and you may copy, move, stretch, scale, and rotate them. You may use **Osnap** and **Grips**, and you may edit them using **Ddedit**.

Feature control frame characteristics are controlled by the dimension variables as follows: color (*Dimclre*); text color (*Dimclrt*); text gap (*Dimgap*); size of text (*Dimtxt*); and text style (*Dimtxtsty*).

See Also   Ddedit; Dimensioning Commands; *Dimension Variables:* Dimclre, Dimclrt, Dimgap, Dimtxt, Dimtxtsty

Toolbar/Tbconfig

Toolbar or **Tbconfig** opens the Toolbar dialog box showing a list of standard toolbars with frequently used commands grouped for easy access. You may display multiple toolbars on the screen at once, and you may hide them when you are not using them. The Toolbars dialog box allows you to create new toolbars, delete toolbars, customize the supplied toolbars by adding or removing commands to meet your current needs, and modify properties on toolbars.

Toolbars may be either *docked* or *floating*. If a toolbar is docked, it locks into position along the top, bottom, or sides of the screen. A floating toolbar can be moved around with your pointing device, and may overlap other toolbars.

To Display a Toolbar

Command Line: **Toolbar** or **Tbconfig**

Menu: View ➤ Toolbars...

Toolbar: Right-click any icon in any toolbar.

TOOLBAR/TBCONFIG

When the Toolbars dialog box appears, check a toolbar name to display it or select an option. You may reposition a toolbar by dragging it across the screen. To close it, click on the upper-left corner.

If you wish to "dock" a **floating toolbar**, drag it by holding your pick button over the title bar to a dock location at the top, bottom, or sides of the screen, and release the pick button.

Some toolbars have *flyouts*, or nested toolbars that contain more tool icons. For example, the Inquiry flyout on the Standard toolbar contains tools for Distance, Area, Mass Properties, List, and Locate Point. For specific tasks you may wish to display the Inquiry toolbar itself on your screen rather than access it repeatedly via the Standard toolbar.

Each tool icon on a tool bar has a *ToolTip* that serves as a label, When you pass your pointing device slowly across the icon, the Tooltip appears and a line of help text is displayed on the status bar.

The position of tools on a flyout customizes itself based upon your usage. The flyout tool most recently used moves to the first position for easier access.

All of the toolbars are flexible and can be customized extensively to meet your specific needs.

Options

Toolbars   The toolbars list box displays all available toolbars, both hidden and shown. Click the box for the toolbar to display and it immediately appears on the graphics screen. Highlight the toolbar whose properties you wish to customize, delete, or modify.

Close   Exits the Toolbar dialog box and implements any changes that you have made.

New   Opens the New Toolbar subdialog box. Enter a toolbar name for the new toolbar. This is the name that will appear above the tools on the toolbar. In the Menu Group drop-down box, select the menu group associated with the new toolbar. The list box contains all menus currently loaded, including the ACAD standard menu and any others you may have created and loaded (see **Menuload**). The internal AutoCAD name, or alias, of a toolbar consists of the toolbar name prefixed by the menu group name—for example, ACAD.*CUSTOM*. When you choose OK, an empty toolbar will appear on your drawing area. You should now use the *Customize* option to add tools to the toolbar.

Delete   Use this option to delete any toolbar. You may create temporary toolbars and then delete them when you no longer need them.

Customize   This option opens the Customize Toolbars subdialog box. The new or existing toolbar(s) that you wish to modify must be visible on your screen. To delete a tool from the displayed toolbar, simply drag it off the toolbar. To add a new tool to a displayed toolbar, select the relevant tool category from the Categories drop-box. When you select a category (for example, Solids or Attributes), all of the tool icons for that category appear in the Categories box. Click on any tools that you want and drag them to the onscreen toolbar that you are customizing. You may also move and copy tools from one displayed toolbar to another. To *move* a tool from another toolbar, drag the tool to the new toolbar. To *copy* a tool from another toolbar, press the Ctrl key as you drag the tool to the new toolbar. During all of the above operations, the displayed toolbar resizes itself as tools are added or deleted. Choose the Close button to save the toolbar changes. Use the Customize category to add an empty icon to a toolbar, then right-click your mouse button over the icon to display the Button Properties toolbar for editing it.

Properties   Opens the Toolbar Properties subdialog box and allows you to change the toolbar name, or help string and identify that particular toolbar's alias.

Large buttons   This check box allows you to change the icons on the toolbars from the standard 15(vert.)×16(horiz.) pixels to 22(vert.)×32(horiz.) pixels.

Show Tooltips   This check box allows you to turn on or off the display of the tool name each time a pointing device passes over any tool icon. It is controlled by the system variable *Tooltips*.

You can open the Toolbars dialog box directly from a displayed toolbar by clicking on a tool icon with the Return button (right button) of your pointing device. Right-clicking on a tool icon will open the Button Properties dialog box for that tool. You may change the name, command, and tool icon associated with that tool. If you click on a flyout toolbar icon while the Toolbars dialog box is displayed, the Flyout Properties dialog box, will open. You may change the flyout name, toolbar, and icon.

You can edit the .MNS file with an ASCII text editor and any changes made to toolbars are saved to the associated compiled menu (.MNC) file.

If you have used **Menuload** to load the Ac_Bonus and Inet menu files, then the Menu Group popup box will display the Bonus and Internet Utilities toolbars.

See Also   Toolbar; *System Variables:* Tooltips

-Toolbar

-Toolbar is used at the command line and helps you to display, hide, relocate or dock a toolbar.

To Use the Toolbar Command

Command Line: **-Toolbar**

1. **Toolbar name (or ALL):** Enter the full alias for the toolbar, and press ↵.

2. **Show/Hide/Left/Right/Top/Bottom/Float <current>:** Enter an option or press ↵.

Options

All   Type *All* to activate this option. Choose *Hide* or *Show* all toolbars. If you choose Show, every toolbar both top level and lower level will display on your screen. If you choose Hide, every toolbar including your default toolbars will close.

Show   Displays the named toolbar.

Hide   Closes the named toolbar.

Left/Right/Top/Bottom   Docks the named toolbar at the left, right, top, or bottom of the screen. The "Position" prompt sets the position of the toolbar relative to an existing docked toolbar.

Float   Changes the named toolbar from docked to floating. The "Position" prompt sets the position of the floating toolbar in XY coordinates. The "Rows" prompt allows you to define the number of rows in the toolbar.

Trace

Trace can be used where a thick line is desired. Alternatively, you can accomplish the same thing using the **Pline** command. If you draw a series of Trace line segments, the corners are automatically joined to form a sharp corner.

To Draw a Thick Line

Command Line: **Trace**

1. **Trace width <default width>:** Enter the desired width.

2. **From point:** Pick the start point for the trace.

3. **To point:** Pick the next point.

As with the **Line** command, you can continue to pick points to draw a series of connected line segments. Trace lines appear only after the next point is selected.

> **NOTE** If you draw a series of Trace line segments, the corners are automatically joined to form a sharp corner. For this reason, traces do not have an Undo option, and the starting and ending segments will not join and bevel properly. To make traces bevel properly for the start and end segments, begin the trace not on the desired corner/endpoint but at any point midway on the desired first segment, and then make the end segment complete the actual first segment.

See Also Fill; *System Variables:* Tracewid

Tracking/Track/Tk

Tracking helps to locate points based on a reference point in your drawing. Use **Track** or **Tk** to initialize tracking during execution of a command.

To Start Tracking

Command Line: **Tracking**

Object Snap Toolbar: Tracking

To draw a circle centered within a rectangle, you could set tracking on to locate the rectangles vertical and horizontal midpoints and use these as reference points. For example, enter the **Circle** command, then use the middle button or hold the Shift key and right click your mouse button to display the cursor menu and select Tracking. Open the cursor menu for the midpoint option, pick a line (perhaps the vertical line) on the rectangle, then reopen it again and select midpoint again and pick the opposite (the horizontal line) and the circles center point will start at the center of the rectangle. To end tracking, press ↵.

The following describes the command sequence for the example above:

1. circle 3P/2P/TTR/<Center point>: Press the Shift key and right mouse button, then select tracking.

2. **First tracking point:** Press the middle button or use the Shift key and right click the mouse button to open the cursor menu, select midpoint, and pick the vertical line of the rectangle.

3. **Next point (Press ENTER to end tracking):** Press the middle button or use the Shift key and right click the mouse button, then select midpoint and a horizontal line of the rectangle.

4. **Next point (Press ENTER to end tracking):** Press ↵.

5. **Diameter/<Radius>:** Specify radius, or enter **D** for the diameter of circle.

Transparency

Transparency allows you to set background pixels in an image as transparent or opaque so that graphics on the screen shows through those pixels.

To Set an Image's Transparency

Command Line: **Transparency**

Menu: Modify ➤ Object ➤ Image ➤ Transparency

Reference Toolbar: Image Transparency

1. **Select image:** Select an image to set its transparency.

2. **ON/OFF <OFF>:** Enter **ON** or **OFF**.

> **TIP** **Transparency** is available for both bitonal and non-bitonal (Alpha RGB or gray-scale) images and is determined on a per object basis.

Transparent Commands

The transparent commands can be used while AutoCAD is still executing another command. Control is transferred temporarily to the transparent command until it is completed, or until you terminate it by pressing Escape. Not all commands can be used transparently. See Table 11 for a list of transparent commands.

TABLE 11: AutoCAD Transparent Commands

Transparent Commands

About	Dragmode	Redraw
Aperture	Elev	Redrawall
Appload	Fill	Regenauto
Attdisp	Grid	Resume
Base	Graphscr	Script
Blipmode	Help / ? / F1	Setvar
Cal	Id	Snap
Color	Isoplane	Spell
Ddgrips	Layer	Status
Ddlmodes	Limits	Style
Ddosnap	Linetype	Textscr
Ddptype	Ltscale	Treestat
Ddrmodes	Ortho	Time
Ddselect	Osmode	Units
Ddunits	Osnap	View
Delay	Pan	Zoom
Dist	Qtext	

To Use a Command while Another Is Executing

Type an apostrophe preceding the command name. (This only works for commands that are identified as transparent commands in Table 11 and throughout this book.)

Treestat

Treestat displays data regarding the drawing's current spatial index, allowing you to improve drawing efficiency via the *Treedepth* system variable. Information is provided separately for model space and paper space.

To View the Tree

Command Line: **Treestat**

The number of nodes being reported is shown in the Modelspace branch and Paperspace branch. Each node requires approximately 80 bytes of memory. Setting the *Treedepth* system variable to a large number increases disk swapping, negating the performance benefits of the spatial index. The objective is to have fewer objects per node to take advantage of spatial indexing, the optimum number being dependent on the amount of memory your computer has. The more memory you have, the more you can take advantage of spatial indexing. The use of *Treedepth* and *Treestat* is best suited to large drawings in order to optimize performance.

AutoCAD indexes objects in a region by recording their positions in space. The result is called a spatial index.

See Also   *System Variables:* Treedepth

Trim

Trim shortens an object to meet another object or objects. One or more objects may also be trimmed to a point of *implied* intersection—that is, to the point at which they *would* intersect with the cutting edge if the cutting edge were extended out. Additionally, objects may be trimmed to the current UCS plane or along the current view direction—that is, to an apparent intersection in the current view. These options are controlled by the system variables *Projmode* and *Edgemode*.

To Trim an Object

Command Line: **Trim**

Menu: Modify ➤ Trim

Modify Toolbar: ⌁ Trim

1. **Select cutting edge(s)(Projmode - UCS, Edgemode - No extend:** Choose object(s) that define the cutting edge(s) at which you want to trim other objects.

2. **<Select objects to trim>:** Pick the objects you want to trim, one at a time or using the Fence selection set option, or select an option:

    *   If you type **P**, you will be prompted **None/Ucs/View/ <current value>:**.

    *   If you type **E**, you will be prompted **Extend/ No extend <current value>:**.

Options

Project   Specifies the projection mode for AutoCAD to use when trimming objects: **None** specifies that only objects that actually intersect the cutting edge will be trimmed; **UCS** specifies projection onto the XY plane of the current UCS; **View** trims all selected objects which intersect with the cutting edge in the current view. The system variable *Projmode* settings control the projection mode.

Edge   Allows cutting edges to be extended to the point where they *would* intersect with an option. You may select either **Extend** or **No Extend** (system variable *Edgemode* settings 1 and 0). If you choose No extend, only objects that *actually* intersect the cutting edge will be trimmed.

> **NOTE**   Objects that may be trimmed include arcs, circles, elliptical arcs, lines open 2D and 3D polylines, rays and splines. These same objects may be selected as cutting edges. Regions, floating viewports, text, and xlines may also be used to define cutting edges.

> **TIP**   At the "Select cutting edge:" prompt, you can pick several objects that intersect the objects you want to trim. Once you've selected the cutting edges, press ⏎ and the "Select object to trim:" prompt appears, allowing you to pick the sides of the objects to trim. You cannot trim objects within blocks or use blocks as cutting edges.

See Also   Break, Change, Extend; *System Variables:* Edgemode, Projmode

---

U

U reverses the most recent command. You can undo as many commands as you have issued during any given editing session.

To Reverse a Command

Command Line: **U**

Menu: Edit ➤ Undo

Standard Toolbar: 🔄 Undo

The Auto, End, and Control options under the **Undo** command affect the results of the **U** command. **U** is essentially the **Undo** command with 1 as the parameter.

See Also   Redo, Undo

UCS

UCS, the user coordinate system, is a tool for creating and editing 3D drawings. A UCS can be described as a plane in 3D space on which you can draw. Using the **UCS** command, you can create and shift between as many UCS's as you like. It determines the orientation in which 2D objects are drawn and the direction in which objects are extruded.

To Modify a UCS

Command Line: **UCS**

Menu: Tools ➤ UCS ➤ Preset Options

UCS Toolbar: [icon] UCS [icon] Named UCS [icon] Preset UCS [icon] UCS Previous [icon] World UCS [icon] Object UCS [icon] View UCS [icon] Origin UCS [icon] Z Axis Vector UCS [icon] 3 Point UCS [icon] X Axis Rotate UCS [icon] Y Axis Rotate UCS [icon] Z Axis Rotate UCS

Origin/ZAxis/3point/Object/View/X/Y/Z/Prev/Restore/Save/ Del/?/<World>: Enter or select an option.

Options

Origin   Determines the origin of a UCS.

Zaxis   Determines the direction of the Z-coordinate axis. You are prompted for an origin for the UCS and for a point along the Z axis of the UCS.

3point   Allows you to define a UCS by selecting three points: the origin, a point along the positive direction of the X axis, and a point along the positive direction of the Y axis.

Object   Defines a UCS based on the orientation of an object. Objects not eligible for selection include a 3D solid, 3D polyline, 3D mesh, viewport, mline, region, spline, ellipse, ray, xline, leader, mtext.

View   Defines a UCS parallel to your current view. The origin of the current UCS will be used as the origin of the new UCS.

X/Y/Z   Allows you to define a UCS by rotationg the current UCS about its X, Y, or Z axis.

Prev   Places you in the previously defined UCS.

Restore   Restores a saved UCS.

Save   Saves a UCS for later recall.

Del Deletes a previously saved UCS.

?/List Displays a list of currently saved UCS's. You can use wildcard filter lists to search for specific UCS names.

World Returns you to the world coodinate system.

> **NOTE** The world coordiante system, or WCS, is the base from which all other UCS's are defined. The WCS is the default coordinate system when you open a new file. The *UCSfollow* system variable automatically shifts your drawing into the appropriate plan view whenever the UCS is moved. If you use the *Objects* option, the way the selected object was created affects the orientation of the UCS. Table 12 correlates selected objects with UCS orientation.

TABLE 12: UCS Orientation Based on Objects

Object Type	UCS Orientation
Arc	The center of the arc establishes the UCS origin. The X axis of the UCS passes through one of the endpoints nearest to the picked point on the arc.
Circle	The center of the circle establishes the UCS origin. The X axis of the UCS passes through the pick point on the circle.
Dimension	The midpoint of the dimension text establishes the UCS origin. The X axis of the UCS is parallel to the X axis that was active when the dimension was drawn.
Line	The endpoint nearest the pick point establishes the origin of the UCS, and the XZ plane of the UCS contains the line.
Point	The point location establishes the UCS origin. The UCS orientation is arbitrary.
2D Polyline	The starting point of the polyline establishes the UCS origin. The X axis is determined by the direction from the first point to the next vertex.
Solid	The first point of the solid establishes the origin of the UCS. The second point of the solid establishes the X axis.
Trace	The direction of the trace establishes the X axis of the UCS, with the beginning point setting the origin.

TABLE 12: UCS Orientation Based on Objects (continued)

Object Type	UCS Orientation
3Dface	The first point of the 3Dface establishes the origin. The first and second points establish the X axis. The plane defined by the face determines the orientation of the UCS.
Shapes, Text, Blocks, Attributes, *and* Attribute Definitions	The insertion point establishes the origin of the UCS. The object's rotation angle establishes the X axis.

See Also   Dducs, Dducsp, Dview, Elev, Plan, Rename, Vpoint, Wildcard characters; *System Variables*: Ucsfollow, Ucsicon, Ucsname, Ucsorg, Ucsxdir, Ucsydir, Vsmax, Vsmin, Worlducs, Thickness, Ucsicon

Ucsicon

Ucsicon controls the display and location of the UCS icon. The UCS icon tells you the orientation of the current UCS. It displays an L-shaped graphic symbol showing the positive X and Y directions. The icon displays a W when WCS is the current default coordinate system. If the current UCS plane is perpendicular to your current view, the UCS icon displays a broken pencil to indicate that you will have difficulty drawing in the current view. The UCS icon changes to a cube when you are displaying a perspective view. When you are in Paperspace, it turns into a triangle.

To Modify the UCS Icon

Command Line: **Ucsicon**

Menu: View ➣ Display ➣ UCS Icon ➣ On/Origin

Options

ON   Turns the UCS icon on.

OFF   Turns the UCS icon off.

All   Forces the Ucsicon settings to take effect in all viewports if you have more than one viewport. Otherwise, the settings will affect only the active viewport.

Noorigin   Places the UCS icon in the lower-left corner of the drawing area, regardless of the current UCS's origin location.

Origin   Places the UCS icon at the origin of the current UCS. If the origin is off the screen, the UCS icon will appear in the lower-left corner of the drawing area.

> **NOTE**   Instead of selecting the *ORigin* option as shown above, achieve the same affect by selecting View ➤ Display ➤ UCS Icon ➤ Origin. The UCS icon will always move automatically with the origin, unless the origin is not within the drawing view window.

See Also   UCS, Viewports; *System Variables:* Ucsicon

Undefine

See **Redefine**

Undo

Undo allows you to undo parts of your editing session. This can be useful if you accidentally execute a command that destroys part of all of your drawing. **Undo** also allows you to control how much of a drawing is undone.

To Reverse Commands

Command Line: **Undo**

Menu: Edit ➤ Undo

   Auto/Control/BEgin/End/Mark/Back/<default number>:
Enter an option to use or the number of commands to undo.

Options

Auto   Makes AutoCAD view menu macros as a single command. If Auto is set On, the effect of macros issued from a menu will be undone regardless of the number of commands the macro contains.

Control   Allows you to turn off the Undo feature to save disk space or to limit the Undo feature to single commands. You are prompted for All, None, or One. *All* fully enables the Undo feature, *None* disables Undo, and *One* restricts the Undo feature to a single command at a time.

Begin, End   *Begin* marks the beginning of a sequence of operations. All edits after that point become part of the same group. *End* terminates the group. This allows you to mark a group of commands to be undone together.

UNDO

Mark, Back   Allows you to experiment safely with a drawing by first marking a point in your editing session to which you can return. Once a mark has been issued, you can proceed with your experimental drawing addition. Then, you can use *Back* to undo all the commands back to the place that Mark was issued.

> **NOTE**   Many commands offer an Undo option. The Undo option under a main command will act more like the **U** command and will not offer the options described here.

Union

Union creates a composite object by combining the total area or volume of two or more regions or solids.

To Combine Regions or Solids

Command Line: **Union**

Menu: Modify II ➤ Union

Modify II Toolbar: Union

Select objects: Click on the overlapping solids or regions that you want to combine.

> **NOTE**   Union can be used only for regions or solids. You may select both regions and solids at the same time, and you may select objects from any number of planes. AutoCAD will group the selection set into subsets by region/solid and by plane (in the case of regions) before combining them.

See Also   Intersect, Region, Solid Modeling, Subtract

Units

Units sets AutoCAD to the unit format appropriate to the drawing. For example, if you are drawing an architectural floor plan, you can set up AutoCAD to accept and display distances using feet, inches, and fractional inches. You can also set up AutoCAD to accept and display angles as degrees, minutes, and seconds of an arc rather than the default decimal degrees. The dialog box equivalent of this command is **Ddunits**. The units format also appears as a tab in the Setup dialog box for both Quick and Advanced setups.

To Change Drawing Units

Command Line: **Units** (or '**Units** to use transparently)

1. **Report formats: Enter choice, 1 to 5 <2>:** Enter the number corresponding to the desired unit system, as described below. With the exception of the Engineering and Architectural modes, you can use these modes with any basic unit of measurement.

2. **Number of digits to the right of decimal point(0 to 8):<4>:** Enter a number to specify the degree of precision.

3. **System of angle measure: Enter choice, 1 to 5 <1>:** Enter the number corresponding to the desired angle measure system, as described below.

4. **Number of fractional places for display of angle (0 to 8) <0>:** Enter a number to specify the degree of precision.

5. **Direction for angle 0: Enter direction for angle 0 <0>:** Enter the desired angle for the 0 degree direction, as described below.

6. **Do you want angle measured clockwise?<N>:** Enter Y if you want angles measured clockwise, otherwise, press ↵.

Options

System of units   Sets format of units that AutoCAD will accept as input:

Report Format	Example
1. Scientific	1.5500E+01
2. Decimal	15.5
3. Engineering	1'-3.50"
4. Architectural	1'3 1/2"
5. Fractional	15 1/2

System of angle measure   Sets format of angle measurement AutoCAD will accept as input:

Measurement Format	Example
1. Decimal	45.0000
2. Degrees/minutes/ seconds	45d0'0"
3. Grads	50.0000g
4. Radians	0.7854r
5. Surveyor's units	N 45d0'0"E

Direction for angle 0   Sets direction for the 0 angle:

East	3 o'clock = 0
North	12 o'clock = 90
West	9 o'clock = 180
South	6 o'clock = 270

NOTE   You can set decimal or fractional input regardless of the unit format being used. This means you can enter 5.5', as well as 5'6" when using the Architectural format. Decimal mode is perfect for metric units as well as decimal English units.

See Also   Ddunits, Mvsetup; *System Variables*: Aflags, Angbase, Angdir, Aunits, Luprec, Unitmode

View

View allows you to save views of your drawing. Instead of using the **Zoom** command to zoom in and out of your drawing, you can save views of the areas you need to edit, and then recall them using the *Restore* option of the **View** command. The corresponding dialog box command is **Ddview**.

To Save Views of Your Drawing

Command Line: **View**

?/Delete/Restore/Save/Window: Enter an option.

Options

?   Lists all currently saved views. Wildcards filter lists are accepted.

Delete   Prompts you for a view name to delete from the drawing database.

Restore   Prompts you for a view name to restore to the screen.

Save   Saves the current view. You are prompted for a view name.

Window   Saves a view defined by a window. You are prompted first to enter a view name and then to window the area to be saved as a view.

AutoCAD provides a Select Initial View check box to restore a previously saved view in the Select File dialog box when you open an existing drawing. View will save 3D orthographic projection views, perspective views, and Paperspace or Modelspace views. View does not save hidden-line views or shaded views.

See Also Open, Ddview

Viewports

*See **Vports***

Viewres

Viewres controls whether AutoCAD's virtual screen feature is used and how accurately AutoCAD displays lines, arcs and circles.

To Invoke Fast Zoom Mode

Command Line: **Viewres**

Do you want fast zooms? <Y> Enter **Y** or **N**. If you respond with **Y**, the following prompts appear: **Enter circle zoom percent (1-20000) <100>:**. Enter a value from 1 to 20,000, or press ↵ to accept the default.

Options

Yes Sets up a large virtual screen within which zooms, pans and view/restores occur at redraw speeds. You are prompted for a circle zoom percent (based on the current zoom magnification). This value determines how accurately circles and noncontinuous lines are shown.

No Turns off the virtual screen. All zooms, pans, and view/restores will cause a regeneration.

The circle zoom percent value also affects the speed of redraws and regenerations. A high value slows down redraws and regenerations; a low value speeds them up. Differences in redraw speeds are barely noticeable unless you have a vary large drawing.

Use a high percent value for circle zoom to display smooth circles and arcs and to accurately show noncontinuous lines. A low value causes arcs and circles to appear as a series of line segments when viewed up close. Noncontinuous lines, however, may appear continuous. This does not mean that prints or plots of your drawings will be less accurate; only the display is affected.

The default value for the circle zoom percent is 100, but at this value dashed or hidden lines might appear continuous, depending on the Ltscale settings and how far you are zoomed into the drawing. A value of 2000 (i.e., 20x) or higher reduces or eliminates this problem with little sacrifice of speed.

A low circle zoom value causes object endpoints, intersections, and tangents to appear inaccurately placed when you edit a close-up view of circles and arcs. Often, this results from the segmented appearance of arcs and circles and does not necessarily mean the object placement is inaccurate. It may also be hard to distinguish between polygons and circles. Settings the circle zoom percent to a high value also reduces or eliminates these problems.

The drawing limits affect redraw speed when the virtual screen feature is turned on. If the limits are set to an area much greater than the actual drawing, redraws are slowed down.

To force the virtual screen to contain a specific area, set your limits to the area you want, set the limit's checking feature to *On*, and issue a **Zoom**/*All* command. The virtual screen will conform to these limits until another **Regen** is issued or until you pan or zoom outside of the area set by the limits.

See Also   Limits, Redraw, Regen, Regenauto

Vplayer

Vplayer controls the visibility of layers for each individual viewport and allows display of different types of information in each viewport, even though the views are of the same drawing. You can use **Vplayer** in conjunction with overlapping viewports to create clipped views.

To Modify Viewport Layer Visibility

Command Line: **Vplayer**

?/Freeze/Thaw/Reset/Newfrz/Vpvisdflt: Enter the desired option.

Options

?   Displays the names of layers that are frozen in a given viewport. You are prompted to select a viewport. If you are in Modelspace, AutoCAD temporarily switches to Paperspace during your selection.

Freeze   Lets you specify the name of layers you want to freeze in selected viewports. You are first prompted for the names of "Layer(s) to Freeze <>:", then "All/Select/<Current>:" appears for the viewport(s) in which to freeze them.

Thaw   Thaws layers in specific viewports. You are prompted for the layer names to thaw, then the viewports in which the layers are to be thawed.

Reset Restores the default visibility setting for layers in a given viewport. See the *Vpvisdflt* option for information on default visibility.

Newfrz Creates a new layer that is automatically frozen. You can then turn this new layer on for each viewport individually.

Vpvisdflt Presets the visibility of layers for new viewports to be created using **Mview** by prompting:

Layer name(s) to change default viewport visibility <>:
Enter layer name.

Change default viewport visibility to Frozen/<Thawed>:
Enter an option.

NOTE All options that prompt you for layer names allow use of wildcard characters to set multiple layer names. You can also use comma delimiters for lists of layers with dissimilar names.

See Also Ddlmodes, Layer, Mview, Mvsetup, Pspace; *System Variables:* Tilemode, Visretain

Vpoint

Vpoint selects an orthographic, 3D view of your drawing.

To Set a Viewing Point

Command Line: **Vpoint**

Menu: View ➤ 3D Viewpoint ➤ Tripod or Vector

Viewpoint Toolbar: Top View Bottom View Left View Right View Front View Back View SW Isometric View SE Isometric View NE Isometric View NW Isometric View

If you are operating from the command line **Rotate/<View point> <current settings>:**, enter a coordinate value, or enter **R** for the *Rotate* option, or press ↵ to set the view with the compass and axes tripod.

Options

Rotate Allows you to specify a view in terms of angles in the XY plane and from the X axis. You are first prompted to enter an angle in the XY plane from the X axis. Next, you are prompted to enter an angle from the XY plane.

View point/Vector Allows you to specify your viewpoint location by entering an X, Y, Z coordinate value.

⏎/Tripod   Allows you to visually select a view by using the compass and axes tripod.

There are three methods for selecting a view: Enter a value in X, Y and Z coordinates that represents your view point. For example, entering 1, 1, -1 will give you the same view as entering 4,4,-4.

Use the *Rotate* option to specify a viewpoint as horizontal and vertical angles in relation to the last point selected. Use the **ID** command to establish the view target point (the last point selected) before you start Vpoint.

Press ⏎ at the "Vpoint" prompt, and visually select a view point using the compass and axes tripod. To select a view, move your pointing device until the tripod indicates the desired X-, Y-, and Z-axis orientation. A cross on the compass indicates your location in plan. For example, placing the cross in the lower-left quadrant of the compass places your viewpoint below and to the left of your drawing. Your view elevation is indicated by the distance of the cross from the compass center. The closer the cross is to the center, the highter the elevation. The circle inside the compass indicates a 0 elevation. If the cross falls outside of this circle, your view elevation becomes a minus value and your view will be from below your drawing.

Vports/Viewports

Vports or **Viewports** displays multiple views, or tiled viewports, of your drawing at one time. This command is disabled when the *Tilemode* system variable is set to 0.

To Display Multiple Viewports

Command Line: **Vports** or **Viewports**

Menu: View ➤ Tiled Viewports

   Save/Restore/Delete/Join/SIngle/?/2/<3>/4: Enter the desired option or press ⏎ for the "Horizontal/Vertical/Above/Below/Left/<Right>:" default prompt.

Options

Save   Saves the current viewport arrangement.

Restore   Restores a previously saved viewport arrangement.

Delete   Deletes a previously saved viewport arrangement.

Join Joints two adjacent viewports of the same size to make one larger viewport.

Single Changes the display to a single viewport.

? Displays a list of saved viewport arrangements along with each viewport's coordinate location.

2 Splits the display to show two viewports. You are prompted for a horizontal or vertical split.

3 Changes the display to show three viewports.

4 Changes the display to show four equal viewports.

Layout If you are working from the pull-down **View** menu, you may select *Layout...* to open the Tiled Viewport Layout dialog box. This displays an icon menu of predefined viewport arrangements from which you may select the desired layout.

Each viewport can contain any type of view you like. For example, you can display a perspective view in one viewport and a plan view of the same drawing in another viewport.

You can only work in one viewport at a time. To change active viewports, pick any point inside the desired viewport. The border around the selected viewport will thicken to show that it is active. The standard cursor appears only in the active viewport. (When you move the cursor into an inactive viewport, it changes into an arrow.) Any edits made in one viewport are immediately reflected in the other viewports.

Each viewport has its own virtual display within which you can pan and zoom at redraw speeds. For this reason, the **Regen** and **Redraw** commands affect only the active viewport. To regenerate or redraw all the viewports at once, use the **Regenall** and **Redrawall** commands.

NOTE Tiled vports are helpful when working with 3D objects. If you attempt to plot while your screen is arranged in tiled viewports, you will only be plotting the view displayed in the active viewport. Use the **Mview** command in paperspace (tilemode=0) to create, then plot multiple viewports.

See Also Mview, Redraw, Regen; *System Variables:* Cvports, Maxactvp, Viewctr, Viewdir, Viewtwist, Vsmax, Vsmin, Viewres

Vslide

Vslide displays raster image slide files in the current viewport. Slides are individual files with the extension .SLD. You many combine slide files into a slide library by using the extension .SLB.

To Display Slide Files

Command Line: **Vslide**

Slide file <current file name>: Enter the name of the slide file to be displayed. If *Filedia* is set to 1, the Select Slide File box will appear to specify a drive, path and file name.

To View a Slide from a Slide Library

Slide file <current file name>: Enter the slide library name followed by the slide's name in parantheses, as in:

library-name(slide-file-name)

See Also   Mslide, Script, Slidelib.EXE

Wblock

Wblock lets you create a new file from a portion of the current file or from a block of the current file. The equivalent dialog box command is **Bmake**.

To Write a Block to Disk

Command Line: **Wblock**

1. In the Create Drawing File dialog box, enter the file name, directory and drive letter for the new drawing file.

2. **Block name:** Enter the block name or press ↵ to select objects for creating a block.

    The block or set of objects will be written to your disk as a drawing file.

NOTE If you are exporting a block from your drawing and you want the file name to be the same as the block name, enter an equals sign at the "Block name:" prompt, or enter the same block name again. If you enter the name of an existing file at the "File name:" prompt, you receive the prompt:

A drawing with this name already exists. Do you want to
replace it! <N>:

You can replace the file name or return to the command prompt to restart **Wblock**.

To write a portion of the current drawing view to a file, press ↵ without entering anything at the "Block name:" prompt. You receive the following two prompts:

Insertion base point: Enter a coordinate or pick a point.

Select Objects: Select objects using the standard AutoCAD selection options.

The objects you select are written to your disk as a drawing file. The point you select at the "Insertion base point:" prompt becomes the origin of the written file. The current UCS (user coordinate system) becomes the WCS (world coordinate system) in the written file. When you save a block to disk, the UCS active at the time you create the block becomes the WCS of the written file.

Entering an asterisk (*) at the "Block name:" prompt writes the entire current file to disk, stripping it of all unused blocks, layers, line types, text styles. This can reduce a file's size and access time. (See **Purge**.)

Objects are placed in the Modelspace of the output file unless the asterisk is used. In that case, objects are placed in the space they are in. Also whatever layer is set current at the time of the **Wblock** will be the current layer in the new file.

See Also Base, Bmake; *System Variables*: Expert, Handles, Insbase

Wildcard Characters

Wildcard characters allow you to list file names by using a filter to include or exclude files according to similarities in their names. AutoCAD wildcard characters are extensions of the standard DOS wildcard characters. Here are the wildcard characters you can use:

Character	Description
#	Matches any number. For example, **C#D** selects all names that begin with C, end with D, and have a single-digit number between.
@	Matches any alphabetical character. For example, **C@D** selects any name that begins with C, ends with D, and has a single alphabetical character between.

Character	Description
.(period)	Matches any character not numeric or alphabetical. For example, **C.D** might select the name C-D.
*(asterisk)	Matches any string of characters. For example, ***CD** selects all names of any length that end with CD.
?(question mark)	Matches any single character. For example, **C?D** selects all names of three characters that begin with C and end with D.
~(tilde)	Matches anything but the set of characters that follow. For example, **~CD** selects all names that do *not* include CD.
[ ] (brackets)	Typing any set of characters between two brackets matches any one of the characters enclosed in brackets. For example, [CD]X selects the names CX and DX, but not CDX. Brackets can be used in conjunction with other wildcard characters. For example, you could use **[~CD]X** to find all names except CX and DX.
-(hyphen)	Lets you specify a range of characters when used within brackets. For example, **[C-F]X** selects the names CX, DX, EX, and FX.
`(single quote)	Forces the character that follows to be read literally. (The reverse quote is the character that is located to the left of the 1 key on most keyboards.) For example, ` selects the name *CD, instead of all names that end in CD.

Xattach

Xattach attaches an external reference to the current drawing. When first invoked it displays the Select file to attach dialog box, then displays the Attach Xref dialog box. Subsequent attachments only display the Attach Xref dialog box, which contains insertion options similar to the **Image** and **Xref** commands.

To Attach an Xref File

Command Line: **Xattach**

Reference Toolbar: External Reference Attach

Xattach can be used to quickly insert an xref file into the drawing, otherwise, select the **Xref** command and click the *Attach...* button to display the same Attach Xref dialog box. (See **Xref**.)

Options

Xref Name   Displays names and paths of attached xref files.

Reference Type   Identifies whether xref is an attachment or overlay.

Include Path   Check box indicating xref path is saved in the drawing database or saved in the database without a path.

Parameters   Specifies insertion point, X,Y, and Z scale factors, and rotation angle.

See Also   Image, Xref

-XBIND

-**Xbind** imports a block, dimension style, layer, line type, or text style from an external reference (xref). The equivalent dialog box command is **Xbind**.

To Bind Symbols into Your Drawing

Command Line: -Xbind

1. **Block/Dimstyle/LAyer/LType/Style:** Enter the desired option.

2. You are then prompted for the name of the item to import. Enter a single name, a list of names separated by commas, or use wildcard characters to specify a range of names.

> **NOTE**   Named variables from an xref file must be prefixed with their source file name. Be sure to include the full xref file name, including the vertical bar symbol, or pipe character (|), for example, xref-*filename|blockname*. When you use -Xbind to import the named block, its name will change to xref-*filename0blockname* to reflect its source file. If a block of the same name already exists, the 0 is replaced with a 1, as in xref-**filename1blockname.**

See Also   Xbind, Xref

Xbind

Xbind opens the Xbind dialog box to import a block, dimension style, layer, line type, or text style from an external reference (xref).

To Bind Symbols Using a Dialog Box

Command Line: **Xbind**

Menu: Modify ➤ Object ➤ External Reference

Reference Toolbar: External Reference Bind

Opens the Xbind dialog box to graphically assist you in selecting a block, dimension style, layer, line type, or text style to bind into your drawing.

Options

Xrefs   List box displaying xref files in your drawing in a DOS tree format. Highlight, then double-click and Xref file name to display named objects: *Block*, *Dimstyle*, *Layer*, *Linetype* and *Textstyle*. Double-click an object, such as Layer, to expand the branches and display specific xref layer names to bind. The layer names will appear in the xref-*filename|blockname* format. If you highlight a layer and click *Add->*, the definition is transferred into the Definitions to Bind list box.

Definitions to Bind   List box displaying name of item to import into your drawing. If you wish to remove a selected item or definition, highlight it and click the *<-Remove* button.

See Also   -Xbind, Xref

Xclip

Xclip allows you to create a user defined clipping boundary, consisting of planar straight line segments, for one or more external reference files or blocks. You can also set front or back clipping planes.

To Create a Clipping Boundary

Command Line: **Xclip**

Menu: Modify ➤ Object ➤ External Reference

Toolbar: External Reference Clip

1. **Select Objects:** Select one or more xrefs or blocks to clip.

2. **ON/OFF/Clipdepth/Delete/generate Polyline/<New boundary>:** Press ↵ or specify an option. If you pressed ↵ at the **Delete old boundary(s)? No/<Yes>:** prompt, a prompt appears to **Select polyline/Polygonal/<Rectangular>:,** offering you additional choices: enter **S** to select an existing polyline, **P** to draw a new polygonal shape or accept the default **R** to draw a rectangle.

3. If you pressed ↵ to create a new boundary using the **P** or **R** option, the external reference file is clipped to the boundary edge, then the polyline disappears. To restore the polyline, reissue the command and type **P** or **Polyline** for the *generate Polyline* option.

Options

Polygonal   Pick a point at the "First point:" prompt, then continue to select or adjust points at the "Undo/<Next point>:" prompts to define the clipping boundary.

Rectangular   Specify two corner points to create a rectangular boundary.

ON   Displays the clipped portion of the xref or block.

OFF   Restores the entire xref or block that was clipped.

Clipdepth   Displays prompts "Specify front clip point or [Distance/ Remove]:" and "Specify distance from boundary:" to set front and back clipping planes on an xref or block preventing objects outside the clip- depth range from being displayed. Use *Remove* option to delete the clipdepth specifications.

Delete   Removes the clipping boundary on one or more selected xrefs or blocks.

Generate Polyline   Recreates the polyline, using the current layer, line- type, and color settings, that define the edge of the clipping boundary. You can edit the polyline with **Pedit** or **Grips**. If you wish to use this new polyline as the new boundary edge, then reissue the **Xclip** com- mand and enter **S** as descibed in item 3 above.

NOTE   If you can use the *spline* option of the **Pline** command to create a smooth curved clipping boundary; the fit curve or arc options are decurved prior to being used as a clip boundary.

See Also   Xclipframe

Xclipframe

Xclipframe sets the visibility of xref clipping boundaries ON or OFf.

To Display an Xref's Clipping Boundary

Command Line: **Xclipframe**

Menu: Modify ➤ Object ➤ External Reference ➤ Frame

Toolbar: 🔲 External Reference Clip Frame

> **New value for XCLIPFRAME <0>:** Enter a value of 0 to turn the clipping boundary Off and 1 to make it visible. The Clipping Boundary is a block in the drawing that has the name of the xref.

See Also   Xref, System Variables

Xline

Xline allows you to create construction lines anywhere in 3D space. By default, **Xline** creates an infinite line based on two input points. The first point specified, the root, becomes the "midpoint" of the infinite line. You may specify the **Xline**'s orientation in a variety of ways.

To Draw a Construction Line

Command Line: **Xline**

Menu:Draw ➤ Construction line

Draw Toolbar: ◢ Construction line

1. **Hor/Ver/Ang/Bisect/Offset/<From point>:** Pick a first point (the Xline "root" or midpoint) or select an option.

2. **Through point:** Pick a second point or enter coordinates to orient the Xline. Continue to pick additional through points as required to create additional construction lines radiating from the midpoint.

Options

Hor/Ver   Allows you to draw a construction line parallel to the X axis (Hor) or Y axis (Ver). You need only pick a single point to define Xlines of this type. Continue picking through points to create as many parallel construction lines as are required.

Ang Allows you to draw an Xline at a specified angle to the X axis by either entering an angle value or by dynamically picking two points. Continue picking through points to create as many parallel construction lines as are required.

Bisect Creates a construction line that bisects a specified angle. First pick the angle vertex point, then points to mark the lines of the angle.

Offset Allows you to draw a construction line parallel to a selected line object (including plines) at a specified offset. First specify the offset by picking two points or entering a numeric value. Then select a line object and pick a point to indicate the side on which to offset the construction line.

NOTE Xlines are ignored by commands that display the drawing extents.

See Also   Line, Ray

Xplode

Xplode lets you explode multiple compound objects and blocks, including non-uniformly scaled objects. You may also control and change the color, layer, line type, either of individual objects or of all of the objects globally.

To Explode Compound Objects

Command Line: **Xplode**

Menu: Bonus ➤ Modify ➤ Extended Explode

1. **Select objects to XPlode. Select objects:** Use an object selection method to pick all of the objects you wish to explode. (AutoCAD will show how many were selected and how many are valid compound objects.)

2. **XPlode Individually/<Globally>:** Press ↵, or enter **I** if you wish to control color, layer, or line type individually.

3. **All/Color/LAyer/LType/Inherit from parent block/ <Explode>:** Press ↵ to explode all of the selected objects without changing any of their characteristics. Type in an option **A/C/LA/LT/I** if you wish to change all or any of the selected object's characteristics.

Options

Global/Individual If you choose the default global option in step 2, Xplode will apply your choices to all objects in a single pass. If you chose the **I** option in step 2, **Xplode** will cycle through each of the selected objects one at a time.

All If you select this option, **Xplode** will prompt you through all of the other options in turn, allowing you to select or enter new values.

Color Allows you to specify any of the standard colors, or to chose color BYLayer or BYBlock. The prompt "New color for exploded objects. Red/Yellow/Green/Cyan/Blue/Magenta/White/BYLayer/BYBlock <BYLAYER>:" lists the options.

Linetype Allows you to specify a new line type at the prompt "Enter new linetype name. <BYLAYER> :".

Layer **XPlode onto what layer? <0>:** Enter a new layer name, or press ↵ to explode the block into the current layer.

See Also Block, Explode, Wblock, Xbind, Xref

-XREF

-Xref lets you attach and detach, list and reload or bind external drawing files to your current drawing file. You may also overlay external files over your current drawing to check the consistency or relationship between the drawings. Xrefs should be regarded as read-only files for reference purposes only. The equivalent dialog box command is **Xref**.

To Import an External File

Command Line: **-Xref**

?/Bind/Detach/Path/Unload/Reload/Overlay/<Attach>: Enter the desired option.

Options

?/List Displays a list of cross-referenced files in your current drawing. The name of the file as well as its location on your storage device is shown. You can filter the Xref'd file names by using wildcard characters.

Bind Causes a cross-referenced file to become a part of the current file. Once Bind is used, the Xref file becomes an ordinary block in the current file and AutoCAD replaces the pipe character (|) with a number (usually 0) between two dollar signs ($$).

Detach   Detaches a cross-referenced file, so it is no longer referenced to the current file.

> **Xref(s) to detach:** Enter name or names separated with commas or wildcard.

Path   Lets you specify a new DOS path for a cross-referenced file. This is useful if you have moved a cross-referenced file to another drive or directory. You are prompted for the file's name:

> **Old Path:** Enter old path.
>
> **New Path:** Enter new path.

Reload   Lets you reload a cross-referenced file without exiting and reentering the current file. This option is useful if you are in a network environment and you know that someone has just finished updating a file you are using as a cross-reference. A temporary lock is created if the drawing you are editing is externally referenced during an Xref Reload operation and, if it encounters an error while reloading, ends the **Xref** command undoing the entire reload sequence:

> **Xref(s) to reload:** Enter name or names separated with commas or wildcard.

Attach   Lets you attach another drawing file as a cross-reference. The Select file to attach dialog box opens to identify the file name, path and drive letter, then you are requested for an insertion point, scale factor(s), and rotation angle for the cross-reference.

> **Insertion point:** Specify an insertion point for the xref file.
>
> **X scale factor <1> / Corner / XYZ:** Enter a new value or press ↵.
>
> **Y scale factor (default=X):** Enter a new value or press ↵.
>
> **Rotation angle <0>:** Pick a rotation angle dynamically or enter a value.

Overlay   Lets you overlay another drawing file as a cross-reference for comparison purposes. It operates in a very similar way to the *Attach* option by opening the Select file to overlay dialog box. You are prompted, in the same way, for a file name, notified if the file exists, then requested for an insertion point, scale factor(s), and rotation angle for the cross-reference. However, overlay cross-references cannot be nested—that is, if you reference a drawing with an overlaid cross-reference, the overlaid cross-reference will not be referenced into your drawing. The *Overlay* option allows multiple users to access the same drawing without circularity of Xrefs.

Xref'd files act like blocks; they cannot be edited from the file they are attached to. The difference between blocks and Xref'd files is that Xref'd files do not become part of the current file's database. Instead, the current file "points" to the Xref'd file. The next time the current file is opened, the Xref's file is also opened and automatically attached. This has two advantages. First, since the Xref'd file does not become part of the current file, the current file size remains small. Second, since the Xref'd file stays independent, any changes made to it are automatically reflected in the current file whenever it is reopened.

In most of the options, you can enter a single name, a list of names separated by commas, or a name containing wildcard characters. Named variables from the Xref'd files will have the file name as a prefix. For example, a layer called "wall" in an Xref'd file called "house" will have the name House|wall in the current file.

At a file name prompt, you can assign a name to an Xref'd file that is different from its actual name by appending to the file name an equal sign followed by the new name. For example, at the prompt, enter a statement in the form of:

newplan=oldplan

where *newplan* is the new name and *oldplan* is the file name of the Xref'd file.

AutoCAD keeps a log of Xref activity in an ASCII file. This file has the same root name as your current drawing file and has the extension .XLG. You can delete this file with no effect on your drawing. It can be set by checking *Maintian a Log file* in the General tabbed section of the Preferences dialog box.

See Also Block, Insert, Preferences, Xbind, -Xbind, Xref; *System Variables:* Xrefctl

Xref

Xref helps to manage how you attach, detach, reload, unload, bind and locate external drawing files in your current drawing. Use **-Xref** to display prompts at the command line.

To Manage Insertion of Xref Files

Command Line: **Xref**

Menu: Insert ➤ External Reference

Reference Toolbar: External Reference

Draw Toolbar: 🔲Insert Block Flyout 🔲External Reference

Insert Toolbar: 🔲External Reference

Xref opens the External Reference dialog box, similar to the **Image** command, to manage your xref files. Select the desired function from the dialog box.

Options

List View Click the List View box or press the F3 function key to display external reference files in a columnar format with headings as described below. Based on their function, the six drag division headings sort information in ascending and descending order.

Reference Name Names of xref files in block definition symbol table.

Status Identifies if an xref file is loaded, unloaded, unreferenced, not found, unresolved, orphaned, or marked for unloading or reloading.

Size Shows the size of the xref file.

Type Specifies if xref file is an overlay or attachment.

Date Displays last modified date of xref file. If xref is unloaded, not found or unresolved, this field is empty.

Saved Path Shows you the saved path for xref file, but does not update the path if the xref file may actually have been relocated.

Tree View Displays the xref files in a DOS directory tree format with branches identifying subdirectories. The *Xref Found At* edit box below shows you its full path. You can also press the F4 key to display the Tree View.

Attach Displays the Attach Xref dialog box executed with the **Xattach** command. (see **Xattach**).

Detach Detaches one or more highlighted external reference files from your drawing. You can only detach those xref files that are directly attached or overlaid in your drawing. It does not detach nested xrefs.

Reload Reloads xref files that have been unloaded.

Unload Unloads, but does not remove, xref files. Unloading prevents the display and regeneration of the xref to improve editing and drawing performance.

Bind   Displays the Bind Xrefs dialog box to *Bind* or *Insert* an xref file. Bind will insert the xref file as a permanent object using the block-name$#$symbolname syntax. Insert is similar to the insert command where an object assumes the current properties defined in the drawing. For example, if a layer named Wall in the xref file was defined with the color yellow, and your drawing contains a Wall layer with the color green, the inserted xref would assume the color green.

Zoom

Zoom controls the display of your drawing dynamically in real time.

To Use Zoom

Command Line: **Zoom**

Menu: View ➤ Zoom ➤ Realtime/Previous/Window/Dynamic/Scale/In/ Out/All/Extents

Zoom Toolbar: 🔍Zoom Window 🔍Zoom Dynamic
🔍Zoom Scale 🔍Zoom Center 🔍Zoom In 🔍Zoom Out
🔍Zoom All 🔍Zoom Extents

All/Center/Dynamic/Extents/Previous/Scale(X/XP)/Window/ <Realtime>:

Press Esc or Enter to exit, or right-click to activate pop-up menu. Press ⏎ for real time **Zoom** or enter the desired option.

Options

In/Out   The Zoom In and Zoom Out icon tools on the Zoom toolbar or the Zoom flyout on the Standard toolbar allow you to zoom in and out by a predefined scale factor. Zoom *In* doubles the size of the drawing display; Zoom *Out* shrinks the display to half of the current size so that you can view double the drawing are.

Realtime   Displays a magnifying glass with a plus and minus sign for real-time pan and zoom. Combines **Rtzoom** and **Rtpan** into a single command allowing you to switch between pan and zoom. Right-clicking your mouse displays a cursor menu to alternate among **Pan**, **Zoom**, **Zoom Window**, **Zoom Previous**, **Zoom Extents** options or **Exit** the **Zoom** command.

All   Displays the area of the drawing defined by the drawing's limits or extents, whichever are greater (see **Limits**).

Center   Displays a view based on a selected point. You are first prompted for a center point for your view and then for a magnification or height. A value followed by an X is read as a magnification factor; a lone value is read as the desired height in the display's drawing units.

Dynamic   Displays the virtual screen and allows you to use a view box to select a view. The drawing extents, current view, and the current virtual screen area are indicated as a solid white box, a dotted green box, and red corner marks, respectively. You can pan, enlarge, or shrink the view by moving the view box to a new location, adjusting its size, or both. When the view box appears, press the pick button to adjust the view box size, then pick again to restore the X in the view box. Press enter to set the new view.

Extents   Displays a view of the entire drawing centered on the screen. In Release 14, this option no longer causes a regen.

Previous   Displays the last view created by a **Zoom**, **Pan** or **View** command.

Window   Enlarges a rectangular area of a drawing, based on a defined window.

Scale(X)   Expands or shrinks the drawing display. If an X follows the scale factor, it will be in relation to the current view. If no X is used, the scale factor will be in relation to the area defined by the limits of the drawing. A value of .5x displays a view half the size of the current view.

Scale (XP)   Sets a viewports scale in relation to the Paperspace scale. For example, if you have set up a title block in Paperspace at a scale of 1"=1" and your full-scale Modelspace drawing is to be at a final plot scale of 1/4"-1', you can enter **1/48xp** at the Zoom prompt to set the viewport at the appropriate scale for Paperspace. You must be in floating Modelspace to use this option.

> **NOTE**   **Zoom** can be used transparently as long as the *Viewres Fast Zoom* option is on. **Zoom** cannot be used transparently while viewing a drawing is perspective. Use the **Dview** command's *Zoom* option instead. **Zoom** cannot be used transparently in Paperspace.

See Also   Limits, Mspace, Mvsetup, Pspace, Redraw, Regen, Regenauto; *System Variables:* Viewsize, Viewres

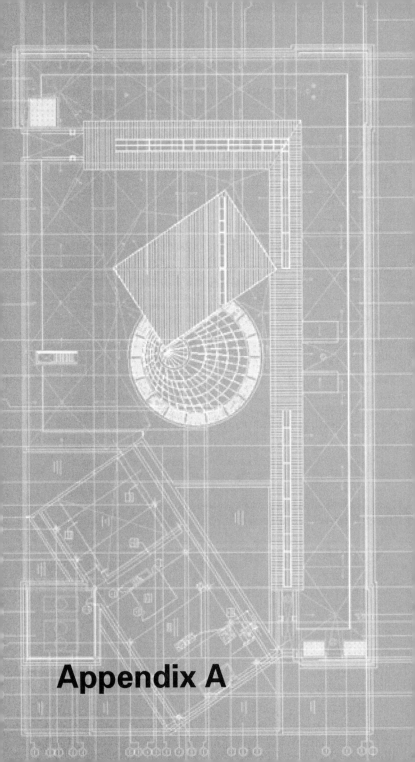

Appendix A

Bonus Toolbars

The Layer, Text, and Standard Bonus Toolbars offer routines that expand the capabilities of some AutoCAD commands. They have been contributed from various sources and are not officially supported by Autodesk. These and more commands can also be selected from the Bonus pull-down menu.

Select the Full installation option or pick the *Add* button and check Bonus in the Components list box in the Custom Components dialog box to install the bonus commands. The commands are stored in the Bonus subdirectory in your default Acadr14 directory.

NOTE If you are interested in knowing the names of the individuals on the Bonus Team, pick Bonus ➤ About Bonus Tools... to open the Bonus Tools Information dialog box. Double-click the red dot located at the bottom of the dialog box in the word Bonus to open the Bonus Contributors dialog box.

BONUS LAYER TOOLBAR

Icon and Tooltip Name	Description
Layer Manager	Helps you to save and restore layer configurations into 'layer states' in your drawing. Exports and importS saved settings from a .LAY file.
Match Object Layer	Matches layer of selected object.
Change to Current Layer	Changes layer of selected object(s) to current layer.
Isolate Obect's Layer	Select object(s) to only display or isolate their layer.
Freeze Object's Layer	Select object(s) to freeze their layer.
Turn Object's Layer Off	Select object(s) to turn off their layer.
Lock Object's Layer	Select object(s) to lock their layer.
Unlock Object's Layer	Select object(s) to unlock their layer.

BONUS TEXT TOOLBAR

Icon and Tooltip Name	Description
Text Fit	Places text between selected points
Text Mask	Hides entities behind text
Change Multiple Text Items	Changes attribute height, justification, location, rotation, style, text, and width for one or more objects
Explode Text	Explodes text into multiple polyline entities
Arc Aligned Text	Aligns text along an arc
Find and Replace Text	Globally or individually searches and replaces text strings
Explode Attributes to Text	Converts attributes to text entities
Global Attribute Edit	Edits attribute values globally

BONUS STANDARD TOOLBAR

Icon and Tooltip Name	Description
Extended Change Properties	Changes properties of multiple objects
Multiple Entity Stretch	Allows multiple selection windows for stretching objects
Move Copy Rotate	Combines move, copy, rotate, and scale into a single command
Extended Trim	Multiple trim for a polyline, line, circle or arc object
Extended Clip	Curved clipping of block or xref with arc, circle and polyline
Multiple Pedit	Pedit multiple polylines
Trim to Block Entities	Trim entities using nested blocks or xrefs
Extend to Block Entities	Extend entities to nested blocks or xrefs
Wipeout	Hides entities for display and plotting
Revision Cloud	Draws arc segmented revision cloud on current layer

BONUS STANDARD TOOLBAR (CONT.)

Icon and Tooltip Name	Description
Quick Leader	Draws leader lines with text; leader settings controlled from a dialog box
Pack 'n Go	Copies files associated with a drawing to specified directory; useful for xref exchanges.
List Xref/Block Entities	Displays entity information nested in external references or blocks

Index

Note to the Reader:
Throughout this index, **bold** page numbers indicate primary discussions of a topic. Page numbers in *italic* indicate illustrations.

Numbers

H

M

N

Q

R